Marxist Ideology in the Contemporary World– Its Appeals and Paradoxes

Hoover Institution Publications

Edited by Milorad M. Drachkovitch

Marxist Ideology in the Contemporary World— Its Appeals and Paradoxes

Contributors

Sidney Hook

Lewis S. Feuer

Joseph M. Bochenski

Daniel Bell

Gottfried Haberler

Yuan-li Wu

Peter T. Bauer

Published for the
Hoover Institution on War, Revolution, and Peace
Stanford University, Stanford, California
by Frederick A. Praeger, Publishers
New York — Washington
Pall Mall Press
London

FREDERICK A. PRAEGER, *Publishers*
111 Fourth Avenue, New York, N.Y. 10003, U.S.A.
77–79 Charlotte Street, London W.1, England

Published in the United States of America in 1966
by Frederick A. Praeger, Inc., Publishers

Library of Congress Catalog Card Number: 66–13961
Printed in the United States of America

Preface

The seven essays in this volume represent edited versions of original papers, expanded comments, and one public address presented on the third day of the international conference organized by the Hoover Institution on War, Revolution, and Peace at Stanford University on October 5, 6, and 7, 1964, entitled "One Hundred Years of Revolutionary Internationals."

The material which follows complements two independently published books * which contain papers offered at the various sessions of the first two days of this conference. In the first book, eight prominent experts from the United States and Europe analyze the impact of Marxism in the twentieth century, or more precisely the fundamental historical characteristics of Communist "isms"—from Leninism to Maoism—in their relationship with the original Marxism and explore their mutual connections, continuity, and contradictions. Whereas in the second, another team of recognized experts from both continents survey the general nature and the historical destinies of each of the three internationals which, despite differences, acted in the name of Marx.

The current volume serves to complete the cycle since it deals with Marxist ideology in the contemporary world. An attempt is made here to cast light on the appeals of Marxism in the non-Communist world and on the role of Marxism-Leninism in the Communist-ruled countries. The three separately published compilations combined offer a panoramic view of the three fundamental aspects of Marxism during

---

* (1) *Marxism in the Modern World*. Edited by Milorad M. Drachkovitch. Published for the Hoover Institution on War, Revolution, and Peace by Stanford University Press, Stanford, California, 1965. (Hoover Institution Publications, 38); (2) *The Revolutionary Internationals, 1864–1943*. Edited by Milorad M. Drachkovitch. Published for the Hoover Institution on War, Revolution, and Peace by Stanford University Press, Stanford, California, 1966. (Hoover Institution Publications, 45).

the last one hundred years: the protean nature of its ideological message; the historical developments of the movements fighting in its name; and the characteristics of the political regimes which tried to put Marxist ideas in practice.

Mr. James McSherry has been most helpful in the editing of this book and I wish to express my sincere thanks for his cooperation.

January 1, 1966   M.M.D.

Contents

Contributors

PETER T. BAUER is Professor of Economics (with special reference to Under-developed Countries and Economic Development) in the University of London, at the London School of Economics. He was formerly Smuts Reader in Commonwealth Studies at Cambridge University, as well as Fellow of Gonville and Caius College, Cambridge. His publications include: *The Rubber Industry* (1948), *West African Trade* (1954), *The Economics of Underdeveloped Countries* (with B. S. Yamey, 1957), *Economic Analysis and Policy in Underdeveloped Countries* (1957), *Indian Economic Policy and Development* (1961), and articles on economic subjects in many periodicals.

DANIEL BELL is Professor of Sociology at Columbia University and a Fellow of the American Academy of Arts and Sciences. He is the author, among other works, of *The History of Marxian Socialism in the United States* (1952) and *The End of Ideology* (1960).

JOSEPH M. BOCHENSKI, Swiss philosopher of Polish origin, was Professor in the Pontifical University (Angelicum), Rome, and is now Professor, Director of the Institute of East European Studies and Rector of the State University of Fribourg. He is the author of *Contemporary Philosophy in Europe* (1947), *History of Formal Logic* (1956), among other works, and Editor of *Sovietica* (1960 ff.) and of *Studies in Soviet Thought* (1961 ff.).

LEWIS S. FEUER is Professor of Philosophy and Social Science at the University of California, Berkeley, where he was from 1957 to 1964 Chairman of the Social Science Integrated Course. He was an Exchange Scholar at the Institute of Philosophy in the Soviet Academy of Science in Moscow during the spring semester of 1963, and is the author of *Spinoza and the Rise of Liberalism* and *The Scientific Intellectual*.

GOTTFRIED HABERLER, a graduate of the University of Vienna, came to the United States in 1936 and has since then been Professor of Economics at Harvard University. During 1934–1936 he was a member of the League of Nations Secretariat in Geneva. He has since held positions in Washington and has lectured in various universities in the United States, Europe, Latin America and South Africa. Among his publications are *The Theory of International Trade* (1955), *Prosperity and*

Depression (last edition 1958), *Consumer Installment Credit and Economic Fluctuations* (1942), *Money in the International Economy* (1965).

SIDNEY HOOK is Professor of Philosophy and Head of the All-University Department of Philosophy at New York University. He is the author of several works on the philosophical development of Karl Marx and on related themes. Among them are *From Hegel to Marx* (second edition 1963), *The Ambiguous Legacy: Marx and the Marxists* (1957), *Political Power and Personal Freedom* (1959).

YUAN-LI WU, a graduate of the London School of Economics, is the author of numerous articles and books on Communist China. His recent publications are *The Economy of Communist China, An Introduction* (1965), *The Steel Industry in Communist China* (1965), and *Economic Development and the Use of Energy Resources in Communist China* (1963). Dr. Wu is at present Professor of International Business, University of San Francisco, and Consultant to the Hoover Institution, Stanford, California.

———

MILORAD M. DRACHKOVITCH, an American scholar of Serbian origin, is a graduate of the University of Geneva, and was formerly Director of Studies at the College of Europe, Bruges. He is a Senior Staff Member of the Hoover Institution and Lecturer in the Department of Political Science, Stanford University. His books include *Les socialismes français et allemand et le problème de la guerre, 1870–1914* (1953) and *De Karl Marx à Léon Blum* (1954).

Milorad M. Drachkovitch

Introduction

Karl Loewith's saying that Marx's creed was a "story of salvation in the language of economics" may serve as an epigraph to this symposium. Five of the seven essays reproduced here discuss the appeals of Marxism in the Western, the Communist, and the "third" world; but in none of these essays is the political economy—in Marx's own "scientific" acceptation—suggested as an explanation for the contemporary attractiveness of Marxism. The remaining two essays, written by economists analyzing Marxist economics, also conclude that the non-economic aspects of Marxism explain its continued appeal after its scientific inadequacies have been revealed by the further development of society and theoretical analysis.

Such a paradox explains also the choice of a key word in the title of the book: Marxist *ideology*. It is used in the sense which Marx himself employed in his criticism of intellectual formulations and pretensions which either mystify the given social realities or cover by verbal screens the underlying vested interests. Thus, in the case of this book, its authors practically never speak of the contemporary meaning of Marxism to the proletariat or the working class, but analyze at length the fascination which certain aspects of Marxism exercise on a number of intellectuals in various parts of the world. Furthermore, these studies suggest that the qualitative meaning of political power in the countries ruled in the name of Marx appears as the very foundation of the structure instead of being simply an impersonal reflection of the new forces and relations of production. The significance of the analyses that follow lies in their attempt to go behind the façade of (often mutually exclusive) Marxist official pronouncements, in search of the real forces, social and psychological, that determine commitments to this most dynamic and protean doctrine of our time.

A revolutionary doctrine par excellence, Marxism could not have played the role it played in the past and is playing today if its other fundamental characteristic were not its "multiple ambiguity." The perceptive biographer of Marxism's centennial life, Bertram D. Wolfe, has pointed to the hard core of the problem, to the "ambiguity in the spirit of Marx himself, ambiguity in the heritage he left, and ambiguity in those who claimed to be his heirs." Thus, a part of Marxian thought and action has been absorbed and diluted in the fabric of the Western pluralistic societies: democratic socialism as an emanation of the politically maturing and organized working class was certainly a legitimate heir of the Marx-led First and Engels-blessed Second Internationals. There is also at least a para-Marxist determinism in W. W. Rostow's fundamental thesis that the "stages-of-growth are an economic way of looking at whole societies." One could say, moreover, that the political economy of contemporary Western welfare states has partly negated and partly adopted the views of the founding fathers of "scientific" Socialism, in their mature years, and of the non-Marxist and anti-Marxist labor movements.

On the other hand, as Professor Lewis Feuer indicates in his essay in this book, the "theoretical history [of Marxism] has been a history of syncretisms." In this sense the Leninist merger of the basic postulates of Marxism with the revolutionary and organizational traditions of Russian populism, has resulted in an amalgam, doctrinally barely compatible but politically supremely effective, known as Marxism-Leninism. Furthermore, the recent discovery that the writings of the young, "protohistorical" Marx exhale a spirit congenial to the alienated intellectuals in the contemporary world, has brought together another theoretically uneasy, well-nigh apolitical quasi-union of Marxism and existentialism. We find thus today three sharply distinguishable and mutually hostile "Marxisms": the historical, "robustly materialistic" (in Sidney Hook's words), social-democratic Marxism which belongs to one current of Western thought and political experience, and thus to the common Western cultural heritage; the voluntaristic, militantly anti-Western—and in China even anti-Russian—"bolshevized" Marxism of present-day Communist parties; and the Utopian and anarchistic "neo-orthodox Marxism" (as Lewis Feuer calls it) which is politically a-Communist but which rejects Western civilizational roots. The essays of this book deal with the two latter aspects of Marxist ideology today.

If one passes from these general observations on Marxist poly-morphism to its threefold representations in the contemporary world, the picture becomes even more intricate and paradoxical. Discussing the appeals of Marxism in the Western world today, Professors Hook and Feuer agree that we are witnessing a relatively sudden and totally unpredictable schism in the interpretation of Marxism. It consists in the rejection, by the present generation of Western intellectuals who have plunged into the old master's texts, of the central themes which for decades were considered the alpha and omega of the doctrine, and which are now being superseded by the concept of alienation, sketched briefly by the young Marx and discarded and even mocked at by the maturing and older Marx himself. This "standing of the mature Marx on his head," as Professor Feuer writes, does not mean only a break with "scientific Socialism," and a return to the "millenary, eschatological traditions of primitive socialism" (Hook); it has other significant corollaries. It reflects a dominance of the critical mood among those Western intellectuals who, in their hostility to the established social order and in their predisposition to revolt against or at least reject it, find a much greater satisfaction in the psychological and unmeasurable concept of "alienation" than in the earlier, classical, and much more concrete economic notion of "exploitation." The alienationist trend in Western contemporary Marxism is not centered in the working class or accepted by it, but becomes the doctrine of the intellectuals of middle-class origin who have cut their intellectual and emotional umbilical cord with Western civilization, and are no less hostile to classical liberalism and the reformist social democracy, than to the traditional values of the West. In his analysis of the "generational revolt" of the students at the Berkeley campus against "The System," Professor Feuer notes that it had nothing to do with the older Marxist tradition of class struggle determined by the interplay of the economic forces in society (the students of today being the most affluent in history) but by qualitatively different impulses— "ethical and voluntaristic"—leading to "spontaneous, quickly mounted, guerrilla action against the System." Professor Hook reaches a similar conclusion in the section of his analysis devoted to the "plain Marxism" of the late Professor C. Wright Mills. The latter's claim to be working "in Marx's own tradition" is denied by Professor Hook; instead it is said to be based on a "pre-Marxist, simplistic moralism," whose political counterpart is, under the present circumstances, "an expression of solidarity for 'the new world' extending from China and Russia to Cuba."

This dualism of estrangement from one's own social and cultural milieu and abstract revolutionary solidarity with the Communist experiments of total social engineering, which possesses philosophical neo-Marxism in the West today, bears a direct relevance to the analysis in the essay of Professor Bauer of the appeals of Marxism on intellectuals in the underdeveloped countries. There again the methodology of the Marxist nineteenth-century "social physics" would have a rather demoralizing effect (Professor Bauer notes that Marx regarded the metropolitan countries as a progressive force in promoting modernization of the colonies), without the ideological and emotional reinterpretation of Marxism in its Leninist variant. A violently anti-Western Marxism-Leninism appears then, in these emerging and not yet diversified societies, at a time of erosion of local traditional values and beliefs, both as an "intellectual structure comprising method, analysis and empirical observation" and a "secular messianic faith or creed which promises salvation here but not now." Moreover, the fact that Marxism-Leninism serves as an official guide in the process of economic transformation of two politically successful empires—the Soviet Russian and the Communist Chinese—is bound to influence those in the underdeveloped countries who are more susceptible to being impressed by the effectiveness of political power than by ideological inconsistencies or economic failures. The guilt feeling of the West, exemplified in the already depicted "neo-orthodox Marxism" of Western intellectuals, enhances the ideological appeals of Marxism-Leninism to the intellectuals of the "third" world. Finally, the Communist concept of economic planning as a precondition for speedy economic growth, in contrast to the alleged inefficiency of capitalism as a model for economic development (Professor Wu scrutinizes in his essay the mystifying and the empirical aspects of both propositions) appeals also to many politicians and intellectuals, since it implies the concentration of power in their governmental hands, in lands in which the gap between the educated elites and the rest of the population is of staggering proportions.

Neo-Marxism in the West, and Marxism-Leninism in the underdeveloped countries thus play different roles. In the former case, neo-Marxism acts as a dissolvent of the existing order; in the latter case, Marxism-Leninism is at least a potential basis and justification for the establishment of varying degrees of despotic and totalitarian regimes. In the other parts of the world, there where the Communist parties are in power, Marxism-Leninism performs still another function, that of a state-building doctrine. The role of the ideology in the Soviet Union (and by inference in other Communist-ruled countries) is examined analytically and conceptually in different ways in the essays

written by Father Bochenski and Professor Bell. The distinguished
Catholic philosopher compares Marxism-Leninism to some of the great
religions like Buddhism, Christianity, or Islam during certain periods
of their histories. He insists with equal force on the adjustments and
even partial capitulations of the official doctrine to the necessities of
life (such as the flagrantly anti-Marxist recognition of the value of
patriotism and the stress laid on family life) and he believes that the
principal strength of Marxism-Leninism in the Soviet Union resides
in the fact that it is "the unifying ideology of a great and proud
nation." He recognizes, of course, the difficulties which a dogmatic
ideology encounters in the changing and diversifying realities of Soviet
life, but he urges the reader to ponder the possibility that just this
confrontation with reality may bring not the decay but the purification
and strengthening of Marxism-Leninism conceived as a moral and
metaphysical faith. Professor Bell's approach to the same problem is
quite different. As a sociologist he views the ideology of Marxism-
Leninism in the Soviet Union as a "social cement," a creed whose
function is both "to justify itself and to meet the challenges of (or to
challenge) other creeds." He considers, however, that a chain of international and domestic circumstances has already weakened doctrinal
unity and has put Marxism-Leninism increasingly on the defensive.
Here is a partial listing of these antidogmatic pressures: the role of
science as a powerful challenger of older orthodoxies; the incongruity
between doctrinal anticipations and the real life of society; the psychological reverberations, particularly among the intellectuals, of
Khrushchev's destalinization campaign; a virtual revolution in Soviet
economic theory and practice; the uneven development of Socialism
on an international scale, magnified by the split with the Chinese
Communists, etc. All these factors exercise an eroding influence on
two pillars of Marxist-Leninist ideology: the Soviet "historical mission"
to realize "communism," and the legitimacy of the "chosen instrument"
—the Party—to lead toward the realization of the historical mission.
Professor Bell considers that both of these ideological pillars have already lost their original rigidity and in this sense he applies to the
contemporary Soviet society his well-known concept of the "end of
ideology": "the abatement of the *dynamism* of a creed and the reduction of the role of ideology as a 'weapon' against external and internal
enemies."

There is, moreover, another aspect of ideological erosion which
manifests itself in different forms and with varying degrees of intensity in all Communist countries. It is the discovery on the part of

the younger Soviet intellectuals of the concept of alienation in the years after 1956. During his extensive academic stay in the Soviet Union in 1963, Professor Feuer found that concept to be "most provocative and illuminating to young Soviet philosophers"; it helped them "to articulate their own discontent with the Bureaucratic Society." [1]

All the preceding considerations—only remotely suggesting the scope and richness of the essays in the present volume—lead to a final and central question asked by Professor Haberler: "How a theory with such glaring defects could exert such a tremendous and persistent influence." He notes that Marx deliberately refrained from going into the economics of socialism, and that his was a theory of capitalist development. Thus, since Western capitalism evolved in a sense contrary to Marx's predictions, and Eastern socialism could hardly find in Marx's nineteenth-century writings the operative solutions for the qualitatively different problems of the twentieth century, Marxist "scientific" relevance is negligible, both East and West. We have thus to look elsewhere to find the answer to the question of the sources of the appeal of Marxism. They seem to be twofold. One is, especially in the non-Communist countries, that "Marxism" represents today the contemporary version of the old phenomenon of "revolutionary messianism." In the words of Norman Cohn (from his book *The Pursuit of the Millennium*), it is a revolutionary ideology and movement of a peculiar kind, in that its aims and promises are boundless. It is appealing because it is so utterly apart from the ordinary run of political parties; contrary to all of them, it endows "social conflicts and aspirations with a transcendental significance—in fact with all the mystery and majesty of the final, eschatological drama." But if this side of the Marxist message satisfies the perennial activist and quasi-religious craving for Utopia in many individuals, Marxism in this century has undergone another transformation, particularly in the Communist countries. There, according to Albert Camus, "the will to power came to take the place of the will to justice, pretending at first to be identified with it and then relegating it to a place somewhere at the end

---

[1] While the young Soviet philosophers approach the problem of critique of their own society with understandable restraint, their Yugoslav counterparts proceed with quite a remarkable directness. A group of "angry young professors" of philosophy at the University of Zagreb, who since September 1964 have been editing a review called *Praxis*, wage an open ideological battle against the Yugoslav Communist bureaucracy in the name of the writings of the young Marx. In the words of one of them, the faithfulness to the humanistic spirit of the early Marxian critique requires "a merciless criticism of everything that exists."

of history, waiting until such time as nothing remains on earth to dominate."

Yet if the attractiveness of Utopia and the fascination of Communist power explain to a large extent the appeals of Marxism in the contemporary world, they do not encompass another fundamental aspect of this protean phenomenon. For, if it is paradoxical that a doctrine claiming to be a science assumes in reality the role of a modern mythology, and that a promise of full human liberation transforms itself in practice into its opposite, Marxism performs today another historical function, no less paradoxical. It becomes in the West, in an unexpected form, an intellectual tool of total social critique and total rejection. No less significantly, however, it emerges as a potential dissolvent as well of the very regimes which speak (with discordant voices) in the name of Marxist orthodoxy. The essence of Marxist ideological ambiguity lies in the unpredictability of its historical uses.

Marxist Ideology
in the Contemporary World–
Its Appeals and Paradoxes

Sidney Hook

Marxism in the Western World:
From "Scientific Socialism" to Mythology

Since the death of Stalin, and particularly since Khrushchev's "revelations" at the Twentieth Congress of the Communist Party of the U.S.S.R., Soviet communism has suffered a political eclipse in cultural and left-wing circles in the West. Yet at no time in the intellectual history of the West have so many members of the intellectual classes evinced so strong an interest in the ideas of Marx or considered themselves "Marxists of a sort." The divisions in the Communist camp and the consequent rise of polycentrism, the removal of Stalin from the Communist pantheon, the new varieties of "revisionism," and the growing interest in the early writings of Marx have generated a climate of opinion in which it is no longer paradoxical to contrast Marxism with contemporary communism.

Even in the academies and universities of the West, in the field of scholarship and historical research, there has been a remarkable surge of interest in the ideas of Marx and Marxism. A generation or two ago, among the universities of England, France and the United States, with some noteworthy exceptions, Marxism, when not ignored, was treated as a movement of the intellectual underworld. Today the picture is impressively different. The course of study in the social sciences and the humanities almost everywhere takes note of ideas and approaches characterized as "Marxist," whatever the validity of the textual support offered in justification of the epithet. Almost every thinker of note feels called upon to define his position in relation to the claims of Marxism. In other words, Marxism has become part of the recognized cultural and historical tradition of the West, which is not surprising in view of the fact that so much has happened to the world in the name of Marxism.

By and large the recent treatment of Marx in the academy has been sympathetic, even if critical of his doctrines when literally construed.

The savage criticisms of Bertrand Russell, of Leopold Schwarzschild, of numerous Catholic writers like McGovern who lumped Marx with Lenin and Stalin as cats of a like breed are not much in evidence. There is still an occasional splenetic outburst from the ideologues of "pure" free enterprise. And even they sometimes accord him a respect they begrudge those who, they fancy, are his confused followers. Whether because it is now believed that there must be something to a view of the world and society and human salvation which has stirred more human beings to action, and even sacrifice, than has Christianity, whether because the bitterest enemies of Marx and Marxism have also been enemies of the liberal and democratic tradition, the most frequent contemporary judgment of Marxism has been "there is a considerable measure of truth in it." Hardly much more could be said of the central ideas of any great figure in the history of thought, and much less was said by Marx of some of his great contemporaries. After all, is there not "a considerable measure of truth" in an observation Bagehot somewhere makes that to illustrate or call attention to a principle "you must exaggerate much and omit much"?

Nonetheless some of the recent critical judgments on Marx by avowedly non-Marxists have been surprisingly mild and generous. Despite the ferocity of Marx's critique of all religion, even Christian philosophers of history like Toynbee, Tillich, Niebuhr, and Butterfield have paid him great homage—not merely because of the prophetic zeal and moral indignation in his writings but on the strength of his historical insight and doctrines. [Butterfield, for example, writes: "The Marxists have contributed more to the historical scholarship of all of us than the non-Marxists like to confess." [1] He regards Marx's historical materialism as a remarkable and permanent contribution to our understanding of history because "it hugs the ground so closely," although some might consider this as giving a narrow perspective for things shaping up on the horizon. And then it turns out that for Butterfield, Marx's materialism, considered merely as a *realistic* approach to the conditions under which and the motives out of which men act, is perfectly assimilable to the synoptic view of those who see the finger of God in history.]

Among the reasons for the comparatively sympathetic judgment of Marx's theory of history among non-Marxist historians, despite the fact that massive historical phenomena like Fascism and even Communism as social systems, are hard to account for in its terms, is Engels' restatement of it. By admitting a reciprocity among all social factors, which was part of his Hegelian heritage, and recognizing a plurality of causes, Engels shattered the imposing, yet simplistic, monism of some of Marx's earlier formulations of the doctrine. V. G. Simkhovitch, the Russian-American economic historian who fancied himself in one of his phases as the American Bernstein, used to complain that Engels' letters to Bloch, Mehring, Starkenberg, and others spoiled the game for the critics of Marxism by watering down Marx's original doctrine with common sense imbibed from the English scene. For in Engels' version the "primacy" of the economic factor, its determination in the last analysis of historical events and tendencies, is at best a statistical judgment, although in his programmatic zeal Engels himself did not see this. And since no one has actually worked out a theory of measurement assigning different weights to different factors in specific situations, and then assessed all the "relevant" specific situations which enter into the pattern of history, it became possible for avowed Marxists to defend the validity of Marx's theory "on the whole" and "in the last analysis" even if it failed to explain any particular set of events; and non-Marxists could acknowledge that as a heuristic method it was very useful. It opened up new fields of inquiry and sometimes led to valid conclusions. Instead of becoming *the* scientific method of history, the Marxist theory became an integral part of the scientific resources of inquiry into history, since every historian professing to write a credible account of a period had to seek, and consider if found, the existing economic class interests and their influence on events. But therewith Marxism as a philosophy of history and as the theory and practice of social revolution became irrelevant to the specific inquiries of the working historian. From a philosophy of history it became a method of *making* history, an ideology of a group or a political party speaking on its own authority in the name of a class, allegedly in behalf of all mankind.

We are dealing with a complex phenomenon which invites Engels' pluralistic approach. Among the main reasons, it seems to me, for the hazy and rather lazy affirmative judgments on Marx's theories in some quarters is the dual attraction for intellectuals of political power on the one hand and the humanistic values in the professed ideals of Marx on the other. To some the very existence of the Soviet Union and Communist China and their growing strength presages at least the permanence if not the ultimate victory of communism as a world social system. This is a powerful ground for reconciling themselves to the official theory or ideology—"to see something in it"—an attitude almost required by the imperative necessity of political coexistence. There is so to speak a social analogue to Newtonian "action at a distance" (a phrase Sartre uses to explain the attraction the proletariat has for intellectuals), action exerted by a new constellation of social forces which has achieved sufficient stability to make unlikely any basic change. The ideology of such a system is as much to be regarded and "respected," not believed of course, as the theology of an established church in a society of plural religious faiths. To others, more fine-grained, who are mindful of the living costs of established tyranny and remember past infamies, the humanistic ideals of Marx still have a strong appeal. The betrayal of these ideals is explained by the fact that the leaders in the Kremlin were Russian and those in Peking Chinese before either were Communist which, if true, constitutes another grave difficulty for Marxism.

It is curious to observe the rationalizations offered by those who, despite their professed belief that historical results are the test of historical ideals and movements, hold on to their doctrinal allegiances even when grim historical events have undermined their organizational loyalties. Some explain the total political and cultural terror of Stalinism, more pervasive in its cultural effects than even the profit motive in the West, as due to the cult of personality or Russian backwardness and the heritage of Czarism or other variations of the Russian soul, without realizing that such an explanation rejects Marx's principle of historical materialism in its canonic form. Others, on the contrary, insist that what happened in the Soviet Union *confirms* the validity of historical materialism because the economic unreadiness of Russia made a regime of terror a foregone conclusion as the only substitute for primitive accumulation under capitalism. This falsely assumes that there were no alternatives. And even if this were granted, it fails to explain why socialism in the Soviet Union was ever attempted if historical materialism doomed it in advance. What explains the failure does not explain the *attempt*. And without the attempt, what a different world it would be! And to span the gamut of absurdity, one should preserve for posterity the proud avowal of an unreconstructed English Marxist (Lindsey) who, although morally reprobating the epoch of Stalin, tells us that he "accepts it all" because, among other reasons, of the great liberations of the spirit which were then achieved—"the liberations that now make possible the ending of the Stalinist epoch." This is very much like praising Hitler because without him there would have been no heroism on the part of the Resistance.

Another source of the renewal and rediscovery of Marx is the natural intellectual evolution of those who develop new social views. I have observed this process for forty years. Members of the academy and university in democratic countries become critical of the social and economic order, or become aroused and frightened by certain events on the international scene. If the development of their views is towards socialism, they often tend to reinterpret Marx in such a way as to bring his thought in line with their antecedent intellectual and philosophical commitments. The oddest syntheses result. I have known professors and graduate students, suddenly stirred into a passion of social protest by some current evil, who have convinced themselves after shortly reading Marx that he was *au fond* a phenomenologist, an existentialist, a positivist, a Spinozist, a Kantian, a Freudian, a Bergsonian, an anticipator of Samuel Alexander (all they had in common were their ethnic origin and beard!)—and, of course, an Hegelian. Some Catholic writers rather cautiously suggest that, despite Marx's atheism, Aristotle and Aquinas would not have disowned him. Some Protestants, and not merely pro-Soviet figures like Karl Barth and Niemöller, declare that Marx is essentially a more religious man than many of his religious critics. Such reinterpretations are familiar in the history of thought and subjectively completely sincere. For all that, they sometimes are patently ridiculous, e.g., the attempts of some English scientists converted to communism in the heyday of Stalin to read the theory of relativity and other discoveries of modern physics out of Marx and Engels' unpublished manuscripts.[2] But they create familiar difficulties of exposition and criticism exacerbated in this case by the passion with which almost every distinguished convert to socialism and peace creates his own Marx.

The psychological compulsion to avow one's Marxism may have been intensified by the intellectual *auto-da-fé* conducted against the few individuals who were willing to support the Socialist, sometimes even the Communist, program of social change but insisted on jettisoning the useless ballast of Marxism in order to make faster progress. They were regarded no matter what their subjective intentions as "objectively" agents of the existing Establishment whose role was to throw the working class off its revolutionary course. And, indeed, the term "socialism" had become so degraded by irresponsible use that it was possible for some totalitarians to declare that Marxism must die in order that socialism live.

I

That attitudes towards Marxist doctrines are often inspired by considerations which have little to do with the truth or falsity of the doctrines is perhaps best illustrated not so much by non-Marxists, sympathetic in their evaluation of Marx as a fighter for freedom and social progress, but by some writers, truculent if not influential, who proudly avow themselves to be Marxists. In the United States perhaps the best known among them is C. Wright Mills. In a comprehensive volume on *The Marxists*[3] which consists of readings in, and commentary upon, the chief figures in the Marxist tradition, Mills is caustic and scornful of liberalism and social-democracy. He distinguishes three types of Marxists—the vulgar, the sophisticated, and just "plain."[4] Vulgar Marxists "seize upon certain ideological features of Marx's political philosophy and identify these parts with the whole." Sophisticated Marxists "refine and qualify the doctrines to a point where they cannot be confirmed or disconfirmed." Plain Marxists "work in Marx's own tradition." The exemplars of the first two schools are not named but Mills identifies *himself* as a plain Marxist. He enumerates among the fellow members of this class Gramsci, Rosa Luxemburg, Lukacs, Strachey, Sartre, and Deutscher.

The family of Marxist doctrines, whether vulgar, sophisticated, or just plain, are related by their derivation from classic Marxism. Mills proceeds to list the seventeen "most important conceptions and propositions of classic Marxism"—all of them buttressed by quotations from Marx on whom he lavishes extravagant praise for the remarkable coherence of his thought. But then in an extraordinary critical assessment of these seventeen important conceptions and propositions, all of them, with one single exception, are declared "false" or "unclear" or "unprecise" or "misleading" or "unfruitful" or "careless" or "confused" or "quite clearly wrong." The single proposition (No. 11) which is regarded as true is dismissed as a truism. It states: *"The opportunity for revolution exists only when objective conditions and subjective readiness coincide."*[5] And with respect to this truism, Mills cannot forbear pointing out that objective conditions and subjective readiness have never coincided in any advanced capitalist society, even during the depths of the world's worst depression. The cumulative effect of Mills's criticisms, largely culled without acknowledgment from criticisms made long before him, is so devastating that were it not for his tone of moral earnestness one would suspect that in calling himself "a plain Marxist" he was perpetrating an intellectual spoof.

There is hardly a single notion of Marx which is not severely questioned by Mills—his theory of class, class interest, historical causation, state, political power, economic development, even the newly refurbished notion of alienation. Mills strains wherever he can to give Marx credit by employing emotively overcharged terms, but the reader sees easily through the stratagem. Thus, concerning Marx's theory of alienation, he says: "At any rate, to say the least [in criticism] the condition in which Marx left the conception of alienation is quite incomplete, and brilliantly [*sic!*] ambiguous." [6] Similarly, of the Marxist model of history he says it is "brilliantly constructed," but valid only "for one phase of one society"—in other words it is either no model at all or inadequate to all history which is past or future to Marx's present. What Mills actually writes about Marx's treatment of the theme of alienation leaves the reader with a much stronger impression of Marx's ambiguity and inadequacy than of his brilliance.

As if this wholesale repudiation of Marx's theories, doctrines, and hypotheses were not enough, Mills goes on to reject Marx's *model* of society and history. And this after telling us that "what is great and alive" about Marx is his model. Mills indicts Marx strongly for his "metaphysics of labor" and for violating the principle of historical specificity, the tying down of social abstractions to a specific historical period, which was supposed to be central to Marx's method. Indeed, despite his hearty back-slapping of Marx, Mills offers nothing to support his judgment of him as a great thinker. Expletives aside, Mills's criticisms could be used by schools devoted to the propagation of *anti*-Marxism. If this is what a plain Marxist makes of Marx—one truism out of seventeen important propositions!—what can someone who is not a Marxist of any variety make of him? It is as if Mills were calling himself a Marxist in order to shock or embarrass his colleagues—which was needless, since most of them, I daresay, give Marx a higher batting average with respect to his important propositions and predictions than does Mills.

After all this, Mills tells his readers that although all of Marx's work is false, inadequate or misleading (except for a single truism) Marx's *method* "is a signal and lasting contribution to the best sociological way of reflection and inquiry available." [7] Apparently Mills does not judge a method by its fruits! He is fearfully vague, however, about what distinguishes Marx's method. It is *not* the dialectical method about which he has harsh words. Nor is it the so-called principle of historical specificity, first mentioned by Karl Korsch. [8] The principle of historical specificity is not so much a method as an approach which delimits the scope and context of an inquiry into a social phenomenon. Since whatever exists is individual, this approach notes carefully the historical situation in which it is found and is cautious about extending any conclusions reached to apparently similar phenomena in other historical eras. Thus, if we are investigating the political and economic life of our

times, we may reach certain generalizations or "laws" about the
character of class-struggles or the development of the economy. Unless
we make explicit that we are restricting ourselves to capitalist society,
we may go astray by extrapolating our findings to other societies.
What holds for economic behavior in one type of society or in one
historical epoch may not hold for other epochs. So when we discourse
about man in economics and psychology, and then talk about man *qua*
man, we may be unconsciously identifying man with bourgeois man.
To assume that all human beings would behave like Robinson Crusoe
is to assume that the eighteenth-century Englishman is the eternal
type of man.

It is obvious, however, that this is not a method of inquiry but a
restriction of subject matter plus a commonplace caution. It is perfectly
legitimate to inquire into the social laws or the development of all
societies. It all depends upon our problem and our intellectual concerns. We may be interested in the analysis of value in a commodity-
producing society. We may also be interested in the analysis of value
in all societies in which there are scarce resources. Just as there are
certain biological laws and principles of organization that hold for all
animals, including *human* animals, so there *may* be certain social
laws and principles that obtain in all societies. Some Marxists may not
be interested in such inquiries but they are as legitimate as other
inquiries with a more restricted time span. Further, it can easily be
shown that without the use of general concepts or categories which
apply to more than the specific subject matter or historical event under
analysis, no warranted conclusion of any kind could be reached. A
"law" that applies to an individual presupposes the possible existence
of *other* individuals of the same type or class, indifferent to the space-
time differentia of the individual case from which we take our point
of departure.

The cream of the jest, however, is that Marx himself clearly does
not accept the principle of historical specificity in formulating some
of his propositions. He tells us in the *Communist Manifesto* that "All
history is the history of class struggles." And in the preface to *A Contribution to the Critique of Political Economy,* he states conclusions
which presumably hold for *all* class societies—capitalist, feudal, slave,
Asiatic.

It remains, therefore, mystifying on theoretical grounds why Mills
insisted upon his "Marxism," whatever the biographical explanation
may be. For essentially his affirmation of Marxism is a programmatic
declaration of allegiance, an expression of solidarity for "the new

world" extending from China and Russia to Cuba. Mills's rejection of
the world of liberalism in all its variants is clear and sharp. But his
socialism he defines negatively by what it is *not*—it is not Leninism,
not Stalinism, not Maoism, not Castroism, although it is unmistakably
of the same family. Himself an individualist with a keen if monochro-
matic vision for power conflicts and aware that they cannot all be
reduced to economic class conflicts, he expresses much more hostility
to classical liberalism and its ideals of individual freedom (which as
far as the United States goes he dismisses merely as "empty rhetoric"),
as well as to social-democratic variants and extensions of the ideals of
freedom, than to the ideals of classical Marxism. Stalin is treated as
the convenient scapegoat to explain the degradation of man and culture
in the Soviet Union. Although he formally leaves open the question
whether Soviet Communism will ultimately realize the humanist and
democratic heritage of Marx, Mills leaves the reader with little doubt
that he both hopes and believes that it will. Nonetheless the mass of
evidence against Marxist theories and predictions is so strong that
Mills cannot summon up the will to believe them. His socialism has
nothing to do with what Marx and Engels called "scientific socialism."
It is based on a pre-Marxist, simplistic moralism, a commendable
opposition to poverty and exploitation which, as far as his own analysis
of moral questions go, unfortunately sparse and shallow, possesses the
same validity as if Marx had never written a line. The very grounds
on which Mills rejects liberalism as both an ideology and as rhetoric
indicates how far he is from the historical Marx. First, liberalism "has
become practical, flexible, realistic, pragmatic...and not at all
Utopian." [9] And second, as a consequence it has "become irrelevant
to political positions having moral contents." This moral standpoint,
proudly impractical, inflexible, unrealistic and unpragmatic, has less in
common with Marx than with the millenary, eschatological traditions
of primitive socialism.

II

The case of C. Wright Mills is an extreme illustration of a fetishistic
response to Marxist terms and symbols but in lesser degree the same
phenomenon can be observed among other self-characterized Marxists.
Some are "revolutionists" without a doctrine or cause except the gospel
that the status-quo, politically, economically and culturally, high, low
and middle brow, is in an advanced state of putrescence. Particularly
loathsome to them are the programs and movements of social reform.
In England, which has always been less doctrinaire in its socialism

than the Continent or even the United States, and because of the
Fabians, who have always been indifferent, if not hostile, to Marxism,
the opposition to the *status quo* has not unfurled ideological banners.
The "new left," or what remains of it, is violently opposed to specific
measures like nuclear armament and to attempts to moderate the
scope of the socialization plank in the program of the Labour Party
or to the perversion of culture by the commercial values of capitalism.
But it has left strictly alone the corpus of Marx's work. With the exception of the youthful *Economic-Philosophical Manuscripts,* and its key
passages on alienation, it has made no attempt to defend or refurbish
Marx's historical analyses and predictions. On emotional grounds, it
is much more doctrinaire in its judgments on foreign policy. Despite
the repression of the Hungarian freedom-fighters and Khrushchev's
revelations about the Stalin regime which Kingsley Martin and others
of his kind had staunchly defended, judging by its literature much of
the non-Communist left in England feels much more sympathetic to
"fellow socialists" in the Kremlin and even in Peking than to anti-
Communist "fellow workers" in the American labor movement.

A singularly eloquent example of a non-Communist Socialist who
to the end of his life pleaded for a united front between Socialists
and Communists against the United States is G. D. H. Cole. He
admits without blinking the "innumerable purges and liquidations,"
"the imprisonment and maltreatment of millions of citizens in 'slave
labor camps,'" the extirpation of intellectual, cultural and political
freedom, and the other charges in the formidable indictment democratic socialists have levelled against Communism; he admits the
betrayal of the Hungarian Revolution and the barbarous excesses
against the Hungarian workers; but he remains adamant in his conviction that Communism is a progressive phenomenon on a world
scale and must be supported by socialists who remain critical of
Communist manners. The explanation of G. D. H. Cole's position, as
well as of his judgment that despite their terror and suffering, "the
Russian and Chinese revolutions are the greatest achievements of the
modern world," is to be found in his fetishism of "the mode of
production." [10]

Perhaps the most celebrated recent case of avowed conversion to
Marxism is that of Jean-Paul Sartre. In his previous writings, despite
his career as a political fellow-traveller of Communism, Sartre made no
attempt to link his existentialist philosophy to the doctrine of Marxism.
If anything he was more hostile to Marxian materialism or naturalism,
because of its slighting of the principle of subjectivity, than to traditional idealism of which this principle was an offshoot.

Despite his words to the contrary, Sartre in a sense has remained a consistent existentialist, consistent in his inconsistency. After Khrushchev had revealed the horrors of Stalin's terrorist regime which Sartre had so ardently defended against its critics, some Frenchmen thought Sartre, as an appropriate act of existential atonement, would hang himself. Instead he wrote his gigantic *Critique de la raison dialectique.*[11] In it he not only avows himself a Marxist, implying that he is the only genuine one in the world, but declares that Marxism "is the philosophy of our epoch," the only one which grasps history as "the concrete synthesis of a moving, dialectical totality." Rejecting the official Communist interpretation of Marxism is an aberration due to Stalinist perversions—concerning most of which he had remained silent or supported until Stalin's dethronement—he nonetheless agrees with Garaudy, the French Stalinist hack whom he otherwise cites as a typical offender against the true spirit of Marxism, about the scope of Marxism. "Marxism constitutes today the only system of coordinates which permits the placing and defining of thought in any domain whatsoever, from political economy to physics [*sic!*], from history to morality." [12] And as if to leave no doubt about his orthodoxy, he quotes Engels with approval that it is the mode of economic production which "in the last analysis" (as if there were any such!) determines *every* aspect of culture, the omnipresent red thread that is the clue to the pattern which runs through and unites the details. The matter, insists Sartre, is far more complex than either Garaudy or Engels suspects but for all the complexity, the monistic emphasis is predominant. Dualism is socially reactionary and pluralism reformist.

What Sartre wishes to do is to make the existentialist approach ancillary to Marxism, to emancipate the latter from mechanistic reductions of cultural phenomena to economic equations of the first degree, to abolish its terrorism of dogma which refuses to differentiate between the events and characters it lumps together too easily under the rubric of Marxist explanation. "Existentialism desires to restore the specificity of the *historical* event; it seeks to restore its function and multiple dimensions." [13] Sartre sees correctly that in the Stalinist world the event has become "an edifying myth." But in his own reconstruction of Marxism, the event can never refute or disconfirm the Marxist position for the latter is defended not as an empirical hypothesis but as an *a priori universal method* of showing how the totality of social life is organized and expressed in every particular event, in every particular individual.[14] His criticisms of the schematic interpretations of cultural and political phenomena by the Communists are trenchant and justified, but what he substitutes for it is an Hegelianized version of Marxism in which a mythical, idealized working-class takes the place of the Spirit, and in which the activity of the working class, whose mission is to make the world more reasonable and men more human and free, is focused in the idealized political "group" which for Sartre, despite the weakness of the vessel, is still the Communist Party.

What Sartre is really doing in his *Critique de la raison dialectique* is disguised in terms of technical philosophical doctrine. He rejects the whole notion of abstract truth and the theory of abstract universals as necessarily unjust to the particular and the singular and what he calls "the profundity of the lived." For example, if the theory of historical materialism tries to explain the work and achievement of Flaubert and Baudelaire in terms of economic conditions or class or any other Marxist category, in the nature of the case the differences between them cannot be accounted for by common causal conditions. This ignores the whole project of creation which eventuates in entirely different works. Sainte-Beuve had already made the same kind of objection to Taine and other monistic philosophies of history and civilization without denying the limited usefulness of their approach.[15] Sartre's criticisms are certainly valid with respect to much of the reductionist interpretations of vulgar Marxism. The relative autonomy, the activity and transformative effects of human knowledge had been stressed long before him by the American pragmatists, especially John Dewey, without mythology. It is not necessary, of course, to reject the notion of an abstract universal if it is recognized that an individual may be determined—*not* created, *not* exhausted—by a plural number of relatively independent factors or conditions of unequal weight. These factors or conditions do not lie inertly side by side but operate in interacting historical clusters. No matter how detailed an account be of a life circumscribed by circumstance and social space, it cannot in the same terms do justice to the chemistry and biology of talent and genius whose vision expresses the "magic" of personality. But this pluralistic approach is emphatically condemned by Sartre because it prevents us from understanding a thing, an event, a human being in its "dialectical totality." True comprehension of anything, especially of the human and historical, Sartre insists, can be reached only by seeing it as an aspect or part of a concrete universal. What is true of the part is true of the concrete universal of which it is a part; it, too, is a moment or aspect of another concrete universal of greater comprehensiveness until we reach the one great social and cultural process, the dialectical totality, which constitutes the history of our time.

Sartre's procedure, its difference from traditional Marxism and its own weakness, may be illustrated with his own illustration in the first part of his *Critique de la raison dialectique* (p. 58) devoted to a consideration of his method. Engels had been guilty of the absurdity of assuming that if Napoleon or any other great historical figure had not lived, someone else would have done Napoleon's work. This is intelligible only if we deny genuine greatness to individuals, i.e., claim that anyone could have done the hero's work, or fall back upon a mystical dialectic of nature to establish a bond between human genes, the cosmos, and the social-historical process. If the human need is strong enough, apparently a mutation in the germ-plasm sparks into life to accommodate it.

Sartre does not reject this Marxist ploy but dismisses it as a commonplace that does not go far enough. It is irrelevant to establish that lacking Napoleon someone else would have had to appear to liquidate and at the same time consolidate the Revolution by a military dictatorship. He demands that the necessity of *this* Napoleon, the one and only, who actually appeared, be explained, and the necessity of *this* bourgeoisie, *this* revolution, this train of events to which he responded as he did be explained in the same way. In fact, he demands that the web of necessity be woven around every event which has historical significance.

Sartre's pattern of "concrete totalization," despite his denial, is nothing but the Hegelian *Begriff* for which the contingent, the pluralistic, the chance event reflects only our ignorance. The untenability of Sartre's view becomes evident when we ask whether *this* Columbus was necessary for the discovery of America in *this* historical era? To which the answer obviously is "no" since America was, and would have been, discovered by others. Of course, Napoleon made things happen as they did, but had he been killed by a shell which killed other artillerymen, who would have made or sent another Napoleon—the world spirit or the dialectic in nature? Or do they guarantee that nothing will befall Napoleon until his task is finished? Had Napoleon been killed, Sartre would have demanded that the necessity of *this* death at *this* time be shown.

Engels had the merit of trying to explain historical events by tendencies and laws which remove some of the apparent contingencies in history. Sartre really wants to relive them. Substituting his own sense of dramatic compulsion, he wants to picture events as if they had the same kind of necessity as the events of a story. In most historical situations, the critical mind can discern several alternatives of varying degrees of probability. Rarely can one say that what took place was necessary no matter what had been done to forestall it or bring it about. In the past Sartre would have had us believe that almost anything could have happened in history. Now he seems committed to the belief that almost everything in history *had* to happen as it did.

Sartre starts from the concrete, specific, existential fact, impressionistically perceived yet ofttimes with considerable insight. But by the time he incorporates it into the totality of social and historical relations whose development is history, despite Sartre the individuality of the event or person is lost. It is a highly moot question whether social or historical knowledge can be achieved in this fashion; but what is obvious is that this approach makes explanation tantamount to justification. The given, as well as the result of its development, in the end turn out to be dialectically necessary. They could not be other than what they are. Freedom is no longer to be found in an act of choice between genuine possibilities. It is found in the action or practice by which history itself, so to speak, takes note of, or is conscious of, itself. It is only in the practice of Marxism that freedom can be found. History is not the self-activity of the Hegelian Spirit which develops by inner fission and opposition; nor is it the interplay of interests, ideas, and personality as the pluralistic critics of Hegel contend; it is the *practice* of human beings, expressed in their daily work, a work that until now had led to self-estrangement and alienation instead of self-fulfillment. The liberating force in history for Sartre is the proletariat to which he was originally drawn, he confesses, not by reading Marx but by its very existence, its struggles, its incarnation of Marxist practice.

What is truly amazing in Sartre's book is what he reads into Marx's conception of *praxis* and class. The "group" is made central to the understanding of society and the making of history, the individual is dissolved into the "group" (actually hypostatized into the ideal Party) which speaks in the name of the proletariat, whom it educates and defends by Terror. Sartre admits that the "dictatorship of the proletariat" is a myth, that it never existed in the Soviet Union or elsewhere, and that by its very nature no group like the proletariat, since it is not a hyperorganism, can exercise a dictatorship. (This would make nonsense of the phrase "dictatorship of the bourgeoisie" too.) He frankly admits that the government of the Soviet Union from the very outset was a dictatorship of the Communist Party. He spares us the verbal legerdemain by which Bolshevik-Leninists tried to explain this away. Terror is exalted as the necessary instrument by which men are made whole and human again after being dehumanized by the processes of "alienation" and "serialization." It is *not* attributed to backward political and cultural traditions. "Historic experience of the countries in which Communists took power has revealed undeniably that the first stage of socialist society in construction—to consider it from the still abstract view of power—cannot be anything else than the indissoluble aggregation of bureaucracy, the Terror, and the cult of personality." [16] The entire work has been aptly dubbed by one critic as "The Metaphysic of Stalinism." [17]

Sartre is not alone in regarding the theme of alienation as central to Marxism and interpreting Marxist doctrines as principles directed to exposing and overcoming alienation. He remains unique in the Stalinist grotesquerie to which he has carried his interpretation. But what has impressed him has also impressed one of his philosophical masters. Just as Sartre regards Marxism as "the philosophy of our epoch," as the best means of overcoming alienation, so Martin Heidegger regards "the Marxist view of history as superior to all other views" [18] because of Marx's prescience in discerning the facts of alienation in the experience of modern man. What for Marx was a youthful insight, derived from and shared with others, and subsequently fleshed out into a sociological criticism of contemporary culture, is transformed by Heidegger into a metaphysics of homelessness beyond all social remedies in some respects profounder than that of Husserl and Sartre. [19]

A Marxist thinker influenced both by Husserl and Sartre and who developed from writing sophisticated apologies of Stalinism to fresh criticisms of the mystical abstractions of Marxism is Maurice Merleau-Ponty. In his *Humanisme et Terreur,* although he is careful not to profess an orthodox Marxism, he regards the cruel and barbarous Moscow Trials as *objectively,* i.e., historically and politically, justified even though subjectively, i.e., in the light of the juridical evidence, the accused were not guilty as charged. According to this view, it is only dotting the i's, after Bukharin's political line turned out to be mistaken, to tax him with murder and arson, for the "politician defines himself not by what he himself does but by the forces on which he relies," [20] in this case allegedly the internal and foreign enemies of the regime. Even if by definition, one postulates that differences with the Communist Party constitute an error, the assumption that errors are to be judged as political crimes logically entails the view that sooner or later, since all men are fallible, *all* may be charged with crimes or that one individual, the Leader, is politically infallible.

This smacks of the political logic of totalitarianism, but Merleau-Ponty denies it on the ground that such a judgment overlooks the fact that Marxism based itself on "the theory of proletariat"—*not* on the theory of the citizen—as a universal class, the carrier of all human value. "The power of the proletariat is the power of humanity" and any action which contributes to its victory is valid or politically true. It is false that Communists do not believe in objective truth. It is only necessary to understand that in a class society the truth in political affairs must be a class truth, and a party truth. "It is not chance," he writes, "nor I suppose a romantic prejudice that the chief newspaper of the U.S.S.R. carries the name *Pravda*." [21]

Nor is it chance that in his conclusions Merleau-Ponty calls upon intellectuals "to recall Marxists to their humanist inspiration and the democracies to their fundamental hypocrisy." He asserts that anti-Communism, indeed *any* criticism of the Soviet Union which does not relate the relevant facts to the whole complex of difficulties which the Soviet Union faces, "should be considered an act of war."

A few years later, in consequence of the Korean War and the train of events it set up, and in specific criticism of Sartre's articles on "The Communists and the War" in which Sartre identifies the cause of the French working class with the Communist Party, with the Soviet Union and its strategy of peace, Merleau-Ponty refused to sign the blank check of faith in the Communist Party implied by Sartre's position. He not only renounces Sartre's "ultra-Bolshevism" as a repudiation of the Marxist dialectic and a substitution for it of a "philosophy of absolute creation in the unknown," he reluctantly admits that neither contemporary capitalism, nor contemporary socialism can be understood in terms of traditional Marxism. In the epilogue to his *Les Aventures de la dialectique,* Merleau-Ponty denies that he has betrayed the revolution, denies that he is an apologist for the *status quo,* and appeals vaguely for a new criticism and a program of new action. He remains despite himself very much of a Marxist in his thinking, really helpless before the historical reality which his Marxism did not enable him to anticipate, finally repelled by the practices of the "Marxist" Communist State, and bewildered by the transmutation of doctrinal Marxism at the hands of intellectuals who still believe that the proletariat and the party of the proletariat, although they may be mistaken, can do no wrong.

III

With the publication of the early *Economic-Philosophical Manuscripts* a new Marx has burst upon the world. The most fantastic interpretations have been placed on these groping efforts of Marx towards intellectual maturity. An extensive literature has already developed which on the strength of these writings subordinates all of Marx's published work to Marx's *Ur-philosophie* of alienation. It is widely asserted both that the meaning of Marx's philosophy has remained unchanged from the early to the later years, and that the real key to its meaning can be found only in the early manuscripts. Thus Father Calvez in his massive volume on the thought of Marx presents the Marxist philosophy as "a complete *system* of man, nature and history." [22] This is already questionable. He then goes on to devote by far the major part of his exposition to the doctrine of alienation in its various forms. Erich Fromm boldly claims that "it is impossible to understand Marx's concept of socialism and his criticism of capitalism as developed except on the basis of his concept of man which he developed in his early writings." [23] This might suggest to some unwary readers that no one understood Marx until his early manuscripts were published in 1932.

To the unsectarian mind, to the student of the intellectual history of ideas without *parti pris,* the difference in interest and emphasis between the old and the new Marx is tremendous. The old Marx is interested in the mechanics or organics of capitalism as an economic system, in politics as the theatre of clashing economic interests, and in the theory and practice of revolution. He is so impatient of the rhetoric of piety and morality that he sometimes gives the impression of a thinker who had no moral theory whatsoever, and whose doctrines logically do not allow for considered moral judgment. The new Marx, barely out of his intellectual swaddling clothes, sounds like *nothing but* a moralist, with a religious dedication to the conception of man in a cooperative society which could easily be rephrased in the ethical idioms of Christ, Spinoza, Kant, and Hegel. The traditional view that Marx, the "scientific" socialist, did not have, nor was entitled to have, a moral position is untenable, and not only because of the passion for justice which pervades his writings. But this certainly does not justify the view that all Marx really had was a morality. Nor does the fact that the new interpretation of Marx as a moralist provides a wonderful weapon against Bolshevik Leninism and all its varieties of terror, and at the same time makes it possible to preserve an intransigent opposition to the evils of capitalism, have any relevant bearing upon its validity. What is "useful" in a political or personal context has nothing to do with the criteria of practice or experimental consequences in a knowledge-getting context. Myths and lies may sometimes be useful too. And there is sufficient humanist fire, including the rhetoric of freedom, democracy, and independence, in the *published* writings of the mature

Marx to achieve the same effect. No minority-party dictatorship which
tries to conceal its dictatorship by sleazy talk about "leadership" of the
masses can find the slightest support in the published writings of Marx.
The degradation of man, so apparent in the theory and especially the
practice of Bolshevik-Leninism, runs counter to both the spirit and
letter not only of Marx's social philosophy but of his theory of social
revolution.

How shall we go about determining without question—begging the
truth in this matter? Here is not the place to lay down the objective
methodological criteria for deciding how to establish the basic meaning
of a corpus of writings. Suffice it to say that—in the face of Marx's
explicit repudiation in the *Communist Manifesto* of the verbose
lamentations about "the alienation of man" as "philosophical nonsense," his mordant, indeed needlessly cruel and somewhat unjust,
criticism of the *Liebesdusilei* of the "true socialists" in his other
writings as sentimental vaporings, and his subsequent concentration
on historical and economic analysis—it requires some impressive evidence to reverse the traditional interpretations of his thought. For all
their variations, these interpretations exclude the notion of Marx as
an anguished precursor of existentialism. Certainly it is not sufficient
to claim that "Marxism is anything which can be found in Marx's own
writings" because these writings contain incompatible things. Even
the exegetes of the new Marx must admit that there are some things
which those writings contain which are not Marxist.[24]

To be sure any change in doctrine is an event in a thinker's biography. Even a sudden and violent conversion from one position to
another in any field may disclose elements of psychological continuity.
But psychological continuity is not logical continuity. We may recognize Saul in Paul but it would be absurd to argue that Saul was a
believer in Pauline Christianity. This confusion is illustrated in the
position of Adam Schaff who as *Vertrauensman* between the Political
Committee of the Polish Communist Party and the Polish intellectuals
wants to make the best of both worlds. He asserts that even when a
philosopher abandons idealism for materialism, there must be continuity between the two phases of the process. To deny this, he con-
tends, "is impossible if only for psychological reasons; we still have
to do with one man working on his system, and the transitions from
one stage to another are determined by something and must in some
way be interrelated within a certain whole." [25] This is a ponderous
truism reinforced by a dogmatic apriorism—both irrelevant to what
must be concretely established in any specific case. Obviously a convert

from Christian Science to Catholicism or vice versa is the same man, but this is utterly irrelevant when we seek to ascertain whether, and when, he believes one set of dogmas rather than another. And although anything a man believes is determined, the specific causes of his belief may not be psychological determinants which explain *how* he holds his beliefs but rather the grounds or reasons on which the belief rests.

IV

Let us look a little more closely at the doctrine of alienation which is central to the new conception of Marx. It is perhaps unfair to examine carefully a youthful manuscript which Marx left to "the gnawing criticism of mice." But for its resuscitation by latter-day Marxists its chief interest would be biographical. It breathes a brave and generous spirit and is marked by the same kind of passionate moral indignation against the conditions and nature of labor under early capitalism manifested by Engels in his account of the life of the English working classes after the introduction of the factory system. It is full of interesting insights and striking phrases, shows that Marx had been reading widely in political economy, and that under the influence of Moses Hess looked to communism as an ideal society in which man would be liberated from all his oppressive restrictions. But in the light of Marx's own development, candor requires one to point out that philosophically his whole treatment is incoherent, incompatible with the principles of his own subsequently formulated historical materialism, that the truths it expresses were unoriginal and wildly exaggerated, and that it teems with ambiguities, puns, tautologies and non sequiturs. Parts of it read as if a poet were reacting against the abstractions of political economy. William Blake and William Morris are far more interesting.

Historically the doctrine of alienation is derived from religious and idealistic traditions and in most of its expressions presupposes an abstract, unhistorical notion of natural man. Its very language indicates its origins. In the strictly religious tradition all separation is evil, a consequence of man's disobedience to God. In the idealistic tradition from the time of Plotinus on, otherness and multiplicity result from a mysterious but necessary diremption in the bowels of the One. The alienation of man or the soul lies in its descent into the realm of matter, work, and pain. The life of man or the soul is the career of a fallen spirit whose alienation from its initial bliss is overcome by a pilgrimage in which it returns to God or the One. In Hegel the theological doctrine is deepened and at the same time transformed. Alienation loses its previous connotations of strangeness, lack or deficiency. It is integral to the process of growth, of necessary development in nature, society, self and even the advance of knowledge. The Absolute (God or the One) realizes its potentiality in a continuously enriched differentiation. The world and man, human society and history, appear progressively more reasonable despite, or rather because of, the manifestations of conflict and evil. If anything, it is the unalienated man in the Hegelian view who lacks true virtue and being, for he is someone who has remained petrified in a particular state, without conflict and therefore without the prospects of development. Virtue must overcome vice or temptation to escape from the innocence of arrested development.

In Feuerbach the Hegelian "alienation of the Idea" is demythologized. It becomes the alienation of man, alienated because man has not properly understood his own nature, its needs, wants, disguises and illusions. In religion man worships as transcendental the projections of his own needs. Philosophical anthropology therefore is the secret of theology in all its variations. Inspired by Feuerbach, the Young-Hegelians declared the disregard of man's true nature to be the secret of all human institutions. They embarked upon a program to liberate men from the fetishism of their own abstractions in morals, politics and economics. Alienation became not a metaphysical or theological phenomenon but an intellectual, psychological and ultimately social one. Liberation from the abstractions which obsess the human mind, which result in institutions that seem to have a life of their own and which exact human sacrifice, can be won by exposing the way in which abstractions arise and actually function in social life.

The influence of the Hegelian, Feuerbachian and Young-Hegelian concepts of alienation is apparent on almost every page of the *Economic-Philosophical Manuscripts*.[26] It professes to be a continuation of the Feuerbachian and Young-Hegelian mode of analysis applied to political economy whose precursors have been Weitling, Hess, and Engels. Political economy is viewed as the study of the forms of human alienation which underlie all economic categories. Special emphasis is given to labor and the human laborer as expressions of alienation. But in discussing these latter, Marx confuses different kinds of "alienation." He uses the same term to cover the relatively innocent and inescapable fact that men must work in situations of scarcity with the deplorable exploitation which occurs in factory labor unprotected by welfare laws. The emotive overtones associated with exploitation are carried over to activities in which there is no human exploitation whatsoever. The consequence is that what is distinctive about the alienation of labor under capitalism, or a phase of capitalism, gets lost in a melange of widely different conceptions.

The main thing Marx is trying to say in these manuscripts, it seems to me, may be made clear by asking: Whom, and under what conditions, would he regard as the unalienated man, the man truly himself? The closest we can come to answer is: The man who finds personal fulfillment in uncoerced, creative work. He is the person who under an inner not outer compulsion is doing some significant work. He is the creative artist or the dedicated professional man who in pursuit of some vision or task has found a center around which to organize his experiences, a center which gives a rationally approved and satisfying meaning to his life. As an ideal by which to criticize and modify our social institutions in order to make it possible generally for human beings to find significance in their practical life, a great deal can be said for this notion. As an expectation that the labor of an entire society can acquire this character, even if science succeeds in banishing *material* scarcities, it is as Utopian as any of the ideals of the great Utopian forerunners of Marx and Engels.

That this is what Marx intended may be gathered from what he says about the "alienation of labor" which suggests labor under the factory system. "Work is *external* to the worker, that is to say it is not part of his nature, that he therefore does not fulfill [*bejaht*] himself in his work. His work is not voluntary but coerced, *forced labor* [*Zwangsarbeit*]." [27] This is the alienation which produces the familiar dualism between earning one's living and living one's life. But there are other kinds of alienation distinguished by Marx. Alienation is found in the fact that the objects produced by the worker are not his, he has nothing to say about how they are used, distributed or consumed. They have a life of their own, independent and opposed to his own, a hostile and alien force.[28] Here we begin to tread on dubious ground. Whether anyone except an independent producer can control the use or disposition of his product in *any* society is questionable. And even in capitalist society a man who builds bridges, roads and tunnels, even if he does it merely to earn a living, cannot reasonably regard them as independent powers which threaten him. But there is a third sense of alienation, even more questionable. This is expressed in the phenomenon of "objectification" (*Vergegenständlichung*). By becoming dependent upon physical nature and upon the gratification of his own physical wants in production, man reduces himself to the level of an object or natural thing, and his activity to mere animal activity. But "what distinguishes human life-activity from that of animal life-activity is its awareness." [29]

Man is indeed a part of nature but a distinctive part. When he labors to gratify his hunger, without respect for the elements of beauty, truth, social significance, he is betraying what is human within him. He is converting what should be an expression of his *human* life-activity into a means of satisfying his merely biological existence. This seems very far fetched. Man is human but he cannot always live at the top of his ideal form. Apparently for Marx any production under "the compulsion of physical need" is degrading; so that if a man builds a shelter to protect himself and his own from the elements he is caught in the toils of self-alienation.

Marx distinguishes a fourth type of alienation—the alienation of man from other men.[30] This takes place in two ways: As a consequence of betraying one's own humanity in working to gratify physical need, one acts like an animal toward other men; and further, because of the relationship which man acquires in the process of production, he regards other men not as brothers but as competitors or exploiters. What the worker produces does not belong to him but to someone else—to another man. And this man in the nature of the case must find "pleasure and enjoyment in the activity which the worker experiences as torture."

Alienation now is piled upon alienation. The existence of private property itself is not the cause of alienated labor but the necessary consequence of it—so that private property far from being the means by which man humanizes himself is the primal crime of man against man. The existence of a wage system is another infallible sign of alienation. So long as human beings work for wages they are not fulfilling their true human nature or essence. Even if the workers are better paid this would be nothing but a "better remuneration [*Salierung*] of slaves." Even if *everyone* received the same reward, this would mean that what is true for workers in relation to their specific work would also be true for everyone in society no matter what their task. "Society would then have to be conceived as an abstract capitalist." Everyone would be equally enslaved.

The inventory of alienations is not complete but it is time to bring it to a halt. Suffice it to say that from the primary alienation of labor, that creates private property, is derived the alienation imposed by the division of labor, which fragments man; the alienation embodied in the use of money, especially gold, as a medium of exchange; the alienation of man from the community by the rise of the political state; the alienation of man from a truly human culture and human society by man's greed. It is not difficult to find in this mixture of insight, fantasy and balderdash intimations of the latest varieties of alienation celebrated among the literary sophisticates of Paris and New York.

It can hardly be disputed that in these early manuscripts and particularly in his view that alienation is the fundamental cause of the existence of private property, and not vice versa, Marx is not even a thoroughgoing naturalist or materialist. For what makes man human, according to Marx, is his spiritual nature, his traits of mind and consciousness which differentiate him from the animal and plant world. Indeed, to the extent that man is determined by material conditions and needs, by his body, he is not truly human. To be truly human, his life, like his mind, must be expressed in vital choices which are autonomous. He must function, so to speak, in angelic fashion, free from the compulsions of matter and natural necessity. The dehumanization of man, which in his mature writings Marx attributes to specific historical and social conditions, he characterizes as "alienation," as something foreign to his nature, imposed from without. In the mature Marx what is objectionable about alienation is the consequence of the way in which certain forms of private property operate in a determinate historical society. But in asserting that alienation is the cause of the existence of private property, Marx is unconsciously expressing the fables of Genesis. Man is sentenced to hard labor by God for his disobedience, and therewith his very nature as man, and Eve's as woman, is transformed. Marx surrendered his belief in God but not in the Fall, in the curse of alienation. But whereas the religious believer has an "explanation" of alienation, Marx actually has none.] The very terms "alienation" and "estrangement" are completely foreign to a robust materialism for which man is *at home* in nature, not a stranger, as much at home as any other creature. The image of man which rises from the poetic texts of these early manuscripts of Marx is of a fallen angel struggling to liberate himself from the mire of matter, not of man as a toolmaking, symbol-using animal.

It is an open question whether the various types of alienation enumerated by Marx are always and in every respect morally objectionable. This is obviously true for the division of labor which is held heavily responsible for human alienation under capitalism. And it often is. But historically, and also today, many kinds of specialization have served to liberate and enrich both personality and community. Not all forms of specialization are narrowing; they sometimes presuppose mastery of a whole range of activities. Division of labor like other forms of specialization arises from the fact that not all men can do all things equally well. This does not doom man to the assembly line except where production for the sake of production or for the sake only of profit is the rule. Even where social or personal goals control production, division of labor may be a means of self-integration, not self-alienation. The religious roots of Marx's early thought appear clearly in his interpretation of the division of labor as necessarily a form of self-alienation. Although not omnipotent, man is conceived as a creature capable of doing all the things that God can do to a preeminent degree. If not self-created he is self-creating. As soon as he becomes specialized, he is limited, subject to external restraints, alienated from his true nature of self. Marx believed that sexual reproduction is the most primal form of division of labor, which can be interpreted fancifully as self-alienation only if the ideal of a true unalienated being is a self-copulating creature as some ancient divinities are.

Even the most sympathetic approach to Marx's *Economic-Philosophical Manuscripts* cannot overlook a fundamental difficulty, to which we have already alluded, in the doctrine of alienation and self-alienation. This difficulty appears all the more glaring from the standpoint of the historical approach developed by Marx in his maturer writings. What is man estranged or alienated from? A natural self or an ideal self? It cannot be the former because according to Marx's social psychology there is no such thing as a natural or real self, counterposed to the world of nature and society, to be estranged *from*. Already in these manuscripts, following Hegel, Marx rejects the notion that society is an abstraction which confronts the ready-made individual. "The individual is the *social creature*." [31] By acting on nature and society, man continually modifies his own human nature. Man cannot betray or distort or alienate his true nature because he has no true nature. Whatever his nature is at any definite time, it can be explained in terms of the interacting antecedents out of which it developed. Marx admits that at one time human life needed private property for its development,[32] that alienation therefore was both natural and necessary. If human life now requires that private property and the products and process of alienation be abolished, it can only be in virtue of what Marx conceives man *ought* to be, not because of what man *really* or *naturally* or *truly* is. Precisely because man is a creature who makes his own history, and therefore ultimately his own nature, whenever we deplore the facts of human alienation, it can only be in the light of our *ideal* of man, of what he *should* be. That Marx's ideal of man was influenced by the Greek conception of the liberal minded free man and by the Goethean ideal of the active and creative man does not militate in the least against its normative character.

Another way of making this point is to call attention to a kind of alienation which Marx does not discuss but which his own life superbly illustrates. Preeminently alienated from his own society, Marx would have scorned the notion that he was self-alienated, that he had fallen short of his "true" nature. Marx was the kind of man he wanted to be even though not the kind of man others thought he should be. Alienation from society may be a good thing if one lives in a bad society. Internal emigration is not necessarily a state of self-diremption. In any society short of Heaven, and judging by Lucifer possibly there too, there will be at least two possible kinds of alienation —one in which the individual is rejected by society in such a way that he finds himself degraded in his own eyes, and one in which he rejects society, or the powers that be in it, in such a way as to affirm himself and live with courage and dignity. These are choices open to all men so long as they are not under the compulsions of physical torture or extreme hunger. If the notion of alienation is to have an intelligible, non-Utopian meaning, we cannot therefore set up the absence of alienation as a universally valid moral ideal. There will be times and situations in which we may properly ask: why not alienation? Even if it involves the storm and stress of a personality in conflict with itself and sometimes with society, it may be desirable.

The historical materialist's objection to conceiving of alienation as if it meant a departure from an original or natural norm does not hold against the role played by the doctrine of alienation in a system of historical idealism such as Hegel's. For the empirical self in that system grows by virtue of its alienations until it is absorbed into the Great Self or Totality which functions as a substitute for God. An immanent teleology controls the process, and properly considered there is no place in it for chance, individual decisions, objective possibility, or genuine evil. Marx had not freed himself completely from the Hegelian influences he was combatting when he penned this youthful work. Subsequently, without abandoning the humanist ideal, he shifted the basis of his social criticism from the murky ethics of self-realization to an empirical account of the development of the capitalist economy in an effort to discover what policies and programs would facilitate social revolution and usher in a new social order and a more desirable kind of man.

V

What I am asserting is, first, that the contemporary revival of Marxism in the main has been spurred by the view that the conception of human self-alienation is the key to Marx's philosophy; and, second, that this conception is itself alien to Marx's mature thought. That the theme of self-alienation is Marx's central concern has been affirmed not only by Marxists who regard it as valid but by some scholars who repudiate it as a myth. Far from agreeing that the doctrine of self-alienation is metaphysical tripe or the intellectual rubbish Marx himself declared it to be in the *Communist Manifesto*, Professor Robert Tucker defends the thesis that "human self-alienation and the overcoming of it remained always the supreme concern of Marx and the central theme of his thought." [33] Tucker grants that the doctrine as developed by Marx reveals insight but in contradistinction to latter-day Marxists asserts that it is nonetheless a great myth. Its aberration results from the fact that Marx mistook the true locus or source of human alienation. The alien power which distorts man's nature and against which he must struggle to achieve liberation is man's own inner self of greed, pride, and selfishness. Marx therefore mistakenly substitutes a program of social revolution for the revolution within. According to Tucker, it is human selfishness not capitalism which is the real evil from which men must be liberated.

We can leave to Marx's own dual critique of Christianity on the one hand, and of Stirner and Bentham on the other, the appropriate rejoinder to Professor Tucker's own conception of alienation. What concerns us here, however, is Tucker's contention that there is an obvious answer in Marxist terms to the questions I have posed above. "From what true or natural self is man alienated?" Defending his book against criticism, Tucker asserts that Marx views human nature as "both an historical variable and a constant." Man's variable nature changes with variations in the mode of production; the constant element is "the producing animal, a being whose nature it is to find self-fulfillment in freely performed productive activities of various kinds." [34] The only thing obvious about this distinction between man's variable and man's constant nature is that in the light of Marx's published writings it is obviously wrong. First, this is not a *description* of anything observable in all human behavior, it expresses a normative goal—something man *should* be. Secondly, how can man's constant nature first come into existence at the *end* of the human history of class societies? For according to Marx, in no society of the past has man found fulfillment in freely performed productive activities. What is constant in human nature must be present from the first; it cannot first appear under communism. Third, and most important, what Tucker distinguishes as constant and variable in human nature are for Marx in continuous interaction with each other—so much so that Marx even denies that a clear distinction can be made between man's biological nature and his social-historical nature. Human psychology is not only dissolved in social psychology but even human physiology is radically affected. In the very manuscripts which Tucker cites to justify his discovery of a radical dualism between man's constant and variable nature, Marx declares that

the senses of social man are *different* from those of non-social man; it is only through the objectively developed wealth of the human creature that the wealth of subjective human sensibility is in part first created and in part first cultivated, e.g. a musical ear, an eye for beauty of form, in short *senses* capable of human satisfaction, senses which validate themselves as essential human capacities. For it is not only the five senses but also the so-called spiritual senses, the practical senses (will, love, etc.) in a word *human* sensibility, the human character of the senses, which arises only by virtue of the existence of its object, through *humanized* nature. The education [*Bildung*] of the five senses is the work of all previous history.[35]

Presumably, Marx would be prepared to believe that if there were any toothaches under communism they wouldn't hurt as much, or not in the same way, as in other societies. He carries themes suggested by Hegel and Feuerbach to absurd and Utopian lengths. But nevertheless the citation above shows as conclusively as any text can that the distinction between a constant and variable human nature is untenable. For Marx, human nature or the human self is not something anteced- ently given which finds natural fulfillment in the way in which, loosely speaking, an acorn fulfills itself as an oak. Whether man has one self or many selves he redetermines them to some extent in the light of some reflective ideal. Marx's ideal of the good life in the good society is, as we have already indicated, of great nobility—a community of creative individuals living cooperatively in pursuit of beauty and truth. If *this* is Marxism, Marx need not have published a line. This is pretty much the judgment of Tucker. *"Capital,"* he writes, "the product of twenty years of hard labor to which, as Marx said, he sacrificed his health, his happiness in life and his family, is an intellectual museum piece for us now, whereas the sixteen page manuscript of 1844 on the future of aesthetics, [economics?] which he probably wrote in a day and never even saw fit to publish, contains much that is still signifi- cant."[36] Instead of seeing irony in this observation, I regard it as very weighty evidence of the untenability of Tucker's interpretation. If it is the unknown writings of Marx in which his true significance is to be found, from what source, then, did the great mass movements which centered around Marx's name and doctrines catch fire?

VI

It is not only Marx's concept of "alienation" which has been blown
up beyond reason and evidence in order to provide a basis for revolutionary criticism of the status quo as well as criticism of the revolution
betrayed. There are signs that the same thing is happening to the
Marxist concept of "ideology." I predict we shall hear more about this
in the future but it warrants some attention in this sketch. Here the intellectual phenomenon is not the resuscitation of an abandoned notion
but the inversion of a position taken by the mature Marx, an inversion
so startling that the exegesis reveals seams of incoherence. For Marx an
"ideology" is a set of beliefs or doctrines which rationalize the interests
of a class engaged in struggle with other classes for social and political
power. It conceals the real interests of a class engaged in struggle with
other classes for social and political power. It conceals the interests at
stake in a given period as much from those who hold the ideology
as those who oppose it. The function of Marxist historical and sociological analysis, among other things, is to criticize and unmask
ideologies in order to lay bare the stark clash of economic class interests
beneath the rhetoric and abstractions about God, country, national
honor, universal love, peace and freedom. Marxism itself on this view
is *not* an ideology but a true or valid doctrine which honestly expresses the interests of the working class, and ultimately of all
humanity, on the basis of scientifically valid assertions about the
nature, functioning, and collapse of the economic system. From the
Marxist point of view, if an ideology has a genuinely cognitive meaning, it is false. But cognitive or not, an ideology always has the
meaning of a diagnostic sign. It reveals the way in which the true state
of affairs about the power struggle is being concealed either by overt
deceptions or, more likely, by self-deceptions. And it has an effect on
the behavior of those who believe it. That is why it must be combatted.

If contemporary Marxism is the belief that human beings can be
liberated from the burden of all social evils, which are regarded as the
root cause of most personal problems, merely by the socialization of
the means of economic production, achieved by a social revolution
based on the working-class, it is a triple myth.[37] First, the socialization
of the means of production is not a *sufficient* condition of such liberation. In the absence of deeply rooted and effectively operating democratic institutions, it may become the engine of a more terrible
despotism than Marx ever conceived, and certainly worse than any
experienced under capitalism. Total socialization may not even be a

necessary condition for the realization of the humanistic ideals of socialism. A mixed economy under plural forms of ownership all ultimately responsible to regulatory bodies, subject to independent judicial review, may achieve the best results with the fewest dangers. Secondly, even when *the* economic problem is solved, if this is defined as the abolition of poverty and gross physical want and the achievement of decent minimum standards of existence for all, other grave social problems will remain, aside from new ones which may develop, not to speak of certain classes of personal problems which cannot be settled merely by social rearrangements. Thirdly, the social revolution, if and when it comes, whether peacefully or not, is not likely to be based primarily on the working class, and in some countries it may be begun even in the absence of a developed working class in the Marxist sense.

In the light of the historic experience of the Soviet Union, Red China, and every Communist regime in the world, this triple myth can be held only in the same way as the more traditional eschatological beliefs. Marxism in this sense is an ideology not only of some working class groups but of intellectuals, especially in underdeveloped countries, who see in rapid social change not only a promise of plenty for all but of additional opportunities for their skills and talents.

In recent years Marxist ideology of this variety has increasingly come under attack because of its claims to offer *total* solutions for the problems of poverty, war, peace and meaningful vocations. This *type* of criticism of total solutions in the ideology of free enterprise had been effectively and justly made by Marxists and other social reformers. In rejecting total solutions those who have called attention to "the end of ideology" (an unfortunate because ambiguous phrase) have left open how large the piecemeal approach to problems should be. Some problems *are* interrelated and require bold and fundamental reconstruction of the areas in which they are found. For example, if a government finds it necessary to take over an industry in the interest of social welfare, it may have to change its fiscal and tariff policies. Or if large scale educational reconstruction is planned to improve opportunities for minority or disadvantaged groups, this may require profound changes in housing and in employment policy. Other problems can be met only by radical political action (e.g. complete independence for Algeria). Those who have contributed to the literature devoted to the "end of ideology," Raymond Aron, Arthur Koestler, Seymour Lipset, Daniel Bell, and others, have been notable for their liberal and socialist sympathies. Far from urging resignation towards the acute social problem of the day, they have sought to make social criticism more intelligent and responsible.

It has remained for Henry Aiken, an American Professor of Philosophy, to take up the cudgels to halt the intellectual revolt against ideology. The strategy of his defence is very curious. He begins (1) by accepting Marx's critique of ideology as a genial insight; he continues (2) by attacking as merely a defence of the status quo those current analyses which herald and approve the end of ideological thinking; and he concludes (3) with an interpretation and spirited defence of "ideological" thinking as an expression of concern to improve the lot of man! This would make Marx's rejection of all ideological thinking evidence of hostility to attempts to improve the lot of man. Professor Aiken's zeal, however, is not so much to defend Marx as to denigrate the critics of orthodox Marxist ideology. Despite their professions, all who declare themselves for "an end of ideology" are really committed, he asserts, to the position of "that most determined and most consistent of anti-ideologists Michael Oakeschott," the staunch conservative critic of rationalism in all its varieties.[38]

Aiken's reasoning will not bear close examination for a moment. It reduces itself to the charge that because one denies that there is a cure-all for disease one thereby denies that there is a cure for anything. Because the critics of ideology deny there is one single, overall technique for solving social problems, because they contest the viability of a total plan for the final amelioration of the lot of man, they are rebuked by Aiken as if they were *philosophes fainéants*. "I cannot, as a pragmatist," he writes, "see how one can be said actively to seek a less cruel lot for humanity if one can trust no [*sic!*] technique, and no [*sic!*] plan for its amelioration." What he cannot see was seen very clearly by John Dewey, one of the founders of pragmatism, who long before the current discussions about the end of ideology vigorously criticized orthodox Marxism for its quest of total solutions, its disregard of the continuity between means and end, and of the distinction between ends-in-view and ultimate ends, and its consequent hypostasis of a social ideal into a fixed metaphysical goal.[39]

Like so many others, Aiken wants to have his cake and eat it— explicitly to reject Marxism and even socialism and yet to refurbish it with doctrines that would make all liberals, progressives, men of good will, indeed anyone who sincerely and actively commits himself in the struggle to improve the lot of mankind, "Marxist ideologists" too. As if it were necessary to have an "ideology" in order to have a moral passion for freedom or peace or social equality or the prevention of cruelty to children and animals. This is a kind of popular front conception of crypto-Marxism according to which there are no enemies to the "left." This illusion of perspective reinforces the illusion of those conservatives from Herbert Hoover to Whittaker Chambers who regarded the New Deal and the welfare state, for all their piecemeal solutions, as the piecemeal triumph of communism.

VIII

To the extent that Marx has made contributions to the study of history, sociology, social psychology, economics and politics, they are integral to the scholarly traditions in those fields. But whatever these contributions, they do not explain at all the perennial appeal which Marx and Marxism have exerted on the proletariat of some countries of the West and on certain circles among the intellectuals of the West. For those *constituents* of Marx's thinking which represent abiding contributions—like his historical approach to all social tendencies and "laws," his insights into the development of capitalism, his hypothesis that economic and class influences always limit the alternatives of effective social choice and also influence the choice of different groups among these alternatives—all can be accepted without subscribing to any Marxist revolutionary program. Even nonsocialists like Pareto and Max Weber could regard Marx as an intellectual pioneer, albeit one not free from some of the illusions of those he criticized.

To what then can we attribute the recurrent allegiance to Marx, the battle cries which invoke his name and even when his doctrines are rejected or transformed beyond recognition? I shall conclude by listing a few of the motives which seem to me to account for the phenomenon.

1) The dominant intellectual mood in the Western world is critical. The cultural role of the intellectual is primarily to be "against." Dissent from, and nonconformity with existing traditions and institutions are regarded as virtues even when they do not rise above the level of gut reactions because they seem continuous with the dissenting attitudes of the great figures of the past. Since the enemy is usually assumed to be on the right, no association with the dissenting movements and ideologies from *this* quarter is conceivable. The spectrum of professedly liberal views is unexciting and unheroic. Their sane attitudes appear merely safe and their reasonable programs timid. In consequence, allegiance to Marxism, no longer handicapped by seemingly organic ties to the murderous regimes of Communist police

states, provides the break with the imperfect present, continuity with
the revolutionary past, and absolution for the "excesses" or "mistakes"
of the Stalinist cult of personality. From this arises the complex of
views which are *de rigueur* for the doctrinally well-equipped intellectual of our times.

2) Non-Marxist or anti-Marxist reformism does not by far exercise
the same attraction for intellectuals because its programs of piecemeal
change strike the impatient as half-hearted, and most intellectuals (not
the scholars so much as the opinion-makers) are impatient. Although
the specific doctrines and principles of Marxism are rarely defended,
nonetheless as a system of total opposition Marxism has a strong appeal. It is against religion, against the state, against the existing family,
against the profit motive, and against the vulgarities of mass culture
which the profit motive breeds. In short, Marxism "explains" everything even if a little vaguely and hazily. Like Thomism, although not
so well-knit, the system gives a resiliency to the attitude of the believer.
He is buoyed up by it enough to float securely despite rents and tears
in the fabric of the argument.

3) Another source of attraction in Marxism is its strong sense of
social justice, its passionate protest against social inequalities rooted
not in reason but in tradition and arbitrary power. And this despite
some of its hard-boiled pronouncements. It opens the vista of a world
in which the exploited, the enslaved and the oppressed—and there are
many such!—come into their own. The balance wheel of history is
set right not by a mythical *deus ex machina* but by processes which
modern man can accept as natural, even if not merely physical, and
to which he can contribute.

4) Marxism is a philosophy which promises fulfillment to age old
dreams of material betterment and justifies hope in man. After all,
there is no point in crying stinking fish in the world if that has always
been the fare of mankind and always will be. The Paretos, Moscas,
and Michelses with their "iron laws" of the circulation of the elite,
political supremacy of minorities, and organizational oligarchy are
unable to account for the phenomena of *degree,* which may make
the difference between the Weimar Republic and Hitler, sometimes
between the very life of the free mind and its death. Marxism, no
matter how reinterpreted, always appears the optimistic variant in the
reading of the future. To the literary mind, indifferent to recent history,
it suggests a dimension of depth because it expects the felicity of the
future to be accompanied by a little blood and tears (of others). In a
world where there has already been so much evil, and in which so

many have scared themselves witless by fears of accidental nuclear holocaust, a view which sustains hope in a triumphant future, and helps cheerfulness to break out, is not without attraction.

5) As a system Marxism is now invalid. Its theory of historical materialism was exploded by those most "orthodox" of Marxists, the Bolshevik Leninists, who demonstrated that politics mainly determines economics in our age not vice versa. Nonetheless there is no rival system freer of difficulties, especially for those who hunger for the emotional security of feeling that they are thinking and living with the true drift of things. In addition, with a little ingenuity, its doctrines can be qualified to make them not obviously wrong. Let him who is without any a priori assumptions throw the first methodological stone! Further, for some periods of history, and in some regions, some of its general propositions about the state or imperialism or the overriding character of economic class struggles appear to be valid. What is easier than to assume that what is true at some time may turn out upon further exploration to be true at any time? Despite the niggling objection that upon further exploration what seemed true at some time may turn out false, there is just enough semblance of truth in the reconstruction of Marxism to give it an aura of intellectual plausibility to those predisposed to revolt against the present in fervent hope for a better future.

6) Another reason for the strength of Marxist ideology is the apparent use of the theory of historical materialism in undergirding the view that the conflict between Communist and non-Communist worlds is gradually disappearing, that there is a growing "convergence" in their economies, and that their cultures are rapidly becoming mirror-images of each other. The view is held by those who deplore it, and who take pride in their lonely feeling of revolutionary integrity against both the democratic philistines and the equally philistine Communist Commissars of People's Culture. That the democratic philistines cheerfully accept their critics when they do not comfortably support them in their role of dissenters, while the Communist philistines purge and punish dissenters severely, is dismissed as an irrelevant philistine observation. The degree of "economic" convergence is hard to establish because of the variety of notions the term "economic" connotes. But in the main, the structural similarities are found in common technological and bureaucratic phenomena which reflect the place of science and the size of the industrial enterprise in the modern world.

Does it follow that the more similar the basic technology of different societies is, or even their modes of economic production with which technology is vulgarly confused, that the more similar will be their cultures? This is an empirical question for which the evidence, although not conclusive, strongly suggests a negative answer. Cultural and political phenomena of vastly differing significance are compatible with similar economic structures. Consider, for example, the difference which free trade unions can make, and have made, to the way in which the economic system itself functions. Consider the variations in religion which can flourish in the same economy. The predictions of Hayek and others that only a free enterprise economy can support a free culture and that the more socialized the economy of a nation, the less cultural freedom and political democracy it can enjoy, have been refuted by events. (Others besides orthodox Marxists are crypto-historical materialists!) The predictions that the Communist and non-Communist worlds will converge and reveal a common cultural and political pattern in the foreseeable future is today a gratuitous piece of dogmatism not warranted by the facts.

7) Finally, I am not aiming at an exhaustive analysis, there is the factor which I previously mentioned. The centripetal influence of established power, Communist power, forged in the name of Marx, exercises a fascination on leftist circles in the West and not only on leftist circles, almost in inverse relation to their own strength. Even the revolutionary pure become weary of being eternally correct and politically impotent, and long for a sense of effectiveness. This they first get vicariously from the triumphs and achievements of Communist powers. They then rationalize their acceptance of the ideology of their Communist Big Brothers with the consoling myth that they can more easily change Communist thought and behavior by joining them than by cultivating perfection on the side-lines or in ivory towers. Similarly, in the middle and late thirties the apparent strength of the Italian and German regimes exercised a fascination on conservative—and not only conservative—circles in Western Europe. The phenomena, of course, are very complex and not identical, but the simple upshot, now as then, of this attempt to influence totalitarians by joining or even cooperating with them is that the pure become more like the strong than the strong become like the pure, with the consequent increase of coarseness and brutality in the world. In the end, the romantic souls become stern realists. Camus has phrased this with his usual felicity: "The will to power came to take the place of the will to justice, pre-tending at first to be identified with it and then relegating it to a place somewhere at the end of history, waiting until such time as nothing remains on earth to dominate." [40]

These motives for the revival of Marxist allegiance are not all consistent with each other. They appeal in different measure to different types of personality. Nor, I repeat, are they exhaustive. They are the main influences I have found among the Marxists and neo-Marxists of the postwar world. From such groups much may be expected in the way of a new literature of Marxist rediscovery, new expressions of dissent, new much needed and, despite exaggerations, praiseworthy exposures and disclosures of the evils and imperfect functioning of our mixed economies and our mixed-up cultures. But one thing in addition may be confidently predicted of them. They are not likely to serve as a basis for an international *revolutionary* movement or organization. This is true not only because of the influence of nationalism which, despite Marx, is as strong today as in the past century, but because current reinterpretations of Marx have stressed the individual, the deviant, the Utopian and the anarchistic aspects of his beliefs. There is no central core of doctrine. There is no agglutinative element to tie or hold the new Marxists together in a Sartrian "group." It is one of the ironies of intellectual history that Marx's early writings are being cried up without much understanding by neo-Bohemian, neo-Freudian elements whose prototypes Marx repudiated because of their social irresponsibility. The economic millenarianism of the first generation of Marxists was crude and naïve, but at least it pointed to specific programs by which economic suffering and political oppression could be removed. The present form of millenarianism which centers around the vague concept of alienation is psychological. It assumes that when all institutional restraints on man's primal nature, especially his sexual nature, have been cast off, all human beings will be free and happy. It is, in a sense, a revolt against civilization itself, a blind cult of non-conformity which overlooks the fact that the greatest nonconformists of the twentieth century were the armed Bohemians who set it afire. The valid ideals which also engage them, such as civil rights and the struggle against poverty, are causes for which genuine liberals, radicals, democrats, and socialists have been fighting all their lives without benefit of the metaphysics of alienation. There are many "young Marxists" in the world who believe that it is no longer necessary to read or study the Marx who influenced the world in which they live. It is sufficient to proclaim him on the basis of what they can read into his early manuscripts or summaries of them.

Interpretations of Marx will proliferate. In Japan there is a temple of the ten thousand Buddhas all shiningly indistinguishable from each other. If and when Marxism becomes a world ideology without becoming the theology of a universal church (an unlikely event but made possible by Communist polycentrism), history is likely to become the temple of the ten thousand Marxes, all distinguishable from each other, at which each culture or group will make its selective obeisance in accordance with its own particular needs, wishes, and hopes. Feuerbach will have revenged himself against Marx. The secret of Marxist ideology will be human anthropology.

Lewis S. Feuer

Alienation: The Marxism of Contemporary Student Movements

It seems to me established that the concept of alienation used by the early Marx was vague and ill-defined, and that therefore critics and neo-Marxists are wrong when they try to make this concept a central one in the mature and historically influential work of Marx. The magisterial essay of Sidney Hook has argued these points convincingly. It seems to me that what we further need is what we might call a Marxist account of the "alienationist" trend. Why does one stream of contemporary Marxism both in the West and the Soviet Union feel impelled to identify itself more with the protohistorical Marx than with the historical Marx? The *Economic-Philosophical Manuscripts* of 1844 are the Dead Sea Scrolls of Marxism; what is astonishing is that in the Marxist case the Scrolls are replacing the Scriptures. This is an unparalleled event in intellectual history, and it calls for explanation.

The Revival of Ideology: Back to the Early Marx

The alienationist trend is in the first place an effort to restore the ethical consciousness to Marxism. It arose after an era of Stalinism in which contempt for ethical considerations had been carried to the last extreme. There was a revulsion too against the historicism which Marx and Engels had used in their repression of the ethical consciousness. Also, postwar thinkers realized clearly that a socialist economic foundation was no sufficient basis for the superstructure of a free society; the concepts of bureaucratic collectivism, managerial control, the organized system, and mass society, were all ways of viewing new forms of human repression. And the common denominator of all the repressive features of social existence seemed to be man's alienation. Those who looked to Marx as the one great social prophet of our time found in this notion a new dramatic metaphor for the mainspring of human striving in history. No longer was history a locomotive on predetermined dialectical rails; rather it consisted of man's own gropings to realize his essence.

In the second place, the use of "alienation" derives from the fact that the emphasis is now on the moral critique of both the capitalistic economy and the bureaucratic order, the societies of both the United States and the Soviet Union. The widespread appeal of the arguments of Karl Popper and Isaiah Berlin against sociological determinism and historicism was founded on the experience of many radicals who finally decided that they had been guilty of methodological immodesty, that the law of motion of modern capitalism had eluded them. The capitalistic system was evidently stable at least during this era. A law of the declining rate of profit was sounding no knell for the expropriators. And yet the will to criticize, the will to revolution, the will to moral protest against the established order persisted. It expressed itself among new student generations especially in a readiness for individual direct action; a historical voluntarism arose to supersede the historical materialism of mass impersonal movements.

According to Marx's social psychology, says Professor Hook, there is no such thing as a natural or real self; a Marxist distinction, he says, cannot be drawn between man's biological and his social-historical nature. Yet one must perforce acknowledge that every child is born with certain drives or instincts or unconditioned responses; every society then educates the child into social forms in which these instincts will be in varying degrees expressed or repressed, fulfilled or frustrated. Human sensibilities, the "spiritual senses" (in Marx's words) arise through "humanized nature," but the "humanization" (or "socialization," as we would say today) proceeds through the operation of social circumstances on the biological organism. All this is not only consistent with but necessary to the understanding of historical materialism. If all history is a history of class struggles, it is because there is a universal, underlying nature of man; in every society he has been inwardly or outwardly rebellious against exploitation because to accept it would always have involved a self-hatred against which his underlying nature rebelled. "The free development of each," the aim of Marx's communism, is unintelligible unless there is a natural human being whose freest, maximal development is sought. It is in this region that Marx's ideas meet with Freud's, for Marx's social science requires a theory of the underlying nature of man of the sort which Freud was trying to develop. The whole basis of the materialistic conception of history, as Engels said in his funeral oration on Marx, was in man's underlying psycho-biological nature, in "the palpable but previously totally over-

looked fact that men must first of all eat, drink, have shelter and cloth-
ing, therefore must work, before they can fight for domination, pursue
politics, religion, philosophy, etc."

Curiously, Professor Hook's argument against the notion of an
underlying human nature is out of keeping with his vigorous critique
of Mills' use of the "principle of historical specificity." [1] There are
biological laws which hold for all animals, including human ones, says
Professor Hook, and there may be laws which hold for all societies.
If so, we ask, why may there not be universal psychological laws
defining a common human nature underlying all social systems?
The restricted laws of social psychology would then be special cases
of such universal, transsocietal laws.

Now Marx, as Professor Hook shows, rejected in his maturity the
concept of alienation. No one has yet explored, however, the political
significance which this concept had for Marx and Engels in 1844 and
1845. During the last months of 1844 and the spring of 1845, Engels
was very active in speaking and writing about the advantages and
practicability of the Community System, particularly on the model of
the American colonies then in existence. He wrote a well-documented
essay on the American communities in which he collated the reports
of English travellers to show that the Community System was far
superior to competitive society, and announced furthermore that his
group was making arrangements "to draw up a plan of organization
and regulations for a practical Community" based on the experiences
of the American communist colonies and the English Harmony Hall.
Engels enumerated the active names of the German socialists; Moses
Hess and Karl Marx were among the six he named.[2] In short, the
political significance of the concept of alienation was the foundation of
Communities, communist colonies. Here all the modes of alienation
would be overcome; men would not be estranged but befriended.
Community was the answer to Alienation. When such thinkers as
Martin Buber find the answer to "collective loneliness" in the communal villages of Israel, they are in effect retracing the thought and
feelings of the young Marx and Engels.[3] When Marx and Engels, however, rejected the approach of voluntary Communities, they at the same
time abandoned the alienationist standpoint. They ceased for the most
part to speak of the moral redemption of man's essence, and dropped
the total hopes of the immediate regeneration of man's nature which
were part of the Community ideology. They shed their youthful
idealism when they took to class struggle and practical politics rather
than communal love as the mechanism for social change. And

"alienation" was the language of the Feuerbachian philosophy of love and the Utopian communist enclaves.

Today the concept of alienation has the same appeal for circles of student activists as it once had for the young Feuerbachians. Those who find a comradeship in direct action for personal rights, peace, and civil rights find its language congenial, and often share the same total hopes for the overcoming of all alienation.

We may thus appreciate why the "end of ideology" doctrine arouses such antagonism among youthful political activists. The "end of ideology" is the doctrine of middle-aged and middle-class post-Marxists. The phrase itself comes from Engels who used it to signify the end of all forms of thinking in which the thinker is unconscious of the underlying, impelling economic source.[4] In contemporary discussion, however, "ideology" has come to be used with positivistic overtones to signify any political philosophy; "the end of ideology" then denotes the demise of all political philosophy, and the instatement of political sociology and managerial science as a sufficient basis for answers to all political problems. Behind this political positivism, young neo-ideologists detect a mood of complacency. The post-ideologist is apt to be, in their eyes, a smug ex-Marxist, now a comfortable Clerk of the Establishment, and one who will be found nowhere near the new battle lines, for instance, of the civil rights movement. In the Marxist usage, the "end of ideology" is precisely the ideology of Establishment Clerks. Then too there is division of generations between the post-ideologists and the neo-ideologists.

Marxism, of course, holds that it is a science, not an ideology. And here is another reason why young neo-Marxists so often turn to alienationism. For what they find lacking in classical Marxism is precisely a philosophy. The mature thought of Marx consists of social science and a political summons, but the ethical-philosophical basis of his individual choice is repressed; indeed, the grounds of individual decision are a kind of "unproblem" for Marxism, and *Capital* regards persons solely as "personifications of economic categories." With all its incoherences, the notion of the recovery of one's essence from the alienated self corresponds to the sense of striving for one's freedom in the liberated community.

Perhaps it is because Marxism has always lacked a genuine philosophy that its theoretical history has been a history of syncretisms. Marx himself in his early writings appealed to "the categorical imperative to overthrow all those conditions in which man is an abased, enslaved, abandoned, contemptible, being.[5] Bernstein explicitly merged Marx with Kant; Sorel joined him to Bergson; Kautsky united Marx with

Darwin; Walling and Hook synthesized him with James and Dewey, just as today Sartre conjoins him with Heidegger. Marxism has never been a philosophy so much as an "over-philosophy," a current among all philosophies; it has made for left Kantians, left Bergsonians, left Nietzscheans, left pragmatists, and left existentialists. As Professor Hook says, almost every distinguished convert to socialism creates his own Marx. Its sociology of class struggle, its vision of a new society, and its faith in working mankind can be attached to a variety of philosophical beliefs. There has never, we might say, been a philosophical Marxist. This, however, is precisely a source of its vitality; it can link itself with protean forms, with tribalism in Africa, with Buddhism in Burma, with anti-Westernism in the West.

The chief basis indeed for neo-orthodox Marxism in the West is precisely hostility to the liberal and democratic values of Western civilization. In the writings of Paul Sweezy, for instance, it shows itself in a disaffection from the American working class and in a self-identification with the historical destiny of the "uncommitted," underdeveloped African and Asian peoples, and, above all, with the Chinese Communists.[6] C. Wright Mills likewise regarded the classical faith in the working class as a "labor metaphysic...a legacy from Victorian Marxism," and was especially attracted by the hegemony of intellectuals in backward areas.[7] In every confrontation of world movements, there have been such internal and external secessions. Not infrequently Romans fifteen hundred years ago affirmed the moral superiority of the barbarian invaders, and as late as the seventeenth century Europeans were defecting to the North African Moslem pirate-states. Neo-orthodox Marxism, as a rejection of one's own roots and civilization, unites Marxism with primitivism; it has a de-civilizing intent. To understand it, we should require all the resources of the psychoanalysis of ideology.

The persistent strength of Marxism is not, however, to be altogether explained by the irrational factors which Professor Hook has lucidly set forth. There is also the impressive fact that Marxist hypotheses and modes of thought still attract social scientists more than those of any other social theorist. Professor Hook writes: "As a system Marxism is now invalid. Its theory of historical materialism was exploded by those most 'orthodox' of Marxists, the Bolshevik-Leninists, who demonstrated that politics determines economics in our age, not vice versa." But the theory of historical materialism has something of the resiliency of the law of conservation of energy; it offers the means of explaining by further research apparent exceptions to itself. A whole school of social scientists today hold, for instance, that communism tends to triumph precisely in underdeveloped areas rather than in advanced industrial societies. Although such a generalization is at odds with a specific Marxist prediction, the generalization is itself a historical materialist explanation; it rests on the primacy of the economic factor. The Bolshevik-Leninists, far then from being regarded as having exploded the theory of historical materialism, are in effect taken as an example of how economics determines politics. In the history of social science, crucial experiments seem harder to come by than in the history of physical science.

Combine Marxism's theoretical power with its vision, and one has a standpoint which can inspire young, idealistic social scientists far more than any theory of Weber or Pareto or Parsons. Weber may have seen himself in the role of a modern Jeremiah, but his forecast of a bureaucratic world does not stir human energies; likewise, Pareto's immutable cycle of circulation of elites imparts a lesson of democratic futility, while Parsons' model has everyone subservient to the controls and equilibrating mechanisms of the social system. Marx's vision, by contrast, seems at the minimum a possible form of social development, a dream which may become reality if one has but the will and resolution. And as a possible form of social development, it seems to each new generation an unrefuted hope.

Are we confronted finally by an antinomy of human progress? The advancement of the human race is brought about through social movements founded on a self-dedication which only irrational, ideological men possess. For scientific, nonideological men lack the irrationality which commitment to social movements requires.[8] Is there a "contradiction" between social wisdom and social progress?

Our new ideological men are emerging in the student movements of the world in which a revival of ideology is taking place. The moral protest of the student movements, with their distinctive emotions born of a generational struggle yet so often merging with class struggle, has been a recurrent theme. As the notion of exploitation was the ground for the theory of class struggle and the ideology of the workers' movement, so the notion of alienation, derived from the youthful Marx, provides the basis for student movements and the theory of struggle between generations.

The Ideological Language of Younger-Generation Revolt

The concept of alienation provides the central meaning of Marxism for the student movements of the world today—whether they be those of the United States, Japan, the Soviet Union, or Africa. A remarkable convergence in ideology is taking place in the discussions of student activists all over the world; the language and metaphor of alienation has captured most poignantly the underlying spirit of younger-generation revolt. The history of Marxism has once more taken a turn which nobody foresaw, and which merits our closest sociological study. We may document briefly the use of "alienation" in the students' protest in the United States, Japan, and the Soviet Union.

During the autumn of 1964, a student movement rose to sudden prominence at the University of California in Berkeley, the largest state university in America. Demonstrations on the campus took place almost daily. There were vigils, sit-ins, speeches, encounters with police, and at one time on October 2, a narrowly averted clash between student demonstrators and more than six hundred police. The issue which provoked these disturbances was one common to all student movements; it concerned the rules which the university promulgates for the governance of students' political organizations. The university, as a public institution, felt that its grounds and buildings should not be used to organize political actions in the community at large; especially did it feel this in the case of actions taken consciously in violation of the law, that is, civil disobedience. No restrictions were otherwise proposed on speech, discussion, publication, or organization. The University's record for the advancement of the academic freedom of both its faculty and studentry was admittedly strong. Nevertheless, in the ensuing months of disturbances, a generational solidarity arose which joined together a student activist cross-faction of a few hundred from all political groupings, from those who were supporting Senator Barry Goldwater for the Presidency to partisans of Khrushchev, Castro, and Mao. The word which was always on speakers' lips was "alienation." The student crowd, fluctuating from several hundred to several thousand, sensed in this word the symbol of their basic discontent. Their chief leader, Mario Savio, twenty-one years old, and a student of philosophy, formulated one evening the ideology of the student movement as he conceived it:

A lot of Hegel got mixed in with Marx's notion of history. Max Eastman pointed this out. The dialectic was a way in which Marx made the course of world history coincide with his unconscious desires. Nevertheless, the most important concept for understanding the student movement is Marx's notion of alienation. Its basic meaning is that the worker is alienated from his product, but the concept is applicable to students too, many of whom don't come from the working class. Somehow people are being separated off from something. We have too many bureaucracies; their mechanical functioning makes for splits in people's personalities. Marx's concept of alienation was worked out from a two-class society. But it applies equally to our bureaucratic society where there are several centers of economic power. The labor movement has taken on the same impersonal quality as management. The students are frustrated; they can find no place in society where alienation doesn't exist, where they can do meaningful work. Despair sets in, a volatile political agent. The students revolt against the apparatus of the university.

This is the motive power of the student movement. I thought about it and my own involvement when I went to Mississippi where I could be killed. My reasons were selfish. I wasn't really alive. My life, my middle-class life, had no place in society, nor it in me. It was not really a matter of fighting for constitutional rights. I needed some way to pinch myself, to assure myself that I was alive. Now we will have to break down the fiction of the separation of student and citizen. We are breaking down the fiction of roles. We are breaking down barriers set up in a lot of people's personalities. That is what drives the student movement on.[9]

Across the Pacific Ocean, leaders of the Japanese student movement found especially from 1960 on that the concept of alienation articulated the consciousness of their movement. Satoshi Kitakoji, president of Zengakuren (the National Federation of Student Self-governing Associations) in 1960-61, and his close friend, Toru Kurokawa, re-iterated to me: "How to overcome alienation? That is our problem. We will not allow alienation. Men are now alienated from their labor. We must analyze it, and overcome it."[10] Neither of these students came from workingmen's families. Kitakoji was the son of a Communist teacher, Kurokawa of a doctor. The one was studying political economy at Kyoto University, the other literature at Tokyo. Both of them admired exceedingly the writings of a young Marxist philosopher, Kanichi Kuroda, who dwells on the importance of alienation as the concept for criticizing all bureaucracies, whether Japanese or Soviet. Their group, the Revolutionary Communist League, traced the degradation of Stalinism to its having suppressed this essential notion of Marx. Shigeo Shima, Secretary-General of the Communist League (also called the Bund) from 1958 to 1961, and a member as well of the Central Executive Committee of Zengakuren from 1956 to 1958, spoke of the motive power of alienation in 1960 in the student movement; the decline of Marxist organization began, he said, when by becoming mechanized and stereotyped, it gave rise to its own species of alienation:

At the time of Ampo (the struggle against the Security Treaty with the United States) in 1960, the world was bright, but we felt ourselves alienated. Out of the sense of alienation, we were driven to do anything. Bund was sympathetic with the early Marxian concept of alienation, which enchanted the minds of the seriously thinking students. The concept of alienation was tied up with the abolition of capitalism ... The original spirit of the Bund was a protest against that type of Marxism characterized by the absence of man, and against the capitalism that alienated man. But when the initial spirit was translated into stereotyped expressions such as "making the vanguard party," "revolution cannot be achieved by students alone," etc., it lost its original inspiration, and that was a major reason why the Bund became bankrupt. There is a parallelism between the Bund and the prewar orthodox rightist movements. They were both revolutionary movements starting from the sense of alienation in man.[11]

Yet on Shigeo Shima's account, the primacy of the concept of alienation in the student movement was comparatively recent. In fact, its rise would correspond to that phase of the student movement which began in 1956 when Japan seems to have emerged from postwar crisis and to have entered the era (as Shima put it) of the "mass society." Before 1956, he said, "economic life was very bitter. It was hard for students to eat."[12] The various student actions against the so-called "Red purge," the increases in tuition fees, the visiting American lecturers, and involvement in the Korean War were all primarily affected by the misery of their material existence. "To eat, however, was no longer the main problem after 1956." The students began to enjoy the unprecedented material prosperity of Japan under the aspect of a "mass society." The Japanese "bureaucracy" itself became the primary enemy for the student movement. And it was since 1956, said Shima, that the theme of the Japanese student movement became the overcoming of alienation.

In the years after 1956, Soviet students also began to discover the concept of alienation. According to Father Joseph M. Bochenski, it first appeared in Soviet philosophical literature in 1958 by way of a review of Calvez's book on Marx. Father Bochenski judges that the use of the concept is "still slight." In the spring of 1963, however, I found it to be the concept most provocative and illuminating to young Soviet philosophers. Their critique of bourgeois society and philosophy was less in terms of the economic contradictions of capitalism than in terms of its alienation of the spirit of man. To their readers was left the unspoken task of testing the achievement of Soviet society in the light of this cross-societal concept, powerful because of its very vagueness.

Pyata P. Gaidenko. a gifted young philosopher at Moscow State University, for instance, contrasted Marx with the Western existentialists:

This is the crux of Marxian criticism of capitalist society. Marx rebelled against capitalism because capitalism crushed the personality and converted

it into a thing . . . In contrast to Marx the existentialists believe that the
alienated mode of being is rooted in the very nature of man; . . . In the
world of commonplaces the individual lives conformingly; responsibility for
his actions lies not with himself but with "one" (i.e., with them), for while
living in such an environment man the individual is not free in his actions,
but obeys certain laws, precepts, dicta of public opinion, etc. . . . But to be
free, to be a person, is far more difficult than to withdraw into a humdrum
world where there is no need for the individual to make his own decisions,
to be responsible to himself.[13]

Existentialism, says the writer, developed when the individual in the
capitalist world became "aware of himself as something alien to this
whole and even inimical to it."

How does the young Soviet student read such a passage? He recognizes in its description of the pressure of bureaucracy, public opinion,
and impersonal institutions the analogue of what he has experienced
in his life. The circumpressures of Komsomol, Party, and faculty committee, circumpressures in lecture hall and seminar which make a
tedium of the curricula in literature, philosophy, and history, circumpressures which impose a Party line on every essay he submits in every
course, and which impose their requirement that he see things falsely
and purvey hollow words that are not his own—of all this the young
Soviet student is aware. Perforce he finds himself a Soviet existentialist,
a protestant against bureaucratic society with its estrangements.

Such a critique is latent in the writing of the young Soviet philosopher, Yuri Davydov, on the concept of alienation:

The essence of this alienation consists in the fact that the human form of
activity of the individual splits away from him (as a given empirically concrete individual), and not only escapes his control but in reality confronts
him as an alien power.

Now "alienation" . . . is a result of the common activity of the people,
which is conditioned by the division of labor. The reason for alienation
then is seen in the fact that common activity originates not voluntarily but
as if by natural calamity. And, thus, the problem of eliminating this
alienation becomes a problem of such a communal activity of people which
would arise not coercively but voluntarily, consciously, and planned.[14]

The young Soviet philosophers, to be sure, always criticize the
bourgeois existentialist thinkers for failing to perceive the social sources
of alienation in the bourgeois society. But the domain of applicability
for concepts cannot be contained. The young Soviet readers value
these writings not for their predictable refutations of the bourgeois
existentialists but for their portrayal of the experience of alienation
itself. They savor its flavor, and compare it with their own experience. They have been given a word with which to articulate their

own discontent with the Bureaucratic Society. Fortunately Marx himself used the word, a youthful Marx, unpublished and unread in the Stalinist era, but now exhumed by a later generation of youth to speak in indirect discourse of its own alienation from the bureaucratized Stalinist generation.

The Socio-Emotional Basis of the New Alienation

Thus the student movements today confront a world which is both bureaucratic and stable. Whether in the United States, Japan, or the Soviet Union, they perceive a society dominated by large, impersonal institutions which impose their norms of conformity. Hierarchy and impersonality loom as hostile, alien forces against the studentry whose life's ways are comradeship and personalism. A student leaflet at the University of California, for instance, echoed in its title the protest against impersonal, mechanized institutions: "Are you a Student or an IBM Card?"[15] It went on to tell of the student de-personalized by institutions which determined his sleeping quarters, his studies, his life, and rendered him impotent. But the System, though hateful, is stable. Marx assailed the bourgeois society because of its "anarchy" of production. There is no anarchy in the System. Its controls, on the whole, work well; there are inefficiencies but evidently no "contradictions." The System achieves an equilibrium which, if not at a maximum level, is nonetheless an equilibrium. The economic foundation of society seems relatively invulnerable to criticism; the students have as yet no basic changes to propose in the economic substructure. Theirs is the "politics of the superstructure," the politics of the quality of life, of human relations, of civil rights, peace, and humanism.[16] The concept of alienation is the key to the critique of the superstructure as that of exploitation was to the critique of the foundation.

It is the very ambiguity of the concept of alienation which lends itself to the Marxism of the student movement. In the thirties, when the depression was at its height, the students identified themselves with the protest of the workers against exploitation. "Exploitation" was a definable economic process, and measures were proposed to eliminate it. The exploiting persons and the devices of exploitation could be located; the bourgeois society seemed visibly founded on the exploitation of the lower classes. An alternative society was envisaged which would be classless, in which no men would exploit others. Surplus value would cease to be an economic category in a socialist society.

The new student movements, however, are utterly vague as to the society they propose. They are against the bureaucrats, but they scarce

know what to say when asked for the lineaments of the nonbureau-
cratic society. They find it more congenial to concentrate on specific
issues of civil rights, peace and disarmament, or compulsory courses
in military science. Indeed, at its revival in America, the student movement claimed to be "issue-oriented" and without ideology.[17] Yet students soon felt that the "end of ideology" was precisely the ideology
of the Establishment, the older generation, the Bureaucracy. The "end
of ideology" was the doctrine of those who left no unfinished business
for the new generation, and who affirmed a pseudo-consensus which
ended all the basic issues of ethics and political philosophy. Left and
right for the older generation had merged into an all-inclusive center; such differences as remained for them were differences as to
means, not as to ends. The elders shared a drab absence of vision.
The Bureaucratic Establishment moreover was scientific and elitist;
those who now rose to the places of power were required to be competent in the administration of an advanced technological society. They
could hardly be expected to show any reverence for the people,
proletariat or peasantry. As a scientific elite, the Bureaucratic Establishment was convinced that the techniques of applied sociology would
suffice to resolve conflicts. Sociological science, not ideology, held the
intellectual allegiance of the Academic Establishment. And when this
fact was perceived by the students, "the end of ideology" became at
once a suspect symbol. It was the ideology of the smug and self-
satisfied, the callous and complacent, those who were Marxists without being revolutionists, and were emasculating the dialectic of its
motive power.

"Scientific socialism" thus lost its appeals for students precisely
insofar as it was scientific. The new "socialism" such students professed
would now be ethical and voluntaristic; the motive power of history,
if they but chose, was not impersonal forces but their own personal
will, not the indirect pervasive effect of economic pressures but their
own direct action, their individual intervention. Every revolutionary
generation re-selects its Marxist passages and texts for its purposes. The
new student generation found the forgotten texts of "alienation."

Above all, the notion of "alienation" could express the varied moods
of younger-generation resentment. For this resentment is not founded
upon the students' place in the mode of production. The students of
today are the most affluent of history—with a richness of scholarships,
fellowships, and assistantships before them. They often linger for many
years in the status of graduate students because their lives are so
comfortable. They marry and re-marry and have families on their

stipends, salaries, and subventions. Undergraduates often drive their own cars and are free from economic concern. This revolt, therefore, cannot be ascribed to economic goals. Students in the thirties who experienced generational resentment sublimated and translated it into concern with theirs and their fathers' economic problems. There was a kind of healing therapy in dealing with the economic problems of themselves and their society. But the new resentment is unable to attach itself to any central exploitation which it experiences. When an energy of discontent floats about aimlessly, unable to find an appropriate object, it requires an equally ambiguous word, equally devoid of any directional definition; such a word is "alienation." Thus the early Marx provided the emotive symbol for idealistic students in generational revolt against the System. In effect, the new student movement is standing the mature Marx on his head, and the alternation of ideological generations persists with each trying to turn the Ideological Father topsy-turvy.

The use of the concept of "alienation" marks in this fashion a regression in the history of Marxism, a reversion to the stage of "philosophical socialism"—when Marx looked to the intellectuals, not the workers, as the bearers of the great socialist renovation. When Marx and Engels began to view the workers as the historical class, they shifted the emphasis to "exploitation," not "alienation." The new student movements, however, as we have mentioned, arise at a time when societies enjoy relatively full employment and affluence. The working class movement is no longer a movement but an interest group which accepts the System; its trade union leaders are part of the Establishment. The concept of alienation expresses also the feeling of the alienation of the students as young intellectuals from the society around them. They are rejected not only by the middle class but by the workers. Hence, there arises a new vocabulary to express the lines of division in society; every bureaucrat has his beatnik, and the enemy is no class enemy but the "square." [18] One is embattled not with the Ruling Class, but with the Establishment, which embraces the bureaucrats of all classes and strata from financiers to union leaders. A historian of the beatniks writes perforce in the language of the early Marx. This is not

the politically oriented alienation of the thirties. The present generation has ... passed on beyond them to a total rejection of the whole society, and that, in present-day America, means the business civilization. The alienation of the hipsters from the squares is now complete ... This is not just another alienation. It is a deep-going change, a revolution under the ribs.[19]

A revolt against the bureaucrats of all classes, including labor, means that the traditional slogans of classical and Leninist Marxism can no longer stand muster. For Lenin was preeminently an admirer of Bureaucracy, Organization, System. The new student movement finds itself at odds with itself as it looks for an organizational form. It finds itself drawn to spontaneous, quickly mounted, guerrilla actions against the System, and it feels an admiration for guerrilla tactics, whether by Fidel Castro or Viet Cong. Yet it has to seek a permanent form of organization, and the devil bureaucracy begins to intrude. Both in Tokyo and Berkeley, the student movements have been described as Blanquist in spirit and tactics.[20] The era of the Automatized Social System is curiously vulnerable to human assaults in its weakest links of dehumanized control.

The alienation of the generations, the mainspring of student movements, involves an immense social tragedy. It brings a resurgence in action of hitherto unconscious impulses of destruction, of one's self and others. Student movements have a propensity to veer from terrorism to suicidalism. It is a noteworthy fact that massive student movements have tended to arise only in countries which have a youth-weighted suicide rate. Japan, with its recent influential student movement, as well as tsarist Russia, exhibited this characteristic. On the other hand, countries such as Sweden and Switzerland which have not had student movements have "normal" suicidal patterns, that is, frequency of suicide tends to increase with age; the older people have the higher rates.[21] Thus in Japan, the suicide rate from 1952 to 1954 for the ages from 20 to 24 years was 60 per 100,000 as compared to 27.4 in Austria and 25.4 in Denmark. "By 1959 suicide in Japan had become the single most common source of death for individuals under thirty." It was during the efflorescence of the Japanese student movement that the suicide rate for Japanese youth reached its highest proportions, "with the period between 1955 and 1960 showing higher rates reported then for youth than at any other time in Japanese history."[22]

The suicide rate in Russia, the land of the classical student movement, was typically youth-weighted. In Moscow, during 1908 and 1909, of one thousand suicides, 381 were between 15 and 20, 179 between 21 and 25, 134 between 26 and 30, 117 between 31 and 40, 73 between 41 and 50.[23] Krupskaia, Lenin's wife, felt called upon to write an article upon suicide among the Russian studentry. She spoke of the alienation of the generations and the terrible psychological state of loneliness which overcame the student: "Is it common," she asked, "for a student to begin to talk with his teacher of his sincere

thoughts and doubts, does he look for moral support from his teacher?
At its worst, the student and the teacher are two enemy camps." [24]

America, of course, has never had a youth-weighted suicide rate but
America, too, it must be remembered, has never had a massive student
movement of the national proportions which existed in Russia and
Japan. The six hundred youngsters who participated in the Mississippi
Summer Project in 1964 were a minute fraction of a total American
studentry of about two million. By contrast, the back-to-the-people
movement in Russia in the eighteen-seventies numbered several thousands at a time when the total studentry itself was only about five
thousand.[25] Countries such as Britain and America which have been
free of massive student movements have also been characterized by
what we may call a "generational equilibrium." But in the one example
of a large American university where a student movement flourished,
during this past generation, that of Berkeley in 1964, student involvement was evidently a channel for emotions which otherwise took more
self-destructive paths. The statistics of the psychiatric clinic of the
Cowell Hospital of the University of California tell that story. The
clinic on an average day would receive twenty patients for counselling,
but on October 2nd and December 4th, the days of maximum activity,
during the students' largest sit-in demonstration and strike, the number
of new patients sank to zero and two respectively. Moreover, student
activists who later came for counselling, "were almost uniformly filled
with euphoria," reported the university psychiatrist.[26] The generational
alienation which gives rise to student movements has psychological
sources which are still ill-understood. But the writer who dares probe
into them awakens powerful resistance-mechanisms on the part of
involved students. When Ivan Turgenev wrote his classic *Fathers and
Children,* he was denounced and reviled by the Russian student movement for his portrayal of the nihilist student Bazarov. "I was (and, for
that matter, still am) bespattered with muck and filth; so much abuse
and opprobrium, so many curses have been heaped upon my head
(Vidocq, Judas, lout, ass, poisonous toad, spittoon—this was the least
that was said of me) that it would be a satisfaction to me to prove
that other nations see the matter in a different light," confided
Turgenev to a friend.[27] Student movements resent the probing of the
unconscious sources of their generational revolt; they prefer to leave
that repressed, and to look upon themselves through their own "false
consciousness," through their own unanalyzed ideological terms.
"Alienation" thus, indeed, became the root concept of the "false
consciousness" of student movements, of generational revolt.

These phenomena of alienation of generations stand notably outside the purview and concerns of historical materialism. The emphasis on "alienation" rather than "exploitation" involves indeed, a vague feeling that a new conception of history must replace the materialist. The primacy of the mode of production and economic factors is displaced; historical materialism is put aside, and with it as well the notion of workingmen as the progressive, history-making class. The mature Marx wrote: "It is not the consciousness of men that determines their existence, but on the contrary, their social existence determines their consciousness." The young Marx, however, could write in Hegelian paraphrase, that history was constituted by man's consciousness transcending his existence, "as an act of coming-to-be it is a conscious self-transcending act of coming-to-be. History is the true natural history of man." [28] The emphasis on alienation, on man's trying to recover his essence, involves a notion of man's consciousness determining his existence. For if the materialistic conception of history were true, if men's psychologies were shaped as superstructural elements to conform to the requirements of the economic foundation, then no revolutionary social movement could arise. The very fact that a class becomes revolutionary, that it rejects in intention the presuppositions of the social system, is proof that the material base does not determine consciousness, that the ruling ideas of each age are not necessarily the ideas of its ruling class. Man, striving to realize his essence, regards the mode of production as an alienating agent insofar as it frustrates his inner aims; hence in critical junctures he transcends the constraints of the mode of production. The materialistic conception of history, in short, applies to those periods of human history where man acquiesces to his alienations, but it breaks down precisely in the revolutionary eras when his consciousness transcends his material existence, and he becomes truly Promethean, more truly man. Thus, the standpoint of alienation leads to a conception of history which if not idealistic involves the primacy of emotional striving; as the driving force in social process, the repressed unconscious seeking a conscious determining role emerges as the primary activator of historical change. The modes of emotion, of consciousness and the unconscious, are the substance of history rather than the modes of technical production.

The Doubts of Mature Marxism Concerning Student Movements

What then has been the attitude of Marxism to so-called student movements? It is quite clear that Marx and Engels regarded them with suspicion and dislike. After a brief period of hope for the student movement, Lenin decided it offered no revolutionary possibilities. Marx, Engels, and Lenin all seemed to have sensed that the material-istic conception of history was belied by the younger-generation up-risings of student idealism. Generational solidarity was a phenomenon which unlike class solidarity obviously required psychological cate-gories. The philosophical-idealistic aims which aroused the self-sacrificial enthusiasm of students were far removed from the motives of economic self-interest of the classes in class struggle. Student move-ments seemed to Marx and Engels a kind of surd in the historical movement toward a classless society. On the one hand, the students seemed to nurture their own ambitions as an elite in the socialist society, as emancipators of the proletariat who would be its new rulers; or on the other hand, they were given to extremes of self-destruction and terrorism, to a politics of the absurd.

Concerned with Bakunin's menace to the International Working-men's Association, Marx and Engels studied the Russian student move-ment which was so much attracted to Bakunin's creed of destruction, secrecy, and authoritarianism. Marx and his supporters on the General Council of the International Workingmen's Association could not bring themselves to admire the revolutionary student activists. They recognized that a new studentry was appearing which was imbued with socialist ideas "which it dreamed of putting into immediate ap-plication," and they believed too that the great majority of the new studentry was composed of "the sons of peasants and other poor people." They described the repressive measures at the University of St. Petersburg, the police surveillance and the abrogation of scholar-ships, which had called forth students' demonstrations, and the closing of the university. Nevertheless, Marx and Engels and their associates felt that "the more serious" students kept out of the secret political societies, and instead organized practical mutual aid societies. The students in the secret societies, wrote Marx and his group, ended up uselessly as exiles in Siberia, whereas the serious mutual aiders, on the other hand, gave the government no pretext for suppressing them, and helped their poorer classmates to continue their studies. Nechaiev, the bizarre and sick terrorist, had achieved a vogue in Russia, said Marx and Engels, as "the ideal type of the student"; he was the prototype of the student leader. With his mixture of fraud and brilliance, deceit and fanaticism, sadism and self-destruction, Jesuitism and amoralism, Nechaiev could electrify Russian student circles, but to Marx and Engels he was an aberration of political psychopathology.

The student youth were too ready to be deceived by the "fictions—lies on the extent and power of the secret society, prophecies on the imminence of the revolution prepared by it."[29] These revolutionary Russian students felt themselves moreover privileged to act without regard to political ethics: they fancied themselves beyond good and evil.

The later socialist student movement, such as it was, in Germany in 1890 aroused little enthusiasm in Engels. The students, to his mind, were arrogant young declassed bourgeois "arriving just in time to occupy most of the editorial positions on the new journals which pullulate and, as usual, they regard the bourgeois universities as a Socialist Staff College which gives them the right to enter the ranks of the Party with an officer's, if not a general's brevet." They seemed to him as had the students of 1848, those "representatives of intellect" who "were the first to quit their standards, unless they were retained by the bestowal of officer's rank."[30] Most of the students who professed themselves revolutionary socialists thus impressed Marx and Engels as either careerist or morally corrupt.

Lenin, like Marx and Engels, began with hope in the student intelligentsia, but as time went on he lost both faith and interest in the student movement as a vehicle of social change, and turned exclusively to the workers. Student movements have been called the "best barometer" of society, and it is true that the Russian revolutionary movement during its formative era was virtually a student movement.[31] "For at least three decades" after 1861, writes Avrahm Yarmolinsky, "the revolutionary movement was to be a youth movement, manned chiefly by undergraduates."[32] Lenin in 1903 characterized the students in words of tribute: "they are the most responsive section of the intelligentsia, and the intelligentsia are so called because they most consciously, most resolutely, and most accurately reflect and express the development of class interests and political groupings in society as a whole." Indeed, he had evidently saluted the assassination in 1901 of the Minister of Public Education by the student Karpovich. He appealed with moving eloquence for society not to stand aside and wait "for the inevitable tragic events by which every student movement has been attended hitherto." He asked the fathers not to desert their sons. "Why do we not hear the voice of the 'fathers,' when the children have unequivocally declared their intention to offer up new sacrifices on the altar of Russian freedom?"[33]

But as time went on, Lenin came gradually to believe that a "tragic" ending was inherent in student movements, that their defeat was ultimately due not to the fathers deserting their sons but rather to the student sons being too bound to their fathers. The student movement did not subordinate itself to the Bolshevik Party as Lenin had hoped, and he looked for a historical materialist explanation for their recalcitrance. Even at the height of his enthusiasm for the student movement, Lenin had objected to any analysis which emphasized the "unselfishness and purity of aims" of the student consciousness; this was a misleading, idealistic interpretation of history since "the students cannot be an exception to society as a whole, however unselfish, pure, idealistic, etc., they may be." [34]

Indeed, the great schism between the Bolsheviks and Mensheviks revolved in part on the question of the revolutionary character of the student movement. Generations of students are short-lived, and each generation in revolt wants to have its own experience of searching into fundamental problems. Lenin, however, had made his own ultimate commitment when his youthful circle merged itself with the Social Democratic Party, and he was tired of each student generation's renewal of its quest. He became disenchanted with the "circle-spirit" of the student movement. As a member of a party, he would tolerate no longer "all the freaks and whims of the old circles;" only the Girondists, the opportunists, would be so concerned with "professors and high school students." [35] Lenin recalled his own experience with typical Social-Democratic circles of students during the years from 1894 to 1901, their discussions, their groping efforts to contact workers, their first actions usually ending "in immediate and complete defeat." [36] It had been a necessary stage but he wanted no re-enactment of it.

The free-thinking and free-deciding student circles simply could not fit into Lenin's notion of a disciplined party, officered by a few intellectuals but with an obedient infantry. True, the student intellectuals had brought the socialist idea to the workers, but according to Lenin that was to be their last act as free intellectuals. From then on a discipline was required of which student movements seemed intrinsically incapable. After the split with the Mensheviks, Lenin's concern with the student movement tended to vanish. By 1908, he no longer professed to see in the student movement the replica of the class struggle in the nonstudent world. The students' strike of 1908 which erupted in St. Petersburg and spread to Moscow and Kharkov aroused only a tepid interest in Lenin, for he now saw the student as essentially linked to the liberal bourgeoisie: "Even the most active elements among the students stubbornly adhere to pure academism and are still singing the Cadet-Octobrist song ... Thousands and millions of threads bind the student youth to the middle and lower bourgeoisie, to the small officials, to certain groups of peasants, clergy, etc." "The mass of the youth," said Lenin resignedly, still "stands closest to the democratic bourgeoisie in Russia." [37]

To Lenin as to Marx and Engels, the students remained an unreliable ally in the socialist movement. Indeed, they did prove hostile to the Bolshevik Revolution. They had traversed a long ideological journey and drew back from the prospect of alienation in the proletarian-bureaucratic, anti-intellectual and anti-individualist society. As Trotsky wrote in his *History:* "The younger generation, the sons, the students? They were almost all hostile to the October revolution. But a majority of them too stood aside. They stood with their fathers awaiting the outcome of the battle." [38]

Such has always been the pattern of the response of Marxists to student movements—an initial enthusiasm for the creativity and idealism of the students in their revolutionary spirit, and then at a latter stage suspicion of the students as always alienated, always critical, always untractable. Take the evolution of Stalin's attitude, for instance, toward the students. The young Stalin in 1901, fresh from his own days at the theological seminary, had admiration for the students as a group relatively independent of economic determination: "Until they have plunged into the sea of life and have occupied a definite social position, the students, being young intellectuals, are more inclined than any other category to strive for ideals which call them to fight for freedom." [39]

Stalin said in tribute to the studentry that "at the present time the students are coming out in the 'social' movement almost as leaders in the vanguard. The discontended sections of different social classes are now rallying around them." Moreover, he said, students had invented a new tactic—the demonstration, and contributed greatly to the armory of revolutionary weapons. The strike was useful only against profit-seeking capitalists; a university was hardly in this category. Therefore, the students had been impelled to develop the tactic of the demonstration: "We must be grateful to the students for the lesson they have taught us: they showed how enormously important political demonstrations are in the revolutionary struggle." Above all a demonstration had a tremendous psychological potency; it attracted "curious onlookers" and lifted "the backward and timid" out of themselves when they saw "courageous fighters," heard "free voices" and "stirring songs denouncing the existing system. That is why the government fears street demonstrators more than anything else," wrote Stalin. It was because of their influence that "so many people offer their backs to the lash of the Cossacks' whip." [40]

Twenty years later, however, the overwhelming majority of student political activists at Moscow University were enthusiastic adherents of Leon Trotsky. In 1923, "of twenty-five university Communist cells, only one had a non-Trotskyist secretary." [41] All were de-activated or destroyed by Stalin's regime.

The Generational Duality in Contemporary Marxism

The will to revolt, the Promethean impulse, is largely founded on generational protest. Modern revolutionary movements characteristically derive from a union of class and generational struggles. The conflict of generations, a universal theme, imparts to the class struggle aims which transcend those of economic class interest. When the Promethean impulse is defeated and dies, it brings a tremendous gloom to the young, who then veer to self-destruction. Even Marx in his last years became pessimistic and melancholy, for the dialectic of history seemed to foreshadow a fatality of decline to which he had hitherto been insensitive. In 1881 Marx was keenly interested in the essay by his physician, Edwin Ray Lankester, on *Degeneration*. "He is a friend of mine," said Marx.[42] And Lankester in his work had questioned the "tacit assumption of universal progress—an unreasoning optimism," and reminded Victorian England "that we are subject to the general law of evolution, and are as likely to degenerate as to progress." "Does the reason of the average man of civilized Europe," asked Lankester, "stand out clearly as an evidence of progress when compared with that of men of bygone ages? Are all the inventions and figments of human superstition and folly, the self-inflicted torturing of mind, the reiterated substitution of wrong for right, and of falsehood for truth, which disfigure our modern civilization—are these evidences of progress? In such respects we have at least reason to fear that we may be degenerate." "With regard to ourselves," said Lankester, "the white races of Europe, the possibility of degeneration seems to be worth some consideration." [43] Such were the melancholy reflections in Marx's mind toward the end of his life. The dialectical philosophy with its eternal rebirth had proved to be largely indeed a generational projection, the ideology of student intellectuals projecting their eternal creative synthesis, the young destroying the old, and the world forever young. This was not a proletarian metaphysics, but a generational one, a projection of a restless, ever questing romanticism, quite unlike proletarian modes of thought. The eternal student rebel could conquer his generational alienation in a philosophical sense by portraying for himself a world which was in a similar eternal revolt. Li Ta-chao, the librarian at the University of Peking who organized a small group of students in 1921 to found the Chinese Communist Party, thus spoke in the metaphysical accents of the youth movement: "The Universe is eternal, hence youth is eternal, hence I am eternal." [44] The contemporary student has a similar metaphysics.

What has happened to Western Marxism today is bifurcation into two ideologies—managerial middle-age and alienationist youth. Social theory, we might say, oscillates for the moment between the two extreme standpoints of the bureaucrat and the beatnik. Managerial Marxism accepts the historical inevitability of a bureaucratized society; it perceives the hierarchy of new administrative skills as the basis for a new class structure, and refuses to be deceived by myths and illusions about the creative capacity of the lower classes. It accepts economic planning, and wishes to reconcile liberal democracy with the leadership of an intellectual elite. It regards the residual anomie of people in our society as the necessary social cost for the unprecedented rise in our standard of living, and would even assert that this anomie or alienation has declined from its level in past societies. Alienationist Marxism, on the other hand, refuses to be reconciled to bureaucratic society; it is historical voluntarist rather than materialist; it affirms the power of the individual will as against historical inevitability; it identifies itself with the lowliest in society in gesture, speech, clothes, and song; it finds a higher virtue in the Negro, or the Cuban, or the Chinese, than in the white American. It believes in its own direct action rather than in the processes of representative democracy. It is against the System, against the Establishment. It seeks a new mutuality in which there is no elite, for every elite involves a corresponding *rejeté*. When the "Free Speech" Movement won its victory at the University of California, many young activists could not reconcile themselves to its disbandment. For several weeks in demonstrations, sit-ins, strikes, and vigils they had found a new political communion, and communion alone conquers the separateness and isolation of alienation. How then to perpetuate this communion? They circulated a leaflet expressing this longing: "Happiness Is A thing Called People...We've Discovered Each Other. We Don't Want to Lose Each Other. We're Having a People to People Rally."

This bifurcation in Marxism is something which was never anticipated. The analysts of industrial and managerial society inherit the scientific content and method of Marxism; the alienationists have exhumed its repressed ethical protest and revolutionary metaphysics. Here is a novel stage in the history of Marxism more profound in its significance than any of the revisionist heresies, and perhaps even the Leninist modifications. For it portends the duality in conflict of that next era of managerial, industrial society to which we are tending, the conflict between managers and managed, the alienators and the alienated, the fathers and sons. Will the science and ethics of Marxism ever be reconciled? It was easy in the bourgeois society to call for expropriating the expropriators, but how will people achieve the alienation of the alienators? Here is an emerging schism in Marxism which is as universal as the dualities in human nature itself.

Joseph M. Bochenski

Marxism in Communist Countries

For the present writer to present Marxism as developed in Communist countries is a well-nigh impossible task, both for objective and subjective reasons. Objectively there is no method of sketching even the most essential characteristics of a domain so vast and diverse. Subjectively the author is one of those underdeveloped people who do not feel universally and equally competent in the fields of philosophy, sociology, political economy, and political science, all of which are integral parts of Marxism in Communist countries. Some limits had to be set: First, this paper is devoted principally to *philosophy,* with only a few remarks about other departments of the doctrine.[1] Second, even in philosophy, attention has been limited to an explanation of the causes of the present state of Marxism in these countries and to a presentation of those most characteristic aspects of the doctrine which distinguish it from classical Marxism. And finally, Soviet Union has been primarily considered while few remarks only have been included about other Communist countries.

Here, of course, a problem arises: *Can* we talk about men having a philosophy when they are prepared to sustain, in spite of everything, certain dogmatic principles? One classical instance is practically the whole of old Hindu philosophy, which nobody would deny is philosophy even though explicitly bound to a set of dogmas. This philosophy was struggling with certain genuine problems in which many contemporary philosophers in the United States and Europe are interested; while doing so, it seems to have brought out some results which, despite their dogmatic allegiances, are of theoretical value. Now, if this is so, there seems to be no reason why we should deny the name "philosopher" to a Communist thinker merely because he is a believing Communist. Of course, many among them do not merit that name because they are not really interested in any problems and are simply making propaganda. But there *are* in the Soviet Union and elsewhere in Communist countries men who, although believers, still think as the old Hindu philosophers did.[2]

Marxism in Communist countries is not simply Marxism, but Marxism-Leninism.[3] There is also some Marxism-Leninism in the doctrine of all Communist Parties, and several of them, like the French and Italian, did in fact develop some theoretical thought. But, on the whole, the representatives of such Marxist-Leninist thought outside the Communist countries are neither many nor very important. Thus an identification of Marxism in Communist countries with Marxism-Leninism seems to be justified for practical reasons. This expression will therefore constantly be used here.

Historical Background

Since the time of Karl Marx and Frederick Engels, several ideological influences have contributed to Communist thought. They are, in chronological order, Western pre-Leninist Marxism, Russian pre-Leninist thought, Lenin's activity, and post-Leninist ideological developments.

Western, and especially German, Marxism profoundly influenced both Plekhanov and Lenin. The latter, it is true, wrote a violent pamphlet against Kautsky,[4] but he is, nevertheless, on the whole an heir of the German socialist leader. Among other things, Lenin took from Kautsky and other German Marxists faith in the unity of thought of Marx and Engels and the practice of seeing Marx through the eyes of Engels. This is, it seems, one major factor in the constitution of contemporary Communist doctrines. In addition, some particular doctrines, like those of Hilferding, are known to have deeply influenced Lenin.

Russian thought is another factor in the formation of Leninism. It is well known that Lenin considered Chernishevsky a major influence on his own thinking. He also owes much to Dobroliubov, not to mention Plekhanov.[5] More important, Lenin was a Russian member of the Russian intelligentsia; even in Western countries, he lived practically in a Russian ghetto. As a consequence, he retained much of the basic attitude of that intelligentsia. It is probably a hopeless task to look for a particular Russian "soul," but there is without doubt a certain frame of mind, a class of assumptions and a class of basic attitudes that were common to the Russian revolutionary intelligentsia at the end of the nineteenth century. Berdiaev, himself a member of that brilliant group, has given us an unsurpassed analysis of that mentality. He stressed, among other things, the highly speculative and metaphysical trend of the "principal 'nost," the curious blend of politics with attitudes which may be called religious, and the profound urge for social change.[6] It is hardly possible to understand present-day Marxism-Leninism without knowing that background of Lenin. Moreover, it seems that not only the passing attitude of the Russian intelligentsia but also other Russian factors were active in framing Marxism-Leninism. To mention just one instance: the reinterpretation of the doctrine concerning the dictatorship of the proletariat is understandable if one considers the traditional Russian way of looking at the relation between the individual and the community, an attitude expressed, for example, in the old Russian concept of elections.[7]

Nevertheless, Marxism in Communist countries is Marxism-*Leninism*. Lenin contributed much not only in details, such as his theory of knowledge or of imperialism, but also in regard to some quite basic philosophical problems. Lenin was, for one thing, an outspoken voluntarist. He stressed the voluntarist element in Marxism to an extent which would probably never have been admitted by Marx himself. He was also an intellectual aristocrat; if his reformulation of the theory of dictatorship is partly due to his Russian background, his own attitude toward the masses, so different from that of Marx, certainly did play here an important role. Harper, moreover, drew attention to the fact that Lenin's attitude toward religion was far more radical than that of Marx.[8] Finally, I should like to mention his stress on means with an almost complete disregard for the ends. In all these ways Lenin introduced new and important changes into the Marxism of his time.

Contemporary Marxism-Leninism, however, evolved after Lenin's death in several respects and in some of them departed still further from Marx. It became the official and exclusive state-doctrine in Communist countries; the development of the material basis in these countries, to use a Marxian term, changed the outlook of their citizens; and in East Central Europe Marxism-Leninism encountered a completely different intellectual climate from that in which Lenin operated.

One result of all this is that a serious study of the field requires specialization in particular periods and factors. Thus we speak about Marxology, i.e., the study of Marx and Engels; about Leninology, research into the thought and background of Lenin; and of Sovietology, post-Leninist developments.[9] We also need more systematic research into the thought of those German and other Marxists who constitute the link between Engels and Plekhanov. And I would like to insist that it is impossible for anyone to be a "general Marxologist," for no one can be sufficiently well up on all of these periods and factors.

Roughly speaking, the history of Marxism-Leninism can be divided into four periods: the NEP period also called the "first period of discussions" (1922–30), the "dead" period (1931–47), the period of liberalization (1947–56), and the contemporary period (since 1956). At the beginning of the NEP period both Lenin and some of his main collaborators, such as Bukharin and Trotsky, were still alive, and Stalin did not yet have absolute power. Marxism-Leninism was already the state-doctrine, but in one country only, the Soviet Union. The doctrine was also very much alive in terms of both historical, Marxologist research and systematic speculation. A. M. Deborin is probably one of the most prominent Marxist-Leninist thinkers up to the present; G. Lukacs' main work also belongs to those years.

With the decree of the Central Committee of January 25, 1931 against Deborin, the so-called "Stalinist" era begins. As M. P. Baskin said in 1947, there was at that time no philosophy in the Soviet Union, but just "quotatology" (*citatologiia*),[10] and the same was true of political economy and political science. There was some historical research, but Marxologist studies ceased almost completely with the death of D. K. Riazanov and the murder of V. Adoratsky. It was the time of the purges followed by war and the difficult reconstruction after the war. Oriental despotism, so feared by Marx, was applied on an unprecedented scale to the whole realm of thought.

This period is incorrectly called "Stalinist" in that Stalin, who was its moving spirit and thus responsible for it, brought it to a close by his two interventions: on June 24, 1947 (through Zhdanov), and on June 20, 1950, by his famous "letters on linguistics" (very inappropriately called so, because they are neither letters, nor do they treat of linguistics: they are oral declarations about language). It was again a period of discussions, of ardent and sometimes valuable and profitable discussions. Marxism-Leninism became alive again, in spite of the fact that the Soviet Party still strictly controlled thought. There were now many more Communist countries. Although they were completely controlled on the ideological level by Russia, Marxism-Leninism was being seriously considered in many foreign nations, and the foundations were laid for future evolution.

Finally, since 1956 we have had new developments, perhaps less spectacular than those of 1947–56, but developments which have brought notable progress. One might be tempted to call the current period a period of pluralism. There are now several different trends, if not quite distinct schools of thought, among Soviet thinkers.[11] On the other hand we can observe a pluralism caused by the plurality of Communist nations with their different cultural traditions. The most spectacular differences are those evidenced by Yugoslavia[12] and Poland.[13] But it also must be mentioned that Czechoslovakia, a most orthodox country, has developed a vigorous Marxist-Leninist thought.[14]

Marxism-Leninism as State Doctrine

Marxism-Leninism enjoys in all Communist countries the status of state doctrine. In most of them it is the only one which can be publicly expressed and taught, while in a few others some exceptions are tolerated, e.g., in Yugoslavia and, to a larger extent, in Poland.[15] If we look for analogies, the position of Marxism-Leninism is best compared to some great religions like Buddhism, Christianity, or Islam during certain periods of their histories. There is, however, one capital difference: the religions did not pretend, at least in principle, to rule everything in the life of the states they were dominating, while Marxism-Leninism does make such a pretention. It is a totalitarian doctrine.

The Marxist-Leninist in Communist countries has to face two problems. On one side he must be able to deduce from his doctrine principles for ruling or governing the state. His Marxism up to now merely a revolutionary doctrine, a theory about how to overthrow existing systems, has to become a state-building doctrine. The Revolution has been accomplished, the adversary destroyed inside the country, and the question "what is to be done?" takes on now quite a different meaning. It no longer refers exclusively to the *means,* but more and more to the *ends.* Therefore, the Marxist-Leninist must now develop a far more concrete doctrine of ends. It was once enough to repeat some vague slogan about the "paradise on earth" and the happiness of everybody. Now it becomes imperative to state in some detail how that paradise is to be constituted and realized. At the same time, because of his totalitarian pretentions, the Marxist-Leninist is obliged to deal with all new developments. He cannot, for instance, disregard cybernetics or genetics; while claiming that they should be Marxist-Leninist, he still has to allow their development. These theories are of vital importance for the state which the Marxist-Leninists have to rule.

Finally, there is one new aspect, a more consoling one for the Marxist-Leninist. He has all the resources of the state at his disposal for the development and dissemination of his teaching. Means in money and man-power, about which no Marxist could ever have dreamed, can and consequently must—given the importance of ideology according to Marxism-Leninism—be put at the disposal of thought.

It is sometimes said that Marxism-Leninism is quite irrelevant from the point of view of the leaders of the Communist parties in power. To refute such an opinion it is enough to state that those leaders not only constantly stress its importance [16] but also care for its development on an unprecedented scale. In all Communist countries the teaching of ideological doctrines and the publication of ideological writings takes on truly enormous proportions. Thus, Yugoslavia, which before 1945 had produced very little philosophy (there is, for instance, hardly anything about this country in *Ueberweg*),[17] is now producing something like a hundred philosophical studies a year.[18] The Fribourg Bibliography of Soviet Philosophy gives for 14 years almost 8,000 titles.[19] During the past few years the output increased considerably and can be estimated at 1,000 a year. Between 1918 and 1959, 301,015,000 copies of the works of Lenin were published, among others 5,034,000 copies of *Materialism and Empiriocriticism*.[20] At one time the main philosophical journal of the Soviet Union printed 50,000 copies. It still prints about 30,000 [21] copies of some 5,000 pages a year. Moscow alone has approximately 100 full professors of philosophy. Nearly 2,000 are teaching in the country,[22] and several hundred specialize in the philosophy of physics. It is said that in China the Party ordered not less than 15,000 graduates to prepare for the career of professor of philosophy.

The Marxist-Leninist Dilemma

Quantitative development, however, is accompanied by what we may term "the Marxist-Leninist dilemma." It stems from the above mentioned character of a totalitarian state doctrine. On the one hand this is a dogmatic, absolutist viewpoint: [23] every Marxist-Leninist must keep to the basic rules and principles; he must also hold that *everything* in science, art, morals, and so on has to conform to his absolute standards. On the other hand he must face the growing body of scientific knowledge and more generally the development of spiritual life. Up to 1947 the all-pervading authority of the doctrine and of the Party was emphasized. In 1948 this was true of Lysenko,[24] and an attempt was made in the 1950's to apply the same procedure to Einstein's theories.[25] But quite obviously this attempt was not successful, and slowly a method was developed which seems to have become one of the most characteristic traits of the contemporary Soviet and, more generally, Communist attitude.

By now the content of the doctrines is tacitly divided into three zones of different dignity.[26] The first we shall term "the basic dogma." It is a class of relatively few statements formulated in a language intelligible to everybody ("Even a Kolkhoz peasant knows that there is no God," said Khrushchev). The second we shall call "speculative superstructure," a vast class of statements formulated in a technical, Hegelian or Marxist terminology and therefore intelligible only to educated men ("there is a dialectical logic" is an example). The third is a set of statements about problems lying, so to speak, on the borderline between ideology and pure science, e.g. the problem of the legitimacy of mathematical logic as logic. We shall call these "declassified doctrines." [27]

Now the situation seems to be this: Everybody has to recognize the basic faith as absolutely true and not to be interpreted except as approved by the Party. The speculative superstructure must also be acknowledged by everybody, but it may be interpreted rather freely. Sometimes this goes so far that the opposite of what was originally meant is arrived at. Finally, there is today a practically unlimited freedom of discussion in the matter of declassified doctrines. For instance, there are philosophers who hold that mathematical logic is pernicious nonsense if applied to philosophy, while others think that it is nothing more than scientific logic and, in fact, the only one.

Dialectics

In Marxist-Leninist terminology the term "dialectics" refers both to a set of ontological theories and to a method. The second aspect, which was most stressed by Stalin for whom the "dialectical" element in dialectical materialism was merely its methodology, is still thought to be of paramount importance. The method of Marxism-Leninism is said to be dialectical and many studies are devoted to the so-called dialectical logic.[28] However, no clear post-Stalin statement of this methodology is known to the author. Dialectical method would be, according to Stalin, one which considers the interconnection of phenomena, looks for the evolutionary trends, is specially interested in the "nodal points" in which rapid changes occur, and concentrates for an explanation of phenomena on "contradictions," that is, on polar oppositions. All that, even if presented with many details and exemplified by concrete cases, supplies hardly more than a few rough rules of procedure which, incidentally, are universally recognized as sound. What is more important perhaps is a truly platonic attitude, an aversion to ready-made concepts and rigid systems. This comes through Hegel from Plato, and implies an anti-Aristotelian frame of mind.

Seen as a whole, contemporary Marxism-Leninism is, however, quite obviously infected by a strong Aristotelian tendency in method. Not only has formal logic, rejected during the second period (1931–47), been solemnly recognized as a valid instrument of philosophical studies,[29] but it now flourishes in most Communist countries. It often (if not always) takes the shape of a truly scientific, mathematical logic.[30] But there is more to it than that. The fabric of Marxism-Leninism is quite obviously thought of as a sort of axiomatic system in which, from certain absolutely true premises, "basic faith," everything else is rigorously deduced. Of course the opposite, more empiricist element is also present, and the need for empirical studies is stressed. But very few such studies are known to have been made, and those only in recent times. In any event, the deductivist approach, very similar to that prescribed in the Posterior Analytics, is mostly practiced.

It is sometimes difficult to understand how such a system can claim, as it constantly does, to be built up on a purely "scientific" method, by which the method of the natural sciences is meant. The explanation has been supplied by Blakeley. The first step in building a scientific system, namely the inductive reasoning, is supposed to have been performed once and for all by the "classics." Consequently, only deduction and the verification of the results obtained is left to the contemporary Marxist-Leninist. And verification serves exclusively in confirming and never in disproving the results of the classics. This confirmation is obtained by the elimination of negative instances. On the whole the "dialectical" or methodological aspect of contemporary Marxism-Leninism is probably the weakest among its elements. It strikes an impartial and informed reader as a curious mixture of emotionally conditioned judgments, explanatory hypotheses, and deduction—all of which represents a level of thought long since left behind in the development of methodology.

It may be finally noticed that some Marxist-Leninist methodologists seem to be aware of the above criticism and try to find a better way of dealing with dialectics. One quite radical solution, the denial of dialectics as a method altogether, is that of a leading Soviet philosopher, Bakradze.[32] Others, like Zinoviev,[33] seem to be of the opinion that dialectics, while having nothing to do with formal logic, may be useful as a set of guiding principles for philosophical research. But the majority retain Engels' and Lenin's confused notion of dialectics, at one and the same time a logic, a method, an ontology, and a theory of knowledge.

Science and Ideology

In one respect, however, there has been a considerable change in basic methodological principles. During the second period (1931–47), every factor which was social *and* spiritual was considered "ideological." This may or may not be a Marxist doctrine (the present writer thinks it is not), but it is for all that a legitimate conclusion from the principles assumed. For the "forms of social consciousness" are nothing else than another name for the Hegelian objective spirit, and this objective spirit comprehends everything that is both social and spiritual including, consequently and above all, the sciences. But the forms of social consciousness are, according to Marx and his followers, superstructures of a given basis, which in turn is coordinated to a class. They all seem, consequently, to be a class affair, an ideology. The great change in this respect was brought about by Stalin in 1950. By declaring that whatever belongs to production (to "the forces of production," would be a more precise formula) is class-free and stating at the same time that language is such, Stalin opened the door to the recognition of social and spiritual factors which are not class-bound, that is, not ideological.

The consequences of this were soon drawn. In 1951 logic was declared nonideological.[34] Since 1954,[35] according to a standard teaching a part of the content of the sciences must also be considered as such, namely, the properly "scientific" part of them, statements of facts and of the "scientific laws," while the most general theories remain ideological and class-bound. But even in the field of most general theories the opinion that they are class-free sometimes prevails, as in the case of the Restricted Theory of Relativity.[36] At least the better Marxist-Leninists declare that the philosopher has to take the results of science as they are. They deny that there is such a thing as, for instance, a proletarian or a bourgeois physics. The role of the philosopher, that is, of the ideologist, consists in the philosophical interpretation of the obtained scientific results.

This does *not* apply to social sciences, however, but only to the natural sciences. As far as the former are concerned, empirical research in sociology has only recently been recognized as legitimate[37] and according to all we know is still considered a very second-rate affair.

In economics there is no other theoretical science than Marxism-Leninism. And of course political science is still more an affair of pure ideology. Yet everywhere a trend toward liberalization seems to be present. It is less apparent the nearer a field is to the political practice of the Party. But by a sort of osmosis the influence of what has been achieved in restricting the field of ideology in theoretical departments seems to be acting also on the more practical sciences of society.

Materialism

The second central doctrine of Marxist-Leninist philosophy is its materialism. Taken to be a doctrine according to which matter has priority over spirit and being over thought, it is traditionally presented in its four applications: to the theory of knowledge (extreme epistemological realism), to metaphysics (atheism), to anthropology, and to sociology (historical materialism).[38] In epistemology there has not been much novelty since Lenin,[39] and historical materialism is still expounded, on the whole, on Marxist lines with, it must be added, some refinements concerning the concept of historical determination and similar things. But interesting developments seem to be present both in metaphysics and in anthropology.

As far as the metaphysics is concerned, a sort of doctrine of emergent evolution has been developed out of some texts of Engels and Lenin. Lenin maintained that matter is infinite in profundity. By this he meant that, just as going beneath the surface of macrocosmic objects we find molecules and beneath these atoms, we can continue the process of delving into matter indefinitely. This statement is now being reinterpreted as meaning that Matter, that is, Nature, contains in its bosom virtually all possible "forms of movement" which emerge out of it successively in time [40]—a view not very much different from that of Lloyd Morgan or Samuel Alexander, nor basically from that of Augustine. In connection with the doctrine of emergent evolution, optimistic evolutionism has been called in question. While it still is a basic dogma in regard to society, a Marxist-Leninist is allowed to deny it for the world as a whole.

The changes made in anthropology are more complicated. Marxism-Leninism has never been a monistic materialism. That is, the existence of mind, which Marxist-Leninists say is nonmaterial, has always been asserted.[41] Of course there is no soul, no substantial spirit, and consciousness (identified in Marxism-Leninism with mind) is said to be dependent on matter causally in so far as it is matter's function, and also in so far as its content is considered to be "a copy, a photograph, a reflection" (*otrazhenie*) of matter.[42] And for all that mind was said to be something nonmaterial. What was meant here was not a materialistic but rather an Aristotelian view of Man conceived as a unit endowed with many different levels of "movement" which were sharply distinguished from one another. That view has been magnificently elaborated by the leading Soviet psychologist, the late S. L. Rubinstein.[43]

But in 1950 something happened which can, I think, be best explained as a victory of the old, pre-revolutionary monistic psychology of I. M. Sechenov and Pavlov. A "reconstruction" (*perestroika*) of psychology was ordered,[44] and Rubinstein submitted.[45] He did it in such an intelligent way that he seems to have been converted interiorly on command. From that time on no distinction was permitted between the physiological (nervous) and psychological (mental) processes.[46] There is only one sort of "movement." At the same time psychology is said to be a discipline quite distinct from physiology. The situation is far from clear. A more monistic materialistic trend seems to coexist with a more dualistic one.

Axiology

The theory of values does not seem to have undergone any significant changes. But Marxism-Leninism is not only a *theory* of values; it is also a *code* of such values, and in that respect the changes are important. In aesthetics one major addition to classical Marxism is the doctrine of socialist realism. This asserts that art should be a sort of reflection of reality, that it should not be formal and should be understandable to the masses. The above has been deduced, in a way which may appear unconvincing, from the principles of historical materialism. In spite of being a part of what we termed "speculative superstructure," aesthetics has not been declassified and is still imposed in most Communist countries by the Party.

In ethics, on the contrary, many and more far-reaching changes have been made.[47] For one, a curious doctrine of the "golden foundation" (*zolotoi fond*) of humanity, namely, of a set of values valid in all periods and formations, has been proclaimed. This would seem to contradict the basic tenets of historical materialism. More flagrantly anti-Marxist are recognition of the value of patriotism and the stress laid on family life.[48] Both, although destined to disappear according to the Communist Manifesto, are now said to be essential for Communist society and are strongly emphasized. In connection with the doctrine of the family a puritan teaching on sexual morality, often expressed in Augustinian terms, is preached. Here more than in any other part of Marxism-Leninism the necessities confronting a state-building doctrine are manifest. There is at present very much activity in the field of ethics and morals throughout the Communist countries.[49] But the situation is far from clear.

We may distinguish two major problems with which contemporary Marxism-Leninism is grappling in this domain. One is the problem of the relative rights of the individual and of society. In that respect, there is a great difference between the rough statements of Lenin, for whom the individual was nothing more than a means toward the attainment of the social aims, and the emphatic claims of Khrushchev in asserting that the individual must be cared for for his own sake. There is a whole body of moral writings in which, alongside the specific social virtues, others such as "respect for the old," "respect for every man," and "opposition against every sort of oppression" are recommended.[50]

Yet there is one area in which Marxism-Leninism did not rise above the level of Engels and Lenin and did not retain even the attitude of Karl Marx himself. This area is the so-called existential problematic, the questions of the *Grenzsituationen,* of death, suffering, failure and the like. Only during recent years does thought seem to have been devoted to such questions by isolated thinkers.[51] It is also characteristic of Marxism-Leninism that the very term "alienation" is seldom used in Soviet philosophical literature and then mostly between quotation marks, as if it were an unusual word. Recently, however, some interest in alienation has been shown, but it is still slight.[52] Marxism-Leninism is, on the whole, a Spinozistic philosophy in so far as it simply disregards such questions. In that respect it is sharply anti-Marxist indeed.

Something similar may be said as far as religion is concerned. The basic attitude of Lenin has been taken over: Religion is a false and socially harmful phenomenon; it must be combated once its basic, class society, has been destroyed. In that respect Marxism-Leninism is very Leninist indeed. But if we consider the teaching of the so-called "scientific atheism" we miss practically everything of Marx's own justification of atheism except his social doctrines. Religion is usually combated with astonishingly superficial arguments (the astronauts did not meet any God, there were many bad Popes, etc.), and apparently no effort is made to give to atheism a positive philosophical foundation. This is linked with the curious fact that very few among the prominent Marxist-Leninists are taking part in the quantitatively enormous and qualitatively deplorable literature on the subject. It may be that they are either disgusted with its low level or consider themselves already mentally at the stage of communism where, according to Marx, atheism will no longer be needed.[53]

Revisionism

In Communist countries and abroad there is at present much talk about so-called "revisionism" (as also about the so-called "cult of personality" or "Stalinism"). Revisionism is defined, in the abstract, as a tendency toward a revision of what should not be revised, namely, those elements of Marxism-Leninism considered as belonging to the basic faith. Considered by whom? The only answer is: by the respective Party. As Lobkowicz pointed out quite correctly,[54] it makes no sense to call a Marxist-Leninist "revisionist" if he is not called so by his own Party, and it makes no sense to deny that someone is "revisionist" if he has been condemned as such by his Party. Even apart from this fact, there are so many things which may be revised in the large body of Marxist-Leninist basic tenets, that the term "revisionism" does not seem to have a very clear meaning.

Most of the so-called revisionists have wanted to come closer to some among the "classics," above all to Marx, and especially to Marx as represented in his earlier works. But this is not always the case. What some Yugoslav theoreticians say about the class struggle, according to Vrtačić, is not only opposed to the now codified Marxism-Leninism but is even quite clearly in opposition to Marx himself. Also, the attempt of Ernst Bloch [55] to introduce teleology into the system, even though it may seem quite a legitimate step, is nonetheless contrary to the spirit of all the classics. And it seems that Kolakowski [56] might well be a sort of Marxist, but hardly a Marxist-Leninist at all.

Perhaps the case of Khrushchev was basically not very different. He was called a revisionist by the Chinese Marxist-Leninists insofar as they consider him unfaithful to the principles of Lenin, and in this they may be right. To the present writer it seems that Lenin would have approved the sacrifice of millions of workers to accelerate the victory of the Party. Did he not state that "morality is that which serves to destroy the old exploiting society?" [57] By admitting the rights of the individual, Khrushchev and his followers are probably nearer to Marx than was Lenin himself.

Roughly speaking the position in regard to revisionism seems to be this. There is no doubt that the Marxist-Leninists in the European "People's Democracies," or at least many among them, would like

to return to a more Marxist and less Leninist or Stalinist doctrine.]
The present writer thinks that they will do so, and all the more readily
the less their thought is controlled by the Soviet Party. Where there
is no such control at all, for instance in Yugoslavia, the result is plain:
Not only most of Leninism seems to have been thrown overboard,
but even some authentic revisionism of Marx himself is under way.
But in the Soviet Union the situation appears different. Leninism
and its later developments were, on the whole, the work of Russians.
It is not improbable that thinking there will adhere more closely
to the established patterns. Surprisingly, however, in spite of the
historical background, some revisionism seems to be present even
there.

All things considered, the present writer sees no reason for over-
emphasizing the importance of revisionism. In the Soviet Union
at present the Party does not even need to enforce its doctrine by many
police interventions. A generation of truly Marxist-Leninist thinkers
has grown up, and their control is strong enough to ensure that no
radical breach with the past will occur. And it is impossible to guess
how long it will be before other European Communist countries,
still more or less under Russian control, obtain sufficient freedom to
express their own thoughts. Of course, everything in history is subject
to the law of change, and Marxism-Leninism is no exception. But the
changes may be slow, and all the slower in that this doctrine has now
become the unifying ideology of a great and proud nation.

We may conclude these remarks with an attempt to answer a question frequently raised in non-Communist countries: What is the real
significance at present and for the future, of Marxism-Leninism? As
to the first part of the question, the present state, it has been maintained in some quarters that Marxism-Leninism is nothing more than
a set of ritual formulae which at most serve to justify any policy a
given Communist Party chooses to follow. In other words, it has no
significance at all.

This opinion, it is submitted, is completely unwarranted. It is true
that we cannot use in this field any of the classical methods prescribed
in similar cases. We cannot carry out any sort of field research concerning the real beliefs of Communist leaders. And this being so,
we cannot have a scientific certainty about the importance of Marxism-
Leninism. But Communist leaders declare most emphatically that
Marxism-Leninism *is* highly significant to them; they spend considerable financial and human resources in studying and spreading it. More-

over, non-Communist scholars personally acquainted with Communist leaders assert that for these men doubting their Communist faith is simply impossible. And a number of facts seem to show that Communist Parties in their concrete actions are motivated not only by political motives, but sometimes and rather powerfully by purely ideological ones. One instance would seem to be their persistency in the collectivization of peasants, a policy notoriously disastrous both economically and politically but still generally applied. Another instance is the religious policy, which in such countries as Hungary or Poland is still enforced according to purely ideological canons even though it creates great difficulties for the Party.

Of course, nobody would say that ideology is the *only* factor determining policy in Communist countries. There has never been in history a case where one such factor alone determined the course of events. Other factors like nationalism or imperialism do play a large role in the life of Communist countries, but everything we know points to the fact that ideology (i.e. Marxism-Leninism) is *also* a factor and, it would seem, a powerful one.

The question which arises then is: How can writers who know the field intimately (i.e., from first hand) maintain that Marxism-Leninism has lost all its importance? The answer seems to be complex. There are sometimes misunderstandings concerning the different elements of contemporary Marxism-Leninism; by not distinguishing between basic faith and other elements, some authors conclude, say, from the fact of the liberalization in cybernetics, that Marxism-Leninism has lost all significance. Another cause is failure to remember that, despite the changes since Lenin, we are still dealing with societies with a particular historical background. Some observers are tempted to project into Communist states the attitudes of their own civilization. And finally, many people seem incapable of realizing that such things as believers can exist in the contemporary world. They themselves are often quite skeptical about everything except the practical efficiency of the means used; they sometimes become quite incapable of attaching any importance to aims and, therefore, think that Communists are behaving as they do.

A quite different problem is that of the future. Prognoses in historical matters are very risky indeed. Is Marxism-Leninism in the stage of decomposition? Will it not disappear very soon, say, in the course of one generation? Those who believe this cite the progressive impact of scientific methods and stress the well-known fact that with the progress of industrialization ideologies traditionally lose their influence. All this is true, and yet one might defend the opposite view, that what is going on now in the Soviet Union is not a decay of Marxism-Leninism, conceived as a moral and metaphysical faith, but rather its purification from spurious and more or less nonsensical elements. If that be true, Marxism-Leninism will come out of the process not weakened but considerably strengthened.

It is really difficult to say who is right here. One remark may, however, be allowed. While talking about Marxism-Leninism, we must compare it with similar phenomena. Without such comparisons we have no basis for any prognosis whatsoever. Now the phenomena most akin to Communism are religions, and what is nearest to Marxism-Leninism are the various religious creeds. But if we consider their history, we see that many among the "great" religions have survived difficulties similar to those mentioned above. Buddhism, for example, has survived for more than two thousand years. Are we obliged to believe that Marxism-Leninism will burn out in two generations? Of course, one may say that we are living in a completely new "scientific" epoch where the course of history will be completely different. This is indeed possible. But we have no data upon which to base such a judgment, and therefore any prediction should be most cautious. Indeed, one wonders if we are entitled to make any prediction whatsoever.

Daniel Bell

The "End of Ideology" in the Soviet Union?

In 1951 the Polish poet Czeslaw Milosz published a book entitled *The Captive Mind*. It told of the magic influence of a new creed, "The Diamat," which was being embraced by the intelligentsia in Eastern Europe because it gave them a powerful world view, one to which the West offered no comprehensive alternative. "The Diamat— that is, dialectical materialism as interpreted by Lenin and Stalin— possesses a strong magnetic influence on the man of the present day," Milosz wrote. "In the people's democracies, the communists speak of the 'New Faith' and compare its growth to that of Christianity in the Roman Empire.... In France, [among the] group of worker priests, who do the regular work in the factories... a large proportion... have abandoned Catholicism and been converted to communism. The example illustrates the intensity of the ideological struggle which is going on today."

Whether the picture Milosz drew in 1951 was wholly accurate is now open to question, but certainly few persons today would think of the Diamat as a dynamic creed capable of sweeping large sections of the intelligentsia into the arms of Marxism-Leninism. In fact, what is extraordinary is how rarely one hears about the Diamat at all these days—particularly in Eastern Europe.

It would be foolish to assume that the decline of the Diamat's appeal is due only to its intellectual weakness as a doctrine. The Diamat had an appeal, in the early postwar years, because it was the world view of an aggressive and powerful state that seemed, at the time, destined to overrun Europe, and which apparently offered the emerging new countries of the *tiers monde* a model for rapid economic

I am indebted to my colleagues Zbigniew Brzezinski and Alexander Dallin for critical comments on an earlier draft.

and social development. The "magic" of Marxism-Leninism for the Soviet intelligentsia of Eastern Europe, if not for the Western world, was destroyed more by Khrushchev's disclosures about Stalin's reign of murder, and the removal of the body of Stalin from the common tomb with Lenin, than by any intellectual debate or political exposé.

The loss of coercive power of the Soviet Union over the Eastern European world, and its declining prestige in the underdeveloped countries, has been due to a combination of socio-political factors: the increasing difficulties the Russians have had in managing a complex economy; the loss of internal dynamism because of the recalcitrant attitudes of a people living for so long under stringent controls; the open expression of counter-nationalisms, as in the case of Rumania; and finally the rise of China as a force in world affairs and as a competitor for the ideological leadership of the Communist bloc.

Clearly, any analysis of Soviet philosophy must also involve a discussion of Soviet politics, for it is Soviet politics—in the unity of theory and practice—that provides the contradictions of the philosophy. Yet one should not minimize the power of ideas. The fact that, all through the late 1930's and 1940's, a growing number of Western intellectuals had subjected the Leninist-Stalinist version of Marxism to critical scrutiny provided incalculable support to many in Eastern Europe who, for moral, sociological, or psychological reasons, were repudiating communism. As Milosz himself admits, it was when "socialist realism" was introduced into Poland as the official esthetic that he made his own painful decision to defect, for such a doctrine not only contradicted the writer's "essential task—to look at the world from his own independent viewpoint," but "itself makes all judgement of values dependent upon the interests of the dictatorship." And once the "absolute" nature of belief is shaken, the debate is then transferred to the intellectual level. New doctrines and new justifications, new demands and new ideas begin to cross swords with the old doctrines, and a sometimes silent, sometimes even public debate takes place (*vide,* the open discussion in Poland between Leszek Kolakowski and Adam Schaff about the nature of class truth).[1]

The deeper erosions of intellectual faith come when the ideologues are forced to square old doctrines with reality. And within the Soviet Union today there is such an erosion. The classic tenets of Marxism-Leninism face the growing challenges of science (particularly as the newer advances in physics and the conceptions of the physical world confront dialectical materialism with some difficult questions) and the spread of "economic rationality," while the structure of intellectual controls is being undermined by the increasing demand of Soviet scientists and writers for freer discussion, for more contact with the West, and for Russian membership in the open community of science and the intellectuals. In these various ways, hitherto sacred elements of the canon have come under attack, and even the assertiveness of the Soviet world outlook has begun to assume a defensive cast.[2]

Khrushchev's successors will in all probability confront not only a great demand for intellectual liberties on the part of the scientists and the intelligentsia, but a more serious crisis in the reformation of basic doctrine. I shall try to specify these developments in an analysis of what constitutes the core doctrine of Marxism-Leninism today and, following that, scrutinize the way the Soviet authorities are being forced to confront some crucial questions about science, ideology, and *partiinost'* that arise out of these developments. To keep the boundaries of this discussion explicit, let me say that I am dealing primarily with the challenges and changes in the *doctrines,* not in the *politics* of the Soviet world, though in fact the dilemmas arising out of "praxis" first called the doctrines into question.

The Question of Ideology

Marxism-Leninism is a world outlook with a specific historical vista. In the Soviet Union today, five elements combine to make up this *Weltanschauung:* (1) the doctrine of class struggle; (2) a conception of world society as having passed through five historical stages; (3) the contemporary existence of two camps—capitalist and socialist; (4) the contention that planning and collective property constitute superior forms of social organization; (5) the inevitable world victory of communism.[3] These elements of doctrine are the constitutive "ground" of the ideological pronouncements by the regime, the "figures" of which are the specific policies or directives. They form the scope of belief and the justifications of doctrine—the doctrinaire certitudes that become guides to action—and these are the defining aspects of ideology.

But the question that is usually raised is: How "real" a role does ideology play in the Soviet Union? Is it a core of beliefs—an orthodoxy proselytized by the leaders (and followers) of the society and, as such, a consistent and accurate guide to Soviet political intentions and actions? Or is the ideology simply a set of rationalizations manipulated cynically by the leadership, while the more "conventional" motives of power and national interest continue to operate?

To pose the question on the political plane, as is frequently done, is to misunderstand somewhat the nature of ideology as a system of belief and the function it serves in a society. (Such a formulation derives, curiously, from a Marxist or a Paretian "tough-mindedness" about politics, which sees ideology only as a "false consciousness" or a myth used by the elite to manipulate the masses.)

The function of an ideology, in its broadest context, is to concretize the values, the normative judgments that are made implicitly or otherwise by members of the society as to what is moral or desirable, as to what is the good society. And in some instances, as in the Soviet Union, ideology indicates the direction of the future and the realization of some further values in that future. In short, one function of ideology, particularly in a coercive society, is to be a "social cement."

The point is that even the most coercive of societies has to establish some justification of the coercion; it has to transform *Macht* into legitimacy in order to govern without turning an entire society into a concentration camp. (As Rousseau wrote, in the third chapter of *The Social Contract,* "The strongest is never strong enough always to be the master unless he transforms strength into right and obedience into duty.") In effect, within every operative society there must be some creed—a set of beliefs and values, traditions and purposes—which links both the institutional networks and the emotional affinities of the members into some transcendental whole. And there have to be some mechanisms whereby these values can not only be "internalized" by individuals (through norms), but also be made explicit for the society—especially one which seeks consciously to shape social change; and this "explicating" task is the function of ideology. It is only, perhaps, by defining the complicated interplay of values with ideology that one can understand the underlying social processes of a modern society which seeks to mobilize its people for the attainment of specific goals.

Ideology and the Value System

Every modern society, in one way or another, has to justify itself to its members. It is in the sense, perhaps, that one understands for our own time the meaning of Emile Durkheim's statement that "every society is a moral order." [4] There is equally the point crucial to Max Weber's conception of religion, that there is no known human society without something which, at its core, would not be classified as religious—some conception of a supernatural order or impersonal force which gives meaning to the unusual or rationally impenetrable aspects of experience. [5] Without arguing the specific question whether the belief system of the Soviet Union might be characterized as religious, there is little question that the Communist world outlook does possess some notion of an "ultimate"—even though this is conceived as realizable in history—and that this sense of an "ultimate" has a sacral status in the society. As Talcott Parsons has put it: "All human societies embody references to a normative cultural order which places teleological 'demands' upon men," [6] an allegiance to something beyond themselves. And this normative order is expressed in the central value system of a society.[7]

The value system of the society is thus the implicit creed, subscribed to or unquestioningly accepted by the members of the society, which defines what is for them the good society, and which shapes the evaluative judgments on actions taken by members of the society. The values are formulated in "sacred" pronouncements (e.g., The French Declaration of the Rights of Man, the U.S. Constitution, the Communist Party program), become exemplified in history, are presented as tradition, and act to facilitate or inhibit change to the extent that the innovation can be reconciled easily with the established doctrine. The values define what it means to be a member of the society (what it means, for example, to say: "I am a Bolshevik," or "I am an American"), just as religious creed defines what it means to be, say, a Catholic or a Moslem, and a professional credo defines what it means to be a physician or a scientist. The value system legitimates the distribution of authority and the performance of roles in a society.

Now, it is true that a creed, broadly defined, can be compatible with a large number of different political policies; that one cannot deduce one, and only one, course of action from necessarily abstract formulations. Societies guided by a belief in natural law or divine justice have as much difficulty defining the moral correlate of an act as secular societies encounter in rationalizing political actions. (And it is equally difficult to link up specific philosophical beliefs with a consistent political attitude: Hobbes was a materialist and a royalist, Burke an empiricist and a conservative, and Tom Paine an intuitionist and a radical.) So one cannot take ideational formulations as a concrete guide to political policy.

But neither can one ignore them. For each society needs some creed, intellectually coherent and rationally defensible, both to justify itself and to meet the challenges of (or to challenge) other creeds. The value system, like the rule of law, provides a set of standards to evaluate or judge specific actions. At the minimum, it provides a language for defining social reality (e.g., "The New Deal was saving capitalism," or "The New Deal was introducing socialism"; "Stalin was betraying socialism," or "Khrushchev is a revisionist") and for behaving accordingly on the basis of these definitions. At the most, the values of the society set the limits of action, e.g., lead one to support one's government in the most crucial of instances (i.e., the declaration of war) or oppose it.

Societal values however, as is evident, are at the highest level of generality of the normative order. They are directions of action, not directives. To this extent, ideologies as codified systems of belief represent the mobilization of values in order to make explicit the normative judgments of the society.[8] An official ideology is both a principle of inclusion and a principle of exclusion. It defines the official creed, and it identifies the enemy or heretic against whom sentiments must be mobilized.[9] By its very formulation as a public creed, it requires an overt statement of allegiance from those who occupy responsible positions in the society.

Thus ideologies are forms of legitimation, a link between the generalized values of the society and the institutionalized action of collectivities (e.g., governments) that set the limits of action. And, if *authority* is defined as the regulative pattern which is relevant to the normative control of political functions, then ideology, too, is a form of authority.

Ideology and Reality

We have accepted the proposition, advanced by Talcott Parsons, that "a system of value-orientations held in common by members of the social system can serve as the main point of reference for analyzing structure and processes" of that system.[10] With this in mind, the value system of the Soviet Union might be characterized as one of "ideological activism," i.e., a self-conscious set of directives to change the society in accordance with a generalized theoretical doctrine.[11] This involves a constant scrutiny of canonical texts, a testing of achievements by the double standard of practical results and concordance with doctrine, and a constant specification of goals in order to spur the people to the ends set by the regime. Such a society has a high, built-in drive towards social change and great flexibility in the choice of means. But the stress on ideological conformity also creates a rigid submission to authority and evasion of responsibility, both of which inhibit change and create great tensions in the society.

Ideologies, as belief systems, also serve as self-conscious mechanisms for internalization of values, in accordance with specific dogmas. They require, from the adherents, a motivational commitment; acceptance of the cognitive validity of the ideas and practical commitment in readiness to put one's own interests at stake in the service of the ideas. But an ideology, to be effective, must be "congruent" with reality. Official actions must conform to the ideological tenets, or be rationalized in some acceptable way. Where elements of the doctrine are "utopian"—i.e., promise performance in the future rather than the present—the present actions must be justified as moving in the expected direction. Where the doctrine conflicts with performance, some "textual answer" must be found to justify a change. This ideology is in constant revision in the society. The discrepancy between ideology and reality becomes a source of strain upon the society.

By their very possession of authority, the elites of a society must maintain a conscious relationship to the official creed. No society, however, is so completely homogeneous, or a creed so monolithic, that different segments of the elite must maintain an allegiance to the creed with the same degree of intensity. In fact, as we shall see in the case of the scientists, the existence of a set of different and even competing norms sets up a conflict in which Soviet scientists (like Galileo) are forced to conform, or, for expediency or other reasons, aspects of the creed after a while become attenuated, mere lip service is permitted, or even a facet of the creed itself changes. Such a change is often dovetailed with other parts of the creed, though the process may be difficult.

Clearly the different social strata within the elite display variable sensitivities to the vicissitudes of ideology. For the hierophants, the interpreters of ideology, the strains are masked—for one of the chief tasks of these pulpiteers is to provide a seeming unbroken line of continuity in the validity of the doctrine. For the scientific and intellectual members of the elite, however, who are subject as members of the wider international scientific and intellectual community to counterdoctrines or independent interpretations, ideology becomes an important source of strain for those who are professed believers or a means of forcing ideological compromises upon the hierophants as the "price" of their overt and continuing, if only formal and perfunctory allegiance to the creed. The differential degrees of attachment, or alienation, on the part of the scientific and intellectual elites to the creed thus become significant indicators of the cohesion of the society and its ability to mobilize support for its stated goals.

The major ideological problem for a regime, then, is to maintain the central core of the creed or redefine it successfully when it is challenged, to achieve a continuity with the past and a realistic orientation to the present. In the Soviet Union the core doctrines have come under increasing attack from within, and the crucial questions are whether the regime can maintain the given doctrine, modify significant sections successfully (i.e., control the consequences to the existing elite's power as well as rationalize it with other elements of the creed), or face an erosion of doctrine that would result in the alienation of a substantial segment of the scientific and intellectual elites from the system as a whole.

To put the questions in more substantive forms: Do the current debates in science, philosophy, sociology, and literature portend a revision of Marxist-Leninist dogma to bring it in line with the mainstream of Western rationalist thought (as much as Marxism actually was in its pre-Stalinist phase)? Will there be a more open forum for intellectual discussion and literary and philosophical "experimentation" so that some new doctrinal commitments will emerge? Or is the current ferment simply an "accommodation" on the part of the regime to momentary pressures, an accommodation that might be revoked by the ruling elite when it feels that the changes have gone too far? In short, is the process of ideological change irreversible, or can it be halted? If the evolution continues, will it be toward the creation of a doctrine sharing a common intellectual foundation with Western thought and values, or will it be toward some new doctrinal formulations of Marxism-Leninism? No complete answer, again, can be given on the ideological plane alone; a "surrender" of the Russians to the Chinese line might result in new controls and the effort to reassert particular dogmas; intensified conflict between Russia and China might result in more rapid changes moving toward newer ideological formulations. One can deal here only with "immanent" tendencies as they unfold out of the "reality" demands of the scientific and intellectual elite against the ideology, rather than with the total political context in which the major changes will be played out.

Let us turn, then, to a consideration of the changes taking place. I shall deal first with the four areas of the core doctrine as these have previously been defined, seek to assess the extent of the changes in the official doctrine, and then turn to the source and nature of the challenges.

Dialectical Materialism—the Absolute and the Relative

Dialectical materialism has been the keystone of Soviet philosophy, for it seeks to provide (as did the Thomist synthesis of reason and faith) a comprehensive set of answers to the most fundamental questions of philosophy: the nature of reality, the nature of knowing, etc., etc. It has been or claims to be the "unifying element" of Soviet thought. The vicissitudes of dialectical materialism—to look at the technical core of the doctrine—provides then an instructive illustration of the doctrine's decline. For in the last decade, Soviet philosophers have been perplexed about how to bring the "Marxist" categories of matter, space and time into consonance with the recent discoveries and theories in the fields of physics, logic and mathematics. In this respect, it has been Soviet philosophy that has been on the defensive.[12]

The fundamental and still unresolvable dilemma of dialectical materialism is whether it is philosophy or science. In his *Dialectics of Nature,* Engels felt that philosophy would disappear into positive science once the scientists and historians employed dialectics in formulating their concepts. For Engels, dialectics was "the science of the most general laws of *all* motion." Yet the physical concepts of matter, motion, space and time were treated as philosophical categories. Motion was described as the mode of existence of matter, and Engels claimed that neither could be created because they are their own final cause. In cosmology, Engels accepted an infinite concept of the Universe in which matter, motion, space, and time have existed eternally in endless space. From a philosophical point of view, in fact, Engels criticized Newton (following Hegel) because the theory of gravitation posited attraction as the chief characteristic of matter without considering the complementary force of repulsion as required by the dialectical law of the interpenetration of opposites, and he attacked the formulation of the second law of thermodynamics, as set forth by Clausius in 1867, because of its implicit argument that matter is creatable and destructible.

When he wrote his *Materialism and Empirio-Criticism* in 1908, Lenin was unacquainted with Engels' *Dialectics of Nature* (first published in Moscow in 1925) and its declaration about science. He was concerned to defend the idea of an objective reality and the idea of materialism primarily against religion, which he felt idealistic philosophy would lead to. For him, the problems of philosophy were distinct from science involving, as Maxim Mikluk puts it, "the creation of a basic framework to deal with fundamental ontological and epistemological issues." He did not want to criticize scientific concepts, as such, but the epistemological conclusions of modern physics.

In January 1931, the Presidium of the Communist Academy decreed that the task of reconstructing science according to the methodology of dialectical materialism had not been fulfilled. It called for the

Bolshevization of science. Though Lenin had never explicitly expounded on the "class nature" of science—he talked of official philosophy which served the interests of the system that hired the philosopher—the Stalinist philosophers denied the objective basis of science. Bourgeois science, they said, was suffering from a crisis stemming from an effort to merge religion with science. Einstein, Planck, Millikan and Eddington were attacked as leading science to mysticism. Relativity physics was decried for denying the absolute foundation of space and time. Quantum physics was attacked for introducing subjectivity—the standpoint of the knower—into the descriptions of reality.

During the beginning of the Stalinist hegemony in philosophy, after the attacks on Deborin, one could find Soviet philosophers, such as the well-known Bammel, compelled to make such pathetic statements in public confession as: "I criticized the bourgeois tendencies in mathematical logic from a methodological point of view and not from that of their idealistic essence.... I distorted the methodology of dialectical materialism in an idealistic fashion by having attempted to derive the theory of mathematical logic from Meinong's philosophy." [13] Until as late as 1954 Einstein's theory of relativity was publicly attacked by Soviet philosophers ("reactionary Einsteinianism") because the theory of relativity had proposed concepts which appeared to be incompatible with dialectical materialism.[14] The rejection was based, in fact, on a confusion, because the word "relativity" contradicted the belief in an absolute space-time continuum.[15] In publicly rejecting the theory of relativity, as Gustave Wetter notes, "the Soviets even went so far as to attack not only Einstein's relativity theory but also, in practice, the principle of relativity established by Galileo, which states, for example, that there is no absolute path traversed by a falling body."

The reaction against the more unintelligent comments about relativity had set in even during Stalin's lifetime, when *Voprosy Filosofii* in 1951, launched a discussion on the question. But the debate was not concluded until after Stalin's death, in 1955, when a new interpretation by two Leningrad mathematicians, V. A. Fok and A. L. Aleksandrov, was accepted. The new interpretation attributed the confusion of the previous writers to the mistaken definition of the word "relative" as "not objective." It affirmed as the central philosophical principle the objective existence of the real world, but avoided any hypothesis that entailed an assumption of the "knowing subject" as contributing to the knowledge of physical reality.

But even this position continues to involve Soviet philosophy in difficulties. One problem is the inheritance from Lenin's *Materialism and Empirio-Criticism* that knowledge is a "reflection" or "copy" of the real world, in which consciousness or mind makes no active contribution (a position modified or partly contradicted by Lenin in his *Philosophical Notebooks*).

A second dilemma growing out of the first, is Engels' conception that all movement in the world is the movement of "matter." And a third involves the challenging discoveries of quantum mechanics and the interpretations of Bohr and Heisenberg: the principle of complementarity (i.e., that light is both wave and quantum), the idea that knowledge of physical reality depends in part on the observing subject, and the rejection of causality in microphysics—for all these theories challenge the idea of a simple "objective," "real" world.

Today the "dialectics" of Engels and of Lenin's *Empirio-Criticism* are no longer the canonical texts for Soviet philosophy, even though crucial questions remain unresolved. But one fact seems clear: Soviet philosophy had intended dialectical materialism to be a working instrument that would guide Soviet scientists, including physicists, to fruitful work, but today the contrary seems to hold. Not only does one find statements like those of Academician S. L. Sobolev decrying those who talk of idealist and materialist theories of science,[16] but Soviet philosophers now formulate their attitude this way: "Dialectical materialism recognizes everything which results from and is proved by science."[17] Indeed, as A. J. Ayer observed in 1962, after giving a series of lectures at the Faculty of Philosophy of Moscow University: "The prestige of science is so great that it is now becoming much more a question of [the philosophers] having to adapt their philosophical principles to current scientific theory than the other way about."[18]

Outside the Soviet Union—particularly in Poland, where logical theory had always been strong—the rejection of dialectics has been more striking. There the efforts of the official party ideologues to impose a "dialectical logic of contradiction" were finally rejected by the majority of Polish Marxist philosophers. As Z. A. Jordan sums it up: "What all the Polish Marxist-Leninists [now] seem to agree upon is the rejection of logical dualism. There is one and only one logic whose importance for science and philosophy cannot be over-estimated.... Dialectical logic is neither logic in the strict sense, nor formal."

But what is now accepted by the overwhelming number of Polish philosophers is still rejected by the Russians.

While in Poland the stand taken by Schaff [who revised his Soviet-held views on logic] is supported by an overwhelming majority of Marxist-Leninists, and Ladosz [who argues for the existence of a dialectical logic] is almost isolated in his views, the position in the Soviet Union seems to be dissimilar. *Voprosy Filosofii* strongly supported the views defended by Ladosz in Poland, and condemned those of Schaff.... What seems to have been finally decided among leading Marxist-Leninists in Poland still remains in the balance in the Soviet Union.[19]

I cannot here seek to assess the validity of the philosophical answers given by the various Marxist-Leninist philosophers to the various challenges they have been asked to deal with since 1955, with the beginning of more open philosophical debate in the Soviet Union. But what is quite clear is that Soviet Marxism has been unable to go beyond a patchy effort to unify the Hegelian dialectic with materialist philosophy and there is still lacking not only a coherent statement of the philosophical foundations of dialectical materialism, but equally, as Maxim Mikluk points out in a review of the literature, "any consistent, positive and unambiguous explications by Soviet philosophers on the exact nature of the bond between dialectical materialism and science." As Mikluk says, further:

In none of the technical-scientific works by Soviet scientists that this writer examined was there any overt use made of the dialectical laws of thought. Eric Ashby [in *Scientists in Russia* (New York, 1947), pp. 100 ff.] did discover one Nikolai Petrovich Kranke who consciously applied the tenets of dialectical materialism to research on plant development. But Ashby stated that Kranke's research could have been conducted without dialectical materialism. Soviet scientific treatises containing remarks pertaining to dialectical materialism as the guiding philosophy or methodology rarely revealed in detail how dialectical materialism was specifically utilized.[20]

Yet the Soviet philosopher has claimed to be in the superior position —at least until the last decade—to judge the validity of scientific theories without recourse to scientific methodology. And, more importantly, Soviet philosophy has claimed the right—and the possibility —of setting down a set of "first principles," like Thomism, which could act as a guide and judge of scientific work. In this it asserts the right, as does classical philosophy, to ground all scientific findings within a set of philosophical frameworks, and to assert the prior claims of philosophy over science. Now few scientists, with the exception of some positivists, would deny the philosophical ground of science. But science cannot accept any philosophical theory, be it Thomism or dialectical materialism, as axiomatic first principles. It may accept them as possible truths. But Soviet philosophy cannot tolerate having dialectical materialism treated as a set of postulates or hypotheses—which Soviet science is prepared to do—nor can science tolerate the imposition of any set of philosophical first principles as binding on its theories and experiments.

It is at this crucial point that Soviet philosophy and dialectical materialism have failed. *At its core doctrine* Soviet thought is apparently on the defensive; the Diamat can no longer be considered an aggressive doctrine sweeping all rival systems before it. Certainly, so far as the scientists are concerned, it is not even the "unifying element" in Soviet thought. And failing a fundamental unifying philosophy, how different, then, can Soviet philosophy and science ultimately be from the stream of Western thought generally?

Historical Materialism—the Law of Uneven Social Development

The idea of a determinate movement of history and of objective "laws of social development" is equally central to the Marxist-Leninist world outlook. Providing a simplified view of human history, it has been a compelling aspect of the Soviet doctrine, for it provides the *Halbbildung* mentality with an illusion of understanding the world.

Historical materialism, as a way of understanding the past, has been questioned by numerous historians, particularly in the application of the doctrine to crucial events.[21] But while the general scheme of social development has often been challenged, there has rarely been a synoptic effort to match the scope and breadth of the Marxist historical drama, and this has remained a source of its strength.[22] The doctrinal dilemma of historical materialism for the Soviet regime, however, arises not out of any academic challenge about the nature of the past but out of its own conception of the future. Can historical materialism, in effect, be used as a "weapon" to claim that socialism and communism are the "inevitable" next stages in society? These are crucial questions. And it is doubtful whether the Soviet theoreticians can meet the challenge.

There are, it seems to me, three questions that Communist doctrine will be called upon to confront in the next years, and they may well be sources of further erosion of the core doctrine: (1) the theory of "industrial society" formulated most clearly by Raymond Aron; (2) the inquiry into Bolshevik history which was opened among Soviet historians in 1956–57, but was quickly shut because of the implications revealed about the "inevitability" of the revolution; (3) the "polycentrism" of the Communist world, which no longer holds the Russian development to be the model for all subsequent social development.

The theory of industrial society has its roots in the ideas of Max Weber.[23] This is the argument that capitalism and socialism are not successive social systems but two aspects of a common underlying process, that of the bureaucratization of society. The Marxist schema posited a sketch of social development whereby socialism would replace capitalist societies whose economies had come into unresolvable crisis. But obviously the Marxist analysis does not correspond to the events of the twentieth century. Capitalism has not led to increased poverty and decline, but has, through state action, maintained economic growth rates. No revolution of the Marxist type has followed the expansion of capitalism or the achievement of "mature" development, while the successful Communist revolutions have taken place, as in China and Russia, in countries only starting on the path of modernization, and have been carried out by intellectuals rather than the working class.

From the developing perspective of the theory of industrial society, it is the common "imperatives" imposed by industrialization and a new attitude to nature and work which is decisive in the formation of modern societies. From this point of view there is little meaning to the idea of "ownership," since even if property remains nominally in private hands it is the social function of management that becomes decisive for the organization of production. Industrial society, therefore, is characterized by a "technical" attitude to nature and work. Management becomes a technical function; there is the application of science to technology in the exploitation of natural resources; a new class, the technical and professional, becomes predominant in society, and the criteria for social mobility is technical skill and education; there is a quantitative "rationalization" of life—an attitude of calculation in the organization of production and in the measurement of work; and industrial society becomes primarily an urban society with small residues of farmers.[24]

While a common technocratic mentality prevails, economics does not dominate politics in industrial society, but the obverse rules. Masses are mobilized politically for the ends decreed by the regimes, or the political system becomes the arena whereby contending groups bargain for allocations of privilege or seek support. It is this supremacy of politics over economics that becomes the final sociological challenge to orthodox Marxist theory.

As developed by Aron, the theory of industrial society does not argue a "convergence" of the social systems of capitalism and socialism, but points to the similar facets, the "requisites" of industrialization, which lead to similar features of development and similar social structures. (To this extent, it is a more sophisticated version of the simplified projections of Bruno Rizzi's *La Bureaucratisation du Monde* or James Burnham's *The Managerial Revolution*.) But the main thrust of Aron's theory is the attack on the theory of a unilinear evolution of society. And it has been an argument that the Soviet theorists have found difficult to answer.

The theory of industrial society, which has had its greatest effect among Western sociologists, can be momentarily "deflected" as bourgeois ideology. More corrosive to Soviet doctrine are the cautious questions that were opened by the Soviet historians V. P. Nasirin and E. N. Burdzhalov about the "inevitability" of the October Revolution and the subsequent pace of industrialization. As Adam Ulam has pointed out: "Central to the legitimacy of the Communist rule is the belief that the Communist seizure of power in 1917–18 was in complete accordance with the Marxist canon. Indeed, the basis of the whole ideology rests upon two axioms: Marxism is the only true science of society, and the seizure of power by the Bolsheviks was the only correct and necessary application of Marxism under the Russian conditions." [25]

It is these axioms which the two Soviet historians implicitly questioned. By dealing with the hesitations of the Bolshevik party before April 1917, and indeed the readiness of a number of its major leaders to join a parliamentary coalition, the Burdzhalov article in effect questioned the standard image promulgated in the party's *Short Course*—that there had been one "correct" line the Bolshevik party had pursued unequivocally since the formulation of *What Is To Be Done?* The essay by Nasirin, as Ulam points out,

simply restated what was known very well to everybody who read the pre-1930 Soviet books on the subject: that the precipitous nationalization of heavy industry in the wake of the November Revolution was imposed upon the Bolshevik rulers, and that the previous Bolshevik program had envisaged a gradual and cautious plan of nationalization of the means of production. The author reclaimed the resolution of the 6th Party Congress ... calling for immediate nationalization of banks and syndicates but *not* of heavy industrial enterprises.... Carried away by his "discovery," the unfortunate seeker after historical truth quoted Marx's dictum about socialism ripening in the bosom of capitalism and Lenin's definition of socialism as "but state capitalist monopoly turned to the benefit of the whole nation."

The implications of these simple statements, at least for the theoretical solvency of Marxism, are quite damaging: Was the October Revolution a true Marxist revolution or a Blanquist-type *coup d'état*? What is the character of socialism in relation to industrialization? In what sense can one say that underdeveloped countries are socialist if what they do is simply to nationalize industry and raise capital by means of "primitive accumulation"?

Freer historical criticism is indeed a Pandora's box for Soviet doctrine. And at a time when the society is increasingly in ferment regarding science and even intellectual liberty, how long can such criticism be suppressed? [26] When it does emerge, what damage will it do to the simplified images of historical materialism that are part of the core doctrine of Marxism-Leninism? The Soviet authorities are acutely aware of these threatening questions.

Yet it is not the academic challenges but the practical developments in the Communist world that most directly challenge the assumptions of the core doctrine. Since 1956 the Soviet Union has had increasing difficulty in imposing its political leadership on the other Communist countries and in controlling their economic and social development. And this raises further questions about a Marxist theory of social development.

In the Communist world, any divergences on the practical level have to be reconciled and given formulation in the ideological sphere. This was particularly true of social transition: How does one know when a society is moving from capitalism to socialism or from socialism to communism? This problem was given its theoretical formulation by no less than Nikita Khrushchev himself in his speech at the Twenty-First Party Congress on the "more or less simultaneous passage" of all socialist countries "to the higher phase of communist society." [27] With the formulation of this new "law of the equalization of development," Khrushchev was seeking to resolve the ideological dilemma posed most sharply by the Chinese who were seeking to shorten the transitional period from socialism to communism by an organizational measure—the people's commune.

Khrushchev's theme became the subject of a book by G. Glezerman, *The Laws of Social Development*.[28] This theoretical work posited "general laws" on the building of communism, in which the Soviet Union stood as the exemplar. Glezerman's book, intended as a standard account, opens with a review of the theory of historical materialism and sets as its specific goals the formulation of the "laws of social development," particularly as they apply in the transition period to socialism.

"The common law of building communism," he writes, "follows

from the single type of economic system in the socialist countries, based on the social ownership of the means of production, from the single type of their class structure." That is why, he continues,

at the Twenty-Second Congress of the C.P.S.U., representatives of the fraternal parties of the socialist countries pointed out that the construction of communism as chartered out in the C.P.S.U. Programme holds forth prospects of development for other countries as well. Comrade Novotny, First Secretary of the Central Committee of the Czechoslovak Communist Party, stated that Communists in Czechoslovakia regard the C.P.S.U. Programme as their own programme.... Comrade Zhivkov, First Secretary of the Central Committee of the Bulgarian Communist Party, said that Bulgarian Communists mapped out the path of their country's progress with due account of the C.P.S.U. Programme.

Revisionism, as it is defined here, is the effort to assert national peculiarities so distinct as to deny the "general character" of the laws:

The views of the revisionists and other opportunist elements clearly reflect the bourgeois reformist ideology of the Rightwing Socialists whose leaders also deny the general regularities applicable to various countries. Suffice it to recall the arguments advanced by Karl Renner to the effect that every epoch, as well as every country, has "its own Marxism." Such assertions are nothing else but an attempt to adapt Marxism to bourgeois nationalism, and consequently to repudiate proletarian internationalism.
These tendencies are very characteristic of the position held by the revisionists. It is not accidental that the main direction in which Marxism-Leninism is being revised at present is exaggeration of national peculiarities and opposition to these general regularities.[29]

At the time this was written, a few short years ago, Tito would certainly have been classified as a revisionist. But now, by these criteria, one would also have to include the Rumanian, Gheorghiu-Dej, and even the Italian, Togliatti. Mao might argue, as he does, that only the Chinese now know the "true" laws of social development.[30] But Tito, Gheorghiu-Dej, and Longo, by emphasizing openly the role of national differences, have opened the way for wholesale changes in the Soviet doctrine about the stages of social development.

But the ways of the dialectic are wondrous and strange. For if it becomes difficult, in Marxist theory as well as practice, to maintain the "leading role" of the Russian party, one can always transform this leadership to a "collective" or bloc basis. Thus, the Russians always have available the doctrinal formulation by T. S. Stepanyan, a leading Soviet ideologist and former head of the philosophy section of the Academy of Science, which opens up the prospect of what Richard Löwenthal has described as the "racial or continental theory of the stages of Communist development." Stepanyan wrote:

In speaking of the prospect for the further development of communist formation, we should bear in mind *a new law of development: the gradual surmounting of the historical inequality of development within the world system of socialism.* The unequal development of countries and peoples which arose historically on the basis of private ownership and became most acute in the period of imperialism is gradually beginning to disappear on the basis of public ownership, in the development of the world socialist system, in the process of mutual aid and collaboration between all socialist countries. *This new law, in the conditions of the scientific-technical revolution which has begun, provides an opportunity for a whole group of countries, obviously according to the economic zones to which they belong, to enter the epoch of communism almost simultaneously.*

It must be assumed that the European socialist countries which are united in one economic council for mutual aid, constitute a special economic zone and will be the first to enter communism. The Asiatic socialist countries, which have much in common as regards their economic and cultural development, constitute another regional zone and will also jointly enter communism.

The mutual assistance and collaboration between all the countries of the socialist camp enormously accelerates the common process of advancing towards the ultimate aim of our movement.[31]

This distinction between the more highly developed European socialist countries and the backward Asian peoples' democracies was repeated briefly in 1962 and early 1963 in the attempts to formulate laws of the uneven development of socialism. Against the Peking view that the storm center of world revolution is to be found in the underdeveloped countries, we find here a doctrinal line, solidly grounded in Marxist texts, which may be used when ideological differences continue to diverge. In this respect, the Russians have left themselves an alternative theoretical doctrine to explain social development when expedient.

Apart from the internal doctrinal squirmings, however, these differences even more broadly raise some crucial questions for the theory of historical materialism. How does one explain on Marxist grounds the sharp difference between the Soviet Union and China on social development? How explain the divergences between the Soviet Union and Yugoslavia, and now Rumania, and so on? Are these differences, as Soviet ideologists put it, only of a "gnosiological" nature—"the failure," as Glezerman says, "to understand the dialectical relation between the general and the specific"? Or do these differences arise from the different class structures and class natures of the regime? Or can one say that other insidious elements, such as power conflicts or national interests, arise despite the "common" socialist character of the different regimes? In all these ways, however, the doctrine of historical materialism and the "laws of social development" are increasingly called into question, and the regime is faced with increasing theoretical—and propaganda—difficulties.

Capitalism and Communism: The Problem of Economic Rationality

In a striking metaphor, Trotsky once said that capitalism was a system in which "each man thinks for himself and no one thinks for all." The implication was that socialism was a superior system because it could provide the economic rationality for society as a whole, which capitalism had failed to do. It is this idea—that planning is more "rational" than the market—which Marxist theorists had insisted is the distinguishing feature of socialism, as opposed to capitalism.

One can put aside the glaring Soviet failures in agriculture and the gross economic waste in the Russian economic system. What is important to note is that in economic theory, as well as in economic practice, hallowed dogmas are giving way, and that the new economic rationality which is being achieved in the Soviet Union more and more resembles the rationality of "bourgeois" economic thought.

Over the last ten years there has been a virtual revolution in Soviet economic theory and practice which has done much to undermine the doctrinal basis of the Marxist economic orthodoxy. One could begin, for example, with the fundamental problem of the use of the interest rate in capital allocation. In accordance with the Marxist labor theory of value, Soviet economic theoreticians saw interest only as a form of exploitation, and refused to consider it as a mechanism that measures the scarcity of capital and serves to allocate it to its most productive uses. Soviet planners had to find some rational way of determining how the available capital should be distributed for maximum effect. As Robert Campbell has written, "The Soviet leaders faced an impasse; one of the central assumptions of Marxist economic theory had been proved wrong by their own experience, and they were faced with a painful choice between ideology and rational expediency."[32] As long as Stalin was alive, no official line emerged to break the deadlock. About a year after his death, the issue was resolved—though the theoretical implications were masked—in a way that constituted a surrender of orthodoxy to reality.

In the last three years a wide range of issues has emerged in Soviet economics, and they have contradicted on a theoretical and practical level many of the earlier tenets of Soviet doctrine. One finds now an acceptance of mathematical models, particularly input-output schemes and linear programming, which for years had been denounced as bourgeois in origin and "formalistic." But the most important challenges involve consideration of a rational price structure, which can reflect both real costs and underlying market demand, and incentives for managers to increase output, principally the use of the profit yardstick as the criterion of success. Under the proposals associated with Professor E. Liberman of Kharkov, proposals which are now being put into limited practice in the Soviet Union, the plant manager would be given just one instruction: to maximize the profitability of his enterprise, computed in relation to its fixed and working capital stock.

What Liberman is saying is that the factory managers should be free to choose their inputs (the best combinations of labor and capital) in order to reach outputs demanded by a central plan. The implication of this move, as Peter Wiles has pointed out, is clear: "For the outputs of innumerable enterprises are not consumer but intermediate goods; i.e., they could hardly be centrally planned at all." In effect, one would return to a system of markets.

I am not arguing that planning is impossible in a large industrial economy. It may well be that the advent of computers and the ability to process large flows of information and synthesize these in input-output schemes may provide the basis for a comprehensive allocation system. But the point is that whatever system finally evolves in the Soviet Union, whether it moves toward a mathematical model as proposed by Kantorovich (who in the 1930's had independently invented the system of linear programming) or the "shadow" market proposed by Liberman, the final result will have little to do with the dogmatism that prevailed in the 1930's and provided the doctrinal aspects of Soviet thought in the fields of political economy. And the ideologists know it. When L. Leontiev, a corresponding member of the Academy of Science and a vocal spokesman for the "mathematical school," voiced his criticisms (in the *Ekonomicheskaya Gazeta* in November 1961) of the "basic economic law" that is derived from Stalin's *Economic Problems of the USSR,* he was warned by Ilyichev, the secretary of the central committee responsible for ideological work, that his ideas might cast *"doubt on the whole political economy of socialism."* When one compares the standard texts of the thirties with the developments today, there is little question that this has indeed been the case.

If one sums up the meaning of Soviet economic "revisionism" to date, there have been two extraordinary changes in the theory and practice of socialism. In the consumer goods field, "command planning" is beginning to die out and is being replaced by a price system (as expressed in *Pravda,* August 23, 1964) "under the direct control of the consumer." Under this system, what is to be produced is determined by users in accordance with their own needs. In effect, and quite openly, the Soviet system has discovered, and is beginning to make legitimate, the simple idea expressed in the title of an article by B. Mochalov in *Kommunist* (no. 12, 1963)—"The Supply of Goods and the Demand of the Population." The appearance of such an article in the main theoretical journal of the Communist Party is a radical move toward the creation of what is now being called the theory of the "socialist" market economy.[33]

The second change is the virtual abandonment of the labor theory of value. The failure to take into account the rational notion that capital has a "price" and that this price is an element in the cost of a product led to serious defects in Soviet planning and cost accounting. In *Izvestia* (Nov. 29, 1962), two Soviet economists, I. Birman and V. Belkin, had written: "Today it is well known that our wholesale prices are formed by adding a small percentage to prime cost without any relation to capital employed. As a result the profit realizable from the price does not reflect the capital investment necessary for the development of the branch, it does not show how much the product is *in fact* costing the economy."

Shortly before his death, the Academician V. Nemchinov, one of the most influential Soviet economists, published an article in *Kommunist* (no. 5, 1964) proposing to end planning from above and suggesting as well that a charge for capital be levied on turnover as well as basic funds. Together with an article in *Izvestia* (Oct. 31, 1964) which proposed a differential "land rent" (in which land would be valued on a scale of profit per hectare) as the basis for selecting land for housing or industrial development, we have here another major step in the direction of economic rationality and away from economic dogmatism in the Soviet Union.

The important theoretical point here is that economic thought in the West, in its own evolution, had defined the central problem of all economics as the allocation of scarce resources among competing ends (thus involving relative prices and relative quantities), and, in the work of Walras and others, had formulated a general equilibrium theory that provided a model for allocation theory. Because of its rigidity Soviet economic thought had cut itself off from Western economic thought and from such specific techniques as input-output analysis, linear programming, and other practical extensions of mathematical economics. At the heart of the "revisionist economics" of Nemchinov, Kantorovich, and others is the adoption of the "relative scarcity" concept throughout the entire economy. It is a move toward the adoption of a *single* economic theory as an analytical system independent of ideological dogmas.

The Future Society

There is an old story about a Soviet agitator who kept promising the peasants that Communism was "on the horizon"—until someone told him that a horizon was an imaginary line that receded as one approached it. It may well be that the "withering away" of the Soviet state is similarly on the horizon. Yet it is important to note that in 1960 there began a new discussion in the Soviet Union about the nature of the future Communist society—a discussion impossible in the heyday of Stalinism—in which serious statements, most notably some from Khrushchev himself, were made about the eventual possibility of the withering away of the State. More than that, the new Program of the Communist Party of the Soviet Union written under Nikita Khrushchev, only the third of its kind (the others being the first program in 1903 and the second in March 1919), promises that by the end of the century the second and higher stage of communism, in which each would receive according to his need, would be reached.

There is little point in repeating here the doctrinal turnabouts of previous Communist dogmas, such as the withering away of the family, which have been so totally reversed that the family is now one of the stable supports of Russian society. The crucial point is that the withering away of the State's coercive authority is the "ultimate" test of the Communist doctrine, and a central question is whether real changes in this direction are taking place in the Soviet Union.

Quite, clearly, one of the chief motives impelling Khrushchev to open up this vista was that naked terror and direct coercion no longer seemed tenable. Persuasion and promise have in some measures replaced outright coercion. At the same time, the explicit guarantee about the future is that judicial legality will replace the "administrative measures" of the present, and the outright violations of person that characterized Stalinism would no longer be tolerated.

Whether the State will wither away, can wither away, is questionable. In his report to the Twenty-First Congress, Khrushchev proposed that certain state functions be transferred to public organizations as one of the first steps in this transition (the "comrade courts" are an instance of this). But even then Khrushchev hedged and noted that in the transition period "of course definite functions will remain with the courts, the militia, and the Prosecutor's Office ... in order to exert influence on persons who maliciously refuse to submit to socialist society's standards of behavior and are not amenable to persuasion." Even under Communism "there will remain certain public functions similar to those now performed by the state." [34]

This is not the place to judge whether real institutional changes in the realm of power and justice are taking place in the Soviet Union. Let us simply say that Khrushchev has given the Soviet people a promissory note, and this has had the effect of renewing many Russians' allegiance to the regime.

Moreover, there is little doubt that, in contrast with the other tendencies, open discussion about the future of the Communist society tends to strengthen Marxist-Leninist doctrine and provide some elements for a unifying ideology. But promissory notes—greater material wealth, more social service, less coercion, protection of legality—imply an empirical test of their negotiability, and it is this element, more than the theoretical disintegration of some aspects of the official dogma, that involves a greater risk, if it fails, of the practical disintegration of the ideology.

Accommodation or Change?

The fact that a doctrine or an ideology is changing does not necessarily mean the disintegration of faith, a loss of the power to hold or move believers, or the inability to sustain an intellectual argument against outside challenges. The history of the great faith-systems of the past—Catholicism, Islam, Buddhism, and others—illustrates their remarkable ability to reorder their doctrines, assimilate diverse intellectual currents (Platonism and Aristotelianism, for example, in the case of Catholicism), and maintain a following among the faithful—though it is a moot question whether the survival of these faiths can be attributed to the intellectual flexibility of their doctrines or to powerful economic and social systems that allowed them to wield temporal as well as spiritual influence.

A number of people, Professor Joseph Bochenski for one, argue that the present changes in Soviet doctrine do not portend the disintegration of a powerful faith, or the loss of allegiance among the elite, but represent simply a complex process of accommodation that is the feature of every doctrine-centered system. In the paper he presented to the 1964 Hoover Institution conference (included in this volume, Dr.

Bochenski sought to demonstrate the process of change. The Communist countries, he admits, face a dilemma in that every Marxist-Leninist "must hold that everything in science, art, morals and so on" has to conform to the absolutist standards of the totalitarian state doctrine, while at the same time "he must face the developing realms of thought, and more generally of spiritual life."

The regime seeks to overcome the dilemma by a tactic, so to speak, of "three truths." First, there is the basic dogma that is stated in simplified terms for public consumption. Second, there is a "speculative superstructure" of statements in a technical, Marxist terminology that must be acknowledged by everybody, but which can be interpreted freely. And finally, there is a third kind of statement "on the borderline between ideology and pure science," "declassified doctrines" (such as the legitimacy of mathematical logic), about which there can be "practically unlimited freedom of discussion." By this balancing act, the regime seeks to accommodate the different elements in Russian society. But Dr. Bochenski is dubious about the prospects of the revision of "basic faiths." "A generation of truly Marxist-Leninist thinkers has been formed," he argues, "and its control is strong enough to assure that no radical breach with the past will occur...changes may be slow, all the slower in that this doctrine has now become a unifying ideology of a great and proud nation."

As a philosopher and a scholastic, Dr. Bochenski assumes that a system of faith containing an intellectually coherent creed has to be articulated in all its parts so as to embrace every aspect of intellectual activity. Like Father Wetter, a good Thomist, he assumes that dialectical materialism, despite its intellectual primitiveness, is a sufficiently articulated, comprehensive system (and for that reason more dangerous, intellectually, than Western thought, with its eclectic hodge-podge of idealism, Kantianism, empiric-criticism, positivism, naturalism, and the like) which, in scholastic fashion, can and does serve as a unifying feature of Soviet thought.[35]

My principal objection to this argument is that the picture is too static. Even the image of "three truths" (one more than Plato's) assumes a settled system that has discovered how to make harmless accommodations and now exercises this device as a subtle means of social control. My own feeling is that Marxism-Leninism as a unified doctrine is becoming disjointed and losing its élan; where significant philosophical changes are in the offing, they point in the direction of rejoining the diverse traditions (naturalism, positivism, philosophy of science) of Western thought.

There are four broad factors, intellectual and sociological, that put Marxism-Leninism increasingly on the defensive these days:

1) The inherent contradictions that appear in the logic of the doctrine (particularly the "dialectics of nature" once this can be openly discussed).

2) The incompatibility of the doctrinal structure with the complex differentiation of Communist society—expressed on the one hand in the inadequacy of Marxist economic theory, and on the other in the idea of the "laws of socialist development" as they apply to different countries.

3) The influence of Western thought, partly through the emergence of a world community of science, partly through the interchange of literature and ideas.

4) The crumbling of the "walls of faith" as a result of Khrushchev's 1956 speech and the bewildering reversal of his own fortunes. The sense of betrayal about the past and the uncertainty about how far present leaders can be trusted undermine the certitudes of faith. Marxism-Leninism is no longer an all-embracing, aggressive ideological doctrine. Like the break-up of Islam, perhaps, different elements of the doctrine may now become of differential importance for different groups in various Communist countries.

Within the Soviet Union, there are three currents of change that work to modify, reshape, or erode Soviet doctrine: one is the role of science as a new legitimating agency in challenging older orthodoxies; the second is the disillusionment of the young intellectuals, particularly the literary ones, with the old doctrines, and the adoption of a negative attitude toward all ideology; third, the need of the new intellectual elites, no longer believing in "historical reason," to confront the existential questions—the meaning of death, suffering, anguish, and the "ultimate" questions about life.

Obviously, the prestige of science is today enormous in the Soviet Union. But the new role of science gains force not only from its spectacular achievements, but because, for theoretical purposes, it has been "redefined" to emphasize a new aspect of the doctrinal canon.

In Marxist theory, science always played an ambiguous role among the basic notions of historical materialism. Marxism itself was "scientific," but science, as a practical and theoretical activity, was held to be a response to economic and material forces. This was, as I noted earlier, the position taken by B. Hessen in the famous debates in 1931 on the nature of science. In Stalin's day, science was considered part of the social superstructure of society. But in the new 1961 program, a new definition appeared. Science, basic research, and applied research are now considered "productive forces" and the "essential factors" for the change of "productive forces."

This is, of course, more than verbal legerdemain. If science is now part of the productive forces rather than the superstructure, there is a basic legitimacy to its activities and to its needs. And it is the norms and claims of science that now become decisive for the test of theory.

The basic change this new definition has effected is a plea—one finds it in the Soviet scientific and technical press (and in other papers as well)—for *experiment* rather than dogma.[36] One instance is the article by Professor V. V. Parin, a member of the U.S.S.R. Academy of Medicine, in *Literaturnaya Gazeta,* February 24, 1962, which is entitled: "The Authority of Facts: Concerning Scientific Heritage and Dogmatism." He writes: "The main harm caused to science by the cult of the individual lay in the proclamation of a single opinion, a single viewpoint, as an 'inexhaustible fount of wisdom,' as the supreme truth."

But what begins as one more routine endorsement of the Twenty-Second Party Congress turns unexpectedly into a plea for genuine experimentation in all fields of science, and particularly into a defense of the revision of Pavlovian theory in physiology—Professor Parin's domain—which had caused anguished cries from the Party dogmatists. The strategy is fairly simple. One opens with a discussion of the revisions in physics, a field which now seems to be sacrosanct, then moves into biology, and from there into the "softer" scientific fields. By counterposing "experiment" and "fact" to "dogmatism" (a word now applied equally to the Chinese), the demand for more scientific freedom is advanced.[37]

The question is not simply whether certain "harmless" fields like mathematical logic are now "declassified," but whether a process is perhaps now at work that extends the domain of experimental inquiry into many fields of Soviet thought beyond science. In his study of *Dialectical Materialism,* Father Wetter has noted that Soviet philosophers

base their inquiries not on a philosophical method but an explicitly theological one; a method which asks, not whether a proposition is true or false in itself, but whether it figures in the corpus of revealed truth issuing from a demonstrably infallible source of dogmatic authority.... This method is employed in Christian thought in *theology* only, and not in *philosophy.* In the latter field, even the Christian thinker recognizes an authority, in the last resort, only to the extent that his arguments carry proof. But the Soviet ideologue also employs this method in philosophy, when he treats certain propositions of Marxism-Leninism as admitting of no discussion.[38]

But the entire thrust of the recent demand for experimentation is aimed precisely at the scholastic and "theological" modes of thought that were so characteristic of the Stalin era. In the most unlikely and surprising places one encounters attacks on exactly such methods. Thus, in the official *History of the Great Patriotic War of the Soviet Union,* the writer reflects on the "deadening" effect of Stalinist orthodoxy on Soviet military thought: "This 'personality cult' led to dogmatism and scholasticism, which impaired the independent initiative of military research. It is necessary to wait for the instructions by a single man, and to look for the confirmation of theoretical propositions, not in life and practical experience, but in ready-made formulae and quotations.... All this greatly reduced the scope of any free discussion of military theory."[39]

This is not the first time, of course, that the difficulties of "squaring" the requirements of "theology" with science has arisen in the Soviet Union. In fact, it is an old story. Alexander Weissberg has given a humorous account of the difficulties he encountered as editor of the Soviet *Journal of Physics* in 1931, when he was told by Joffe to preface the first issue with a genuflection to dialectical materialism. The introduction, after much debate, duly carried the statement that the discoveries reported therein, including some novel experiments on gaseous diffusion, were made through the application of dialectical materialism to physics. As he feared, Weissberg's chief difficulty was how to explain later to the German Academy of Science, which had inquired about this statement, exactly how dialectical materialism had aided such discoveries. "The Germans were quite prepared to pay travelling expenses for two representatives of Russian science who could instruct them in the practical work of Marxist research in the Marxist theory of physics," he recalled. But none of the Communist physicists wanted to go or could be dragooned into going. "The matter dragged on until the Mendeleyev Congress and the Germans still persisted, so that the party put up some individual—I think his name was Romanovsky—and this man said some very obscure things, so obscure that the Germans were unable to put up any arguments. For after all you have to be able to understand something if you want to give an answer. This was the end of the matter."[40]

It was only as late as the 1930's, in fact, that the required practice of introducing all published work in the sciences with some text from the teachings of dialectical materialism was dropped, and a "private accommodation" was reached with the physicists which allowed them to go on with their work without worrying whether their researches were consistent with dialectics or not. It was the party philosophers who were burdened with the task of proving the primacy of the Diamat to science.

What seems to be going on is a change not only in the method of discourse—i.e., emphasizing the result of experiment rather than proceeding from doctrinal text—but, as I indicated earlier, a basic reversal of order, so that dialectical materialism recognizes everything which results from and is proved by science.

What is even more fascinating, however, and how far it can proceed is still questionable, is the effort of some Russian scientists to offer by way of cybernetics an alternative world outlook to dialectical materialism. When cybernetics, the theory of communication and control associated with the work of Norbert Wiener, was first mentioned in Soviet discussion, it was denounced by *Voprosy Filosofii,* in 1953, as a "pseudo-science," and Wiener himself as a "cannibal." But the increasing practical use of cybernetics in electrical engineering, biology, brain research, and economics (where mathematical techniques and the use of computers were assimilated into the general frame of communication theory) forced the dogmatists to retreat. The appeal of cybernetics is that it is materialistic in doctrine (including its theory of consciousness), and, in the words of the Soviet academician K. Zeleniskii, cybernetics "has made it possible to examine, from a unitary point of view, mathematics, physics, biology, physiology, philology and other disciplines which would seem completely unrelated to each other." [41]

What gives an ideological edge to the debate has been the insistence of the cyberneticians on a "two-way" pattern of communication in order to ensure a healthy organism. The tone of the debate may be gauged from the two articles that appeared in the *Literaturnaya Gazeta* of May 29 and June 2, 1962; one, an attack by Doctor of Philology Byalik, is "Comrade, Are You Serious?", and the reply in the following issue, by Academician S. L. Sobolev, is "Yes, Completely Serious."

In the U.S.S.R., cybernetics today is interpreted broadly as the science of control and includes much work in economic planning (data processing, mathematical economics, operations research and automation) as well as fields more often thought of a "cybernetic" in the West—such as automata theory, neural modeling, artificial intelligence, and pattern recognition. There are now three main cybernetic research centers, in Moscow, Kiev and Novosibirsk, as well as a Scientific Council on Cybernetics in the Academy of Sciences.[42]

The party's tendency in dealing with the problem has been to move from its first attempts to stigmatize cybernetics as a "pseudo-science" to stressing the technical limitations of machines, and finally to admitting the limitless possibilities of machines,[43] but attempting at the same time to divorce the philosophical implications from the computer-research aspects of cybernetics. As Byalik put it, he is all for cybernetics except "to the degree that [some cyberneticians] go beyond the confines of their science and concern themselves with general questions of our world outlook." [44] And that is the crucial question: whether the scientists can and will be able to "go beyond the confines of their science." The tendency is for them increasingly to do so.

The efforts of the Soviet writers and poets to free themselves from the direct party yoke—or at least from the decrees about presenting only "party themes" and "positive heroes" in line with the doctrine of socialist realism—have been amply documented in the Western press in the last several years.[45] What seems most extraordinary is that the conflict has been so "institutionalized" that for the past half-dozen years the "liberals" have recognizably had their "own" magazines (i.e., those printing experimental poems, stories and essays, and expressing criticism of the "positive hero"), such as *Novy Mir, Voprosy Literatury,* and *Literaturnaya Gazeta,* the weekly newspaper of the Union of Writers of the U.S.S.R., while the "reactionaries," concentrated in the Union of Writers of the Russian Republic, have answered back in *their* newspaper, *Literatura i Zhizn',* and the journals *Moskva* and *Oktyabr'.*

While two clearly defined literary factions exist, the Party's behavior is less clear. Officially, the line remains as it was reformulated at the Twenty-Second Party Congress by P. N. Damichev, the first secretary of the Moscow city committee—that the function of writers, as specified in the doctrine of socialist realism, is to "reveal in positive artistic images the new type of [socialist] men in all the magnificence of their human dignity." But this attitude does not seem to translate itself into direct bureaucratic support for the "reactionary" faction or into any reprisals or coercive measures against the liberals, even during the period in 1962 and 1963 when Khrushchev openly denounced by name Nekrasov, Yevtushenko, Voznesensky and other writers, and violently attacked the sculpture of Neizvestny ("revolting concoctions" and "deformities") and the painting of Zhutovsky ("who eats the bread of the people" and paints "horrible rots and dirty daubs"). Two weeks after Khrushchev's fall, *Literaturnaya Gazeta* (October 27, 1964) published an article by Alexander Tvardovsky, the editor of *Novy Mir,* which described his publishing program for 1965. Tvardovsky, who is the embodiment of the revisionist movement in the arts, announced that in the forthcoming year he would be publishing works by Solzhenitsyn, Aksenov, Dudintsev, Paustovsky, Nekrasov, Yevtushenko, and other writers from the liberal wing of the spectrum, while the magazine *Teatr* announced that it would publish plays by Aksenov and Voznesensky.[46]

The Party has been unable to act against the liberal writers—and even such a formulation as "the Party" is inadequate. The "instincts" and sympathies of most of the top leadership lie with the conservatives who conceive literature as an ideological weapon for mobilizing the society, but the liberal position also enjoys support among the highest party leaders, especially those from the technical and scientific intelligentsia. The liberals have been able to voice their themes because they strike such strong responsive chords in the Soviet population.

The courageous writers' most important theme is the disclosure of the terrible ravages suffered by Soviet society as a result of Stalin's purges. As Konstantin Paustovsky passionately declared in his famous speech of 1956, when he was discussing Dudintsev's *Not By Bread Alone* before the Moscow Writers Union (he used the occasion not only to discuss the literary merits of the novel but to score the "Drozdovs," a word derived from the novel's vulgar and obtuse bureaucrat): "If these Drozdovs had not existed, our country would still have such great men as Meyerhold, Babel, Artyom Vesely, and many others. It is the Drozdovs who destroyed them. . . . We cannot imagine what an infinite number of talents, minds and remarkable men have disappeared. But if they hadn't disappeared, if these men were still living, our culture would be in full bloom." [47]

The sense of culpability and shame about the Stalin regime runs deep in Soviet life, especially among the intelligentsia who, as Ehrenburg self-defensively remarked, had to grit their teeth to keep quiet. But Khrushchev, having opened Pandora's box, found that it could not be closed so easily. As he complained in his famous speech on culture in March 1963, "I understand that the magazines and publishing houses are being flooded with manuscripts about people's life in exile, in prison, in camps. . . . A sense of proportion is needed here. If all writers were to start writing only on this type of subject, what sort of literature would it be?"

Nor is it only the long shadow of the past that bedevils the regime; equally troublesome is the alienation of the younger generation. This is clearly reflected in the stories printed in the journal *Yunost'* (Youth), whose circulation in the six years after its founding, in 1955, went from 100,000 to 500,000. (In January 1962, V. P. Kateger, the editor of *Yunost'*, was replaced by Boris Polevoi, a shrewd party minion.) Many of these stories, which illuminate the thoughts and aspirations of young Russians, sound the common theme of running away from it all—running away from home, from school, from discipline, from duty. As Alexander Gerschenkron points out, "There is more to this literature than the exposure of the seamy side of Soviet life.... When one of the younger heroes says: 'We have no "theories",' when a young physician in another story expresses his disgust at all those sickening 'high-falutin words,' of all those 'verbal fetishisms,' [such] views are an open challenge to a state that forces every one of its subjects into an ideological strait-jacket. For 'theories' and the 'high-falutin words' obviously refer to the totality of official values." [48]

These moods merge into an implicit demand for freedom to write about Soviet life as it is, rather than about its supposed or idealized virtues. The issues are rarely stated combatively, and there is no overt attack on "socialist realism"—though the concept is no longer sacrosanct; note Tvardovsky's subtle parody of the meanings of the term in his Twenty-Second Party Congress speech. The target is the "lack of artistry" in Soviet literature.

In its typical zigzag fashion, the regime is slowly giving way. In a long editorial on socialist realism, *Pravda* of January 9, 1965, denounced both "overemphasis on sombre colors" and "the painting of idyllic, rose-tinted pictures." But for the first time, *Pravda* openly gave legitimacy to contrasting opinions when it declared that "Soviet artists ... of *different schools and styles*" could be more creative because "the aesthetics of socialist realism have in the last few years been successfully cleansing themselves of dogmatic distortions." A month later, an article in the February 21st *Pravda*, signed by Aleksey Rumyantsev, who was named editor-in-chief after Khrushchev's downfall, condemned "attempts to impose one's subjective evaluations and personal tastes as the yardstick of artistic creation, especially when they are expressed in the name of the party." Rumyantsev assailed what he described as an anti-intellectual trend of the Khrushchev regime, and asserted that "genuine creativeness is possible only through search, experimentation, free expression and clashes of viewpoints."

None of these statements represent *institutional* guarantees of freer intellectual expression (though the existence of competing magazines represents one such step), but it seems unlikely that strict adherence to the single dogma of "socialist realism" will again become the key for publication in the Soviet Union.

The "End of Ideology"?

In the face of all these changes in doctrine, what is the central core of Soviet ideology? It should be clear here, as in my extensive review of the past, that no single element of doctrine is a keystone whose removal would cause the collapse of Soviet ideology. In his book *Soviet Politics* (sub-titled "The Role of Ideas in Social Change") Barrington Moore sought to compare the pre-revolutionary expectations and ideology of the Communist Party with the Soviet reality, and concluded that, among all the aspects of Bolshevik doctrine, the transfer of the means of production to the State represents one of the few instances of congruity between anticipation and fact.[49] In the expectations concerning the organization of industry, social and economic equality, the school, the family, the power of the State—basic themes of the socialist vision—reality has turned out to be far different. Equality of wages and workers' management of industry have turned into sharp differentials and managerial authority. The 1919 Party program demand for the organization of the army as a people's militia faded long ago into stratified organization, ranks and epaulettes, no different from any other army. The schools, once organized along the lines of progressive education, have become authoritarian institutions (in the jargon of sociological pedagogy, "teacher-centered" rather than "child-centered"). The themes of equality and sacrifice, nobly sounded during the revolution, turned into class distinctions so severe that when drastic food rationing was introduced in 1941, in the month after the Germans invaded Russia, the population "was split up into favoured, semi-favoured and un-favoured categories, the rations of the latter being already extremely meagre." Could the abandonment of revolutionary ideology be more dramatic? By 1941 such conditions were accepted as "normal." [50]

But does this mean, as Robert Daniels has maintained, that ideology, or any description of the Soviet system in terms of direction or purpose, is meaningless? In reviewing the trends of Soviet thought, Daniels argues:

The pattern of changes within the core of official ideology, the official-purpose system, cannot convincingly be written off as a series of mere tactical ruses or strategic zigzags. The Soviet regime has no higher conception of society or social purpose or of the objectives of its own existence than the ideology which has been under discussion here—which ideology has been reduced to an instrument for rationalization after the fact. It has apparently lost all long-run directing power, no matter what the direction. There is no fixed star for the Soviets to steer by; they have no ultimate pattern which has not thus been subject to reshaping over the years.[51]

Thus the question is polarized: Is Soviet doctrine a "unifying ideology," or is it only a "rationalization after the fact"? Neither answer is suitable, not because each represents an extreme and the truth is always the happy middle,[52] but because each misunderstands the nature and function of ideology.

Every society, as I have argued earlier, has some value system, implicit or explicit, reflecting the underlying moral core that is the "irreducible" source of legitimacy and emotional affinity. To the extent that a society has to mobilize its people (for war, for economic development, and the like), it has to create an official ideology—some creed, intellectually coherent and rationally defensible, to justify its actions and to meet the challenges of other creeds. To the extent that a society does not mobilize its people, and becomes pluralistic and diverse, the ideology becomes more diffuse. The question of legitimacy remains then on the more general and abstract level of the value system (e.g., in the American system, the belief in equality, achievement, etc.), which is compatible with a wide range of practices and even attenuated loyalties. But some ideological base always remains. In view of all the changes that have taken place in the content of Soviet doctrines, the meaningful question, therefore, is this: What is the persistent or underlying thread of Soviet ideology, and under what conditions might one expect that element to change, if at all?

I think the underlying thread is fairly simple: The claim to an "historic mission" (to realize "communism") and the legitimacy of "the chosen instrument" (the "leading role" of the Party). To this extent, the vicissitudes of ideology in the short fifty-eight year history of the Soviet regime have been no different, in sociological principle, from the vicissitudes of dogma in the history of the Catholic Church. (In comparing the two, of course, the change of time scale must be kept in mind. Owing to the nature of communication and feedback, the Soviet time period has been vastly compressed.)

While the four elements I listed earlier—dialectical materialism, historical materialism, the superiority of collective property, and the nature of scientific communism—remain on a formal level, the doctrinal core, the central fact is not any specific theoretical formulation, *but the basic demand for belief in the Party itself.* Any hierarchically organized movement discovers this primary truth when it is forced, through the pressure of experience or doctrinal challenge, to surrender one or another contradictory element in its creed; it is not the creed but the insistence on infallibility of the interpreters which becomes the necessary mechanism of social control. Thus the crucial feature of Soviet ideology is not any formal doctrine but the idea of *Partiinost'* itself—that Party direction is essential in all fields of work. Only in this way can the Party rationalize the abandonment of once-hallowed doctrines, and adopt new doctrines that may have little justification in the old dogma.

The degree of control—the need to insist on conformity to specific tenets of the creed—is a function, in the basic sense, of the degree of mobilization in the society. Such mobilization may be the product of an intense drive to realize the "historic mission"; it may be a function of the need for internal unity against an outside enemy; it may be a necessary means of masking failures and crises. In the Soviet Union, I would argue, though the need for *Partiinost'* is still strong, the need for conformity to doctrinal aspects of ideology as a control mechanism has begun to weaken.

Much of this change is due to a redefinition of the "historic mission" of the Party. At the revolutionary inception in 1917, two missions were interwoven as one: to actively promote revolution in all parts of the world, and, through the extension of the revolution, to build socialism and then communism. An aggressive world movement requires an aggressive world view. Today, the Soviet regime, if one reads the signs correctly, has "opted out" of the revolutionary game. It does not particularly matter whether this is due to its vast internal problems in managing an increasingly complex and diversified economy and society, or because in a thermonuclear age Russia has learned that the risks of promoting revolution, or expanding its sphere of influence in the classic sense of power politics, are too great. Both elements contribute to the change of attitude. But the political consequence of this change is the doctrine of coexistence and the doctrinal formulation that wars usher in not communism but world destruction.

To accept the genuineness of the Soviet desire for coexistence is not to say that the regime is no longer aggressive in world politics. What it does imply is that the *character* of the aggressiveness has changed—from an attitude that might accept the risk of limited war to an attitude that deals primarily in terms of diplomatic, economic, and political pressure and perhaps subversion.

The Sino-Soviet split thus represents a genuine turning point in the definition of "historic mission" by the two Communist countries. For the Chinese, foreign policy has an aggressive ideological tinge; for the Russians, it has the more conventional aspects of national interest. For the Chinese, the victory of communism is a goal to be pursued aggressively through the support of national liberation movements; for the Russians, to support such movements is a matter of prudence to be decided on the merits of each case. For the Chinese, the "historic mission" is a matter of will and activity; for the Russians, it becomes relegated to the ambiguous realm of "historical processes."

The second, internal dimension of the "historic mission"—the construction of communism—has also changed in character, and this, too, affects the degree of mobilization and consequently the ideological monolithism of the society. For one thing, as is evident in the new Party programme, the "time perspective" has changed. According to the 1961 declaration, the "material and technical basis of communism will be built up by the end of the second decade (1971–1980)," and at that point "Soviet society will come close to a stage where it can introduce the principle of the distribution according to needs." [53] In this respect, the regime has sought to provide a specific date (suitably hedged) when individuals will receive an abundance in the society— a crucial change, as a way of mobilizing a society, from the sanctions and overt terror mechanisms of the Stalin regime to concrete promises.

More important are the structural changes in the breaking up (decentralization) of a complete "command economy," the reintroduction of market principles on the consumer level, and the increasing "differentiation" and multiplication of elites on the organizational level. What these two aspects of a single process suggest is that direct controls, organizational and even ideological, become increasingly difficult in a complex society,[54] and the regime must find mechanisms that allow for more "self-operation" within the power structure of the Party—and state—itself.

One sees this process taking place in three areas: economically, where the proposals for "consumer sovereignty" in the consumption field, and a general principle of profit as the measure of efficiency, require greater autonomy and self-direction on the part of producers; legally, where the development of civil law reduces the role of *direct* intervention by administrative bodies (Boris Shumkin, in a recent book on civil law in the Soviet bloc, has described this process as the efforts of Soviet lawyers to "Libermanize" Soviet society, not primarily to secure human rights but because a society where rights are specified is easier to govern than one requiring continual direct intervention);

and, finally, in the organizational structure of Soviet life where the structural differentiation of society introduces more claimants and more interest groups, a *widening,* in consequence, of the *political arena,* and the greater negotiation of interests rather than direct command.

Much of this can be fitted into the broader theoretical perspective of the relation between "State" and "Society"—a theme which had been so central to classical sociology. In his *Division of Labor,* Durkheim reformulated an enduring insight:

Collective activity is always too complex to be able to be expressed through the single and unique organ of the State. . . . Where the State is the only environment in which men can live communal lives, they inevitably lose contact, become detached and thus disintegrate. A nation can be maintained only if between the State and the individual, there is intercalated a whole series of secondary groups near enough to the individuals to attract them strongly in their sphere of action and drag them in this way into the general torrent of social life.[55]

Pre-revolutionary Russia, like many Eastern social systems, was ruled largely through the state, while society was weak. In Russia society existed in and through the family, the village, and religion, rather than through voluntary associations, corporations, functional groups, civil societies, professional associations, and other such groups which had given Western society such a thick social texture. When the Bolshevik revolution began to break down the essentially *segmental* nature of Russian social life, the Communist Party became the main agency of "society," seeking to transform it by linking up the different sectors of social life. In a curious sense, Stalinist Russia can be seen as a form of Durkheim's "mechanical solidarity," a homogeneous society where leadership and authority are centralized in a single political center— in this instance, the Party. But as society becomes more differentiated and complex, a new "organic solidarity" begins to appear in which activities—primarily intellectual and artistic, and even to some extent economic—seek to detach themselves from the single political system and attain some degree of autonomy. In this sense, the growth of "organic solidarity" of society is the underlying process which begins to erode the direct controls of the Party itself.

In the Soviet Union, the legitimacy of Communist rule derives in great measure from the claim of the Party to know the truth and direction of History. But as Zbigniew Brzezinski has asked, what is the role of the Party in a technical-managerial society, more directly what is the role of the pure Party functionary—*the apparatchik.* He has no functional role in such a society, either as a technically competent person in industry or as an administrator in government.

In the formative years of Soviet society, the role of the Party was (through "Bolshevik man") to provide a coherent social identity, to formulate goals for the future and to rationalize changes in doctrine, to supply the cadres to replace the bourgeois elements, and to set up a "control apparatus" to push and prod functionaries in other sectors. In the army, for example, Party men long served as "political commissars." But the system of "dual power" was inherently unworkable, and the purely political officer has been withdrawn; the Party "trusts" the higher army officer, as a Party member, but his primary role is that of the army man. In factories today, few successful managers listen to the *obkom* Party secretary as a guide or controller. At the top of the Party, in fact, more and more of the leaders are drawn from among the engineers and technicians rather than, like Khrushchev, from the *apparatchik* cadres. But the question is not merely one of social composition, but of structural relations.[56] What remains for the Party when technical functions begin to predominate, and these are located in technical and governmental institutions?

None of this is meant to suggest that "the Party" will disappear. Since the society lacks any other mechanism, the Party remains, crucially, as the arena where factions can coalesce to put forward one policy rather than another as decisive for the society. But a role as a decision-*making* center is already different from one as a decision-administering center; and in all this, the role of the Party—and with it perhaps, the role of mobilizing ideology—may diminish.

All of these are tendencies; in a complex society, their consequences take many years to unfold. But the direction is clear—the break-up, on all levels, of a monolithic society, and the consequent fact that different groups will have, as in any diverse society, a differential degree of attachment to and alienation from the society. This does not mean that ideology, in the sense of a formulated creed or an articulated belief system, will disappear. But it may signify the "end of ideology" in the sense that the idea has been postulated: as the abatement of the *dynamism* of a creed and the reduction of the role of ideology as a "weapon" against external and internal enemies.[57]

Ideology in the Soviet Union, and even more so in the East European countries, has been losing its full coercive and even persuasive power and, to this extent, the "end of ideology" in the Communist world may well be in sight.[58]

Gottfried Haberler

Marxist Economics in
Retrospect and Prospect

The year 1964 marked a double Marxian anniversary—one hundred years have elapsed since the founding of the First International and seventy years since the long delayed appearance of the third and final volume of *Das Kapital* which was published by Friedrich Engels eleven years after the death of its author. For my paper, concentrating as it does on Marxist *economics* exclusively, the second anniversary is of paramount importance.

I shall deal with Marx the economist—not the sociologist, philosopher of history, the powerful pamphleteer, superb journalist, propagandist and prophet (excepting specific economic prophecies). Intellectually his noneconomic activities may be more rewarding than the pure economics, and it would be more entertaining to deal not only with Marxism but also with Leninism, Stalinism, Khrushchevism, Maoism, etc. In fact the fun started already in Marx's time, he was by no means always satisfied with the interpretation of Marxism by his disciples. Engels reports that Marx "used to say about the French 'Marxists' of the seventies: 'All I know is that I am not a Marxist.'"[1] Especially intriguing would be the exploration of some noneconomic aspects of Marxist economics—particularly how a theory with such glaring defects could exert such a tremendous and persistent influence. But I must resist these temptations and concentrate on Marx's economics which is, after all, at the core of the Marxist system. I shall first briefly discuss the theory of Value and Price and then take up some of Marx's economic prophecies.

The Theory of Value and Price

According to the Marxist doctrine, the theory of value and price as systematically expounded in *Das Kapital* (especially in the first and third volumes) forms the basis of the whole structure from which the rest inexorably follows—the laws of evolution of the capitalist system, the accumulation of capital and the specific economic prophecies such as the alleged increasing misery of the working class, the growing severity of depressions, the swelling reserve army of unemployed workers and the eventual downfall of the capitalist system itself. In the first volume of *Das Kapital,* the only one that Marx was able to finish, a labor theory of value, taken over from the English classical economists, Adam Smith and David Ricardo,[2] was presented. The value of each commodity is determined by "the quantity of socially necessary labor" and "commodities exchange according to their value." The law applies to labor itself. The price of "labor power," the wage, is determined by the "quantity of socially necessary labor," that is the labor required to produce the livelihood of the worker. But capitalists make workers work longer hours than is necessary to sustain the workers' existence. This exploitation is the source of "surplus value," of profits. "Surplus value is in substance the embodiment of unpaid working time."

Ricardo knew that the labor theory of value cannot hold literally and precisely. The proportionality of market price to labor content is impossible, if the commodities require different amounts of capital to produce. Marx, too, was aware of the difficulty. If two commodities require the same total amount of labor to produce but different proportions of direct, "live" labor and indirect labor (labor embodied in capital instruments), they cannot conform to the law of value. Marx also had to clear up an apparent internal contradiction of his theory. He claimed in Volume I that the "rate of surplus value" or "rate of exploitation" (i.e. the ratio of "surplus value" to "variable capital," that is to direct labor) tended to be the same in all industries, while in reality the rate of profit tends to be the same for total capital irrespective of its "organic composition" (proportion of fixed and variable capital, in other words "live" and "embodied" labor).

The solution of these puzzles was promised for later volumes of *Das Kapital.* Volume II, which appeared in 1885, two years after Marx's death, did not contain the answer. But Engels, in his preface, promised it for the third volume and challenged Marx's critics to use their wits to guess what the solution would be. A veritable prize essay competition on the "average rate of profit" and "the law of value" developed during the ten years between the appearance of the second and third volumes. According to Engels' view, as expressed in his preface to the third volume, no one succeeded in carrying off the prize.

What was Marx's solution? In Volume III, Marx developed in fact a theory of price based on total cost of production which is entirely different from the labor theory of value in Volume I. But in many pages of involved and tortuous reasoning he tried to reconcile the two and to explain away the contradiction between Volume I and Volume III. This gave rise to endless discussions, criticism, and countercriticism. I do not, of course, intend to go over this ground again. Let me try to summarize the outcome.

Two years after the publication of the third volume, the Austrian economist Eugen von Böhm-Bawerk, who had already given an exhaustive critical analysis of Marx's version of the labor theory and his exploitation theory of interest (profit) as laid out in the first volume of *Das Kapital* and in other writings, presented his final verdict in his celebrated essay *Karl Marx and the Close of His System*.[3]

In my opinion Böhm-Bawerk's is to this day the most convincing and lucid analysis of the Marxist theory of value, price, capital and interest. More than half a century after it was written, it is still surprisingly readable and fresh. Böhm-Bawerk's criticism is all the more telling because it is couched in moderate and dignified language. There are no harsh words, no biting irony or wounding sarcasm, no abusive or vituperative phrases, no venomous and strident accusations—nothing of these which abound on almost every page that Marx and Engels wrote.

Böhm-Bawerk's conclusion was that Marx has not been able to straighten out the confusion. "I cannot help myself; I see here no explanation and reconciliation of a contradiction, but the bare contradiction itself. Marx's third volume contradicts the first. The theory of the average rate of profit and of the prices of production cannot be reconciled with the theory of value." Böhm-Bawerk's criticism which goes, of course, beyond the demonstration of an internal contradiction to showing the basic flaws of theory, is altogether convincing and has never been refuted.[4]

It has been fully confirmed by the latest full dress examination and dissection of the Marxist system in a brilliant article by Paul Samuelson.[5] Samuelson uses modern methods of linear theoretical analysis (linear programming and input-output theory) which are especially suitable because Marx is supposed to have operated with fixed coefficients of production.[6] His analysis goes beyond Böhm-Bawerk's in depth as well as breadth. The latter dealt only with the basic issues and economics has, after all, made some progress since his time. Some of Samuelson's conclusions are "that Böhm-Bawerk, Wicksteed and Pareto were essentially right in their critiques of the Marxian system" and "that the Marxian notions do not achieve the desired goal of 'explaining the laws of motion or of development of the capitalist system.' " [7]

Classical and neoclassical economics, "bourgeois economics," has become much more operational since the times of Marx or Böhm-Bawerk. It was always "operational" in the logical, philosophical sense. Today it is operational also in the policy sense. That is to say it is more and more used for policy purposes both in predominantly free enterprise countries and in more or less extensively planned countries. This is simply a statement of fact and is not meant to be an argument for or against planning.

Marxist economics has proved operationally completely sterile both in capitalist and Communist countries. That the theory does not apply to socialist economies is not surprising, it might be said, inasmuch as Marx deliberately refrained from going into "the economics of socialism." His was a theory of *capitalist* development. He never gave advice on how to run a socialist economy and refused, and said it was idle and inopportune, to speculate what the concrete economic problems of a collectivist economy would be and how they might be handled. But the point is, and it is a fact of great significance, that the theory of the competitive capitalist economy has also proved a very useful tool for analyzing the basic problems of efficient resource allocation in a centrally planned economy. The management of the Soviet economy has been seriously handicapped by the absence of a ready-made theory of resource allocation which could have been provided, at least in part, by the despised bourgeois economics. Doctrinaire adherence to certain tenets of the Marxist doctrine, especially the dogmatic refusal to systematically use an interest rate in economic calculations to insure rational allocation of the scarce factor "capital" (or to use another terminology which avoids the use of the word "capital," to assure a proper time shape of output and avoid unsustainable roundabout ways of production) has impaired efficiency and reduced output below what it could have been.[8]

Some of these deficiencies are being gradually repaired and even interest has been creeping back on the economic scene, thinly disguised, through the back door.[9] Thus Soviet economics is moving away from the dogmas of Marxist economics.

These remarks again are not meant to be arguments for or against planning. In my opinion, the superiority of the free-market, free-enterprise system over the centrally planned economies is clearly visible even to the naked eye. How should one explain the striking contrast in the standard of living between such pairs of Western and Eastern countries as Austria and Czechoslovakia, Greece and Yugoslavia, and especially Western Germany and the Soviet zone of Germany—countries that are more or less similar with respect to resource endowment, both human and physical (stage of development, cultural background, education, and skills of the labor force, climate, soil, etc.) and which have, in the pre-Communist past, enjoyed a roughly equal level of wealth and economic well-being? Furthermore, I did not want to suggest that the basic difference in the efficiency of the two systems could be eliminated by the more intensive application in the planned economies of modern Western methods of economic analysis. On the contrary, I would argue that the greater use of the most up-to-date methods of economic analysis, although it would help the managers of centrally planned economies to avoid some of the most glaring inefficiencies and wastes, can never be a really effective alternative to the incentives provided by real competition in all parts of the economy, especially among the risk-bearing free entrepreneurs. There are no synthetic substitutes in a planned economy for these essential ingredients of rapid progress.

But in the present paper I am not concerned with these broader issues. All I wanted to show is the operational sterility of Marxist economics and the applicability and usefulness, even in collectivist economies, of neoclassical economic analysis and its modern offshoots.

Marx's Economic Prophecies

Marx was a prophet in more than one sense, in the large and in the small—not only of economic development, but of the broad historical, social, political evolution of every country and the world at large. In their innumerable newspaper articles—especially Marx's numerous contributions to the *New York Daily Tribune* (now *New York Herald Tribune*) of which he was for many years a regular correspondent, and Engels' frequent articles in the *Manchester Guardian*—as well as in their very extensive private correspondence, Marx and Engels were continuously making detailed forecasts about coming depressions, revolutions, wars, the outcome of military campaigns, and many other economic and political developments. In innumerable cases these forecasts proved ludicrously wrong, in others they were right, but they were always presented as firmly based on, and scientifically derived from, a comprehensive socio-economic theory.[10]

In the present paper I shall deal only with two specific *economic* prophecies—the "Verelendungtheorie," theory of increasing misery of the working class, "imiserisation" as it is sometimes called, and the theory of increasing severity of economic depressions. Both have shown a tendency to survive though often in a changed, disguised, and attenuated form. According to orthodox Marxist doctrine these secular tendencies can be deduced from the basic Marxist theory, "the law of value," and are therefore part and parcel of the indivisible Marxist system. But since they are logically not incompatible with neoclassical or modern economics, they must be dealt with on their own merits.[11]

The assertion that in the capitalist countries real wages have a secular tendency to decline flies in the face of what everyone knows of economic history. It is therefore not surprising that of late one does not see it often expressed, at least as far as the industrial countries are concerned.[12] It is interesting, however, to observe how Marxist writers have tried, by reinterpreting its meaning, to uphold the law laid down by the master. Some interpret Marx as saying that the share of national income going to labor—not the absolute wage—shows a tendency for secular decline.[13] This makes little sense for two reasons. First, undoctored statistics show that the share of national income going to labor has been remarkably stable.[14] Of course, if one is satisfied with a mild shift, he should be able to make a case by drawing the line between labor and nonlabor income accordingly. Since there are white collar workers, independent artisans, foremen, supervisory personnel, independent professional workers (lawyers, doctors, etc.), in one word a finely graded hierarchy from unskilled manual workers on the one extreme to entrepreneurs and "pure capitalists" at the other (with the order or ranking often uncertain and arbitrary), it is not too difficult to find a not overly implausible classification which yields the desired result.[15] Secondly, although it is possible to find passages in the writings of Marx that support the relative interpretation, it is pretty clear that he really meant it in the absolute sense.[16] For the theory of increasing misery was meant to be and proved to be a most potent propaganda weapon. In a weak and uncertain relative sense it would have failed in that vital function.

In passing, it might be mentioned that in addition to the conflict with the facts of history, Marx got involved in an internal inconsistency. In the Marxist system it is impossible to reconcile the law of falling real wages (in the absolute or relative sense) with his law of falling profit rate. Even good Marxists like Paul Sweezy and strong sympathizers like Joan Robinson have admitted that contradiction.[17]

The next stage is the Marxist theory of economic imperialism. This theory was clearly foreshadowed by Marx himself but was worked out in different versions by Otto Bauer, Rudolf Hilferding, Rosa Luxemburg, Fritz Sternberg, Lenin and others. It has two interrelated aspects or functions. The first aspect is that imperialism, the subjugation and exploitation of backward areas (colonies) by the capitalist powers, gives capitalism another and last lease of life. If it had not been possible for capitalism to push into "noncapitalist space," the backward areas, it would have collapsed long ago. The other aspect is that Imperialism and Colonialism transfer the exploitation, the increasing misery, from the working class in the capitalist countries to natives of the backward areas.

As to the first aspect, it is sufficient to remark that Colonialism and Imperialism have disappeared, but former colonial powers are better off than they ever were. Moreover, countries that never owned colonies, the Scandinavian countries or Switzerland, or whose colonies were economically worthless (e.g. Germany) have developed just as fast or faster than the colonial powers. The Netherlands had a colonial empire, the Dutch East Indies, now Indonesia, which was valuable and contributed about ten per cent to the Dutch national income—and, of course, much more to the national income and economic welfare of the Indonesian people. The colonies are gone, but after a few years Holland was more prosperous than she ever was—whilst Indonesians are probably worse off than before and certainly much worse than they would have been had they enjoyed twenty more years of orderly and efficient Dutch administration.

The second aspect is well brought out by Paul Sweezy, the foremost living American Marxist. He admits that in the developed countries workers have a "tolerable if degraded [!] life" but the advanced countries "increasingly impose the burdens on the colonies and the raw material producing countries." [18] It is significant that a theory very similar to the Marxist theory of imperialistic exploitation of the backward areas has been put forward by non-Marxist economists and widely accepted in less developed countries. In a sense, this new doctrine, of non-Marxist origin, carries the Marxist theory one step forward: it does not require colonial rule as the theory of imperialism did. As far as I can see these authors have not been influenced by Marxist thought, at least not directly, and are even unaware of their Marxist kinship.

In an extreme form this theory has been put forward by Gunnar Myrdal.[19] He tries to show that "trade operates (as a rule) with a fundamental bias in favor of the rich and progressive regions (and countries) and in disfavor of the less developed countries." The thesis is not merely that the poor countries derive less benefit from trade than the rich but that the poor become poorer if and because the rich get richer. In this extreme form the theory is not widely accepted, although its influence in coloring the general thinking on these problems, especially in less developed countries, should not be underestimated.

In a somewhat less extreme and more technical form essentially the same theory has found wide acceptance in less developed countries. It can almost be called the official theory of the United Nations. What I have in mind is the theory that for deep-seated reasons there is a pronounced and persistent secular tendency for the so-called "terms of trade" to change against the less developed countries; in other words, that the prices of raw materials which constitute the great bulk of the exports of the less developed countries, tend to fall relatively to the prices of manufactured goods which the less developed countries import.

This is a highly technical and involved subject. It would lead too far to discuss it here in any detail. I must confine myself to the somewhat dogmatic statement that recent thorough researches have conclusively shown that there does not exist any such secular tendency. The terms of trade of the less developed world in general and for different regions and countries in that vast area are, of course, subject to changes and swings in different directions, length and severity, but have not displayed any secular tendency. For the proof of this statement, I refer to the extensive literature on the subject.[20]

Marx had many interesting things to say on business cycles and depressions. Whether he had a unified theory of the cycle and, if so, what it was, has been much debated. Many of his followers and critics interpret him as having propounded a Keynes-like underconsumption theory. Others, especially Schumpeter who knew Marxist theory very well, objected to what he called the "Keynesianization of Marx." Vitriolic attacks on "vulgar" underconsumption theorizing can indeed be found in Marx's writings. The truth probably is that his views were changing, eclectic and in places even self-contradictory. But I have to leave this question to the business cycle specialists and Marxologists.

Whether it is compatible or not with what is said in *Das Kapital* or elsewhere on the business cycle, Marx did proclaim the theory that under capitalism depressions necessarily have a secular tendency to become more and more severe. This alleged tendency has been one of Marxism's most powerful propaganda weapons and it is an integral part of the allegedly inexorable historical process that leads to the downfall of capitalism. A severe economic depression, a final big crisis will spark the revolution that overthrows capitalism and ushers in the socialist era. Marx's followers, "neo-Marxists" following Marx's lead have embellished the story by weaving imperialistic conquests and internecine wars between capitalistic powers into the picture, but the increasing severity of depressions has to this day remained one of the fundamental tenets of Marxism.

How has this prophecy stood up in the light of more than one hundred years' history since it was first promulgated in the Communist Manifesto? There have been periods and events that seemed to give support to the Marxist forecast, at least to the casual and superficial observer. The severe depressions in the last quarter of the nineteenth century and above all the Great Depression of the 1930's were grist for the Marxist mill.

The depressed years of the 1930's which lasted until the outbreak of the Second World War [21] stimulated the emergence, or at any rate contributed to the vogue, of Keynesian economics, the "New Economics" as it was and sometimes is called.[22] Now Keynesian economics is very different from Marxism and Keynes himself had no sympathy for and little knowledge of Marx. But the Great Depression also gave rise to the Keynes-inspired theory of "secular stagnation." This view blended well with the Marxist doctrine. A fusion of the two, Marxo-Keynesianism was the result. It is represented by such names as J. Robinson, Paul Sweezy, and Shigeto Tsuru, each having his own "organic composition"—mixtures of Marx and Keynes. But, to repeat, Keynes himself and most of his followers did not embrace Marxism and their policy conclusions and visions of future events are, of course, entirely different from Marx's.

The post-World War II period, which brought almost unprecedented prosperity, occasionally slowed but not interrupted by very mild recessions, has all but shattered the Keynesian belief in tendencies of secular stagnation and the Marxist prophecy of ever deepening depressions and more violent crises.

Twenty years is, however, a very short period for judging secular tendencies. The mere fact that things have gone well for two decades would hardly entitle us to conclude that never again will there be a deep depression or serious stagnation. Moreover, the Keynesian stagnationists will reply that things have gone better precisely because their prescriptions have been followed, to wit a rapid growth of government expenditures and public deficits when necessary. Marxists, too, are not shy to use such arguments, however poorly they may fit into their general scheme.

My answer to these strictures is this: The mere fact that for twenty years things have gone well and severe setbacks have been avoided would not be decisive. What is decisive is that it has become increasingly clear that the catastrophe of the Great Depression was due to special circumstances, institutional weaknesses and incredibly inept and timid policies on the national and international level after the depression had started. This has been misunderstood by most Keynesians and Marxists alike, but was realized at the time by such masters as W. C. Mitchell, D. H. Robinson and J. A. Schumpeter. The Great Depression was not an ordinary endogenous cyclical downswing.[23] Earlier deep depressions during the 1870's and 1890's and in 1920–21, too, can be satisfactorily explained in terms of special avoidable monetary disturbances.[24]

But will such monetary disturbances and mismanagement be avoided in the future? As far as the refutation of Marx's theory of the increasing severity of depressions is concerned, it is sufficient to realize that such monetary mistakes and disturbances can be easily avoided. It should be observed that prolonged and violent inflation, although undoubtedly very bad for rapid growth and socially destructive, need not be and rarely are followed by similarly severe deflation and depression.

I believe that on this most economists including Keynesians and even some Marxists or Marxo-Keynesians will agree. What the latter now say is that the "capitalists" or "ruling classes" will not, in fact, permit the financial policies to be adopted which would be necessary to avoid or mitigate severe depressions. Inasmuch as profits more than any other type of income suffer in a depression, this argument is singularly unconvincing and at any rate a far cry from the original Marxist position. Marx surely did not want to say that capitalism could go on forever if it were not for the stupidity and shortsightedness of "the ruling capitalist classes" in not permitting the adoption of financial policies which would prevent profits from tumbling in severe depressions.

There persists, of course, serious disagreements on such questions as to whether monetary policy alone could do the job and if the answer is "no," whether variation of taxes is sufficient or changes in expenditures ("public works") are required. Some writers favor "automatic mechanisms," others insist on the necessity of "discretionary" policies in the monetary and fiscal area. Some are optimistic and believe that the cycle could be eradicated altogether, while others think that because of unavoidable lags and lack of foresight mild cycles will persist even with optimal financial policies. Needless to add, some recommend doing no more than eliminating the business cycle as far as possible (excepting possibly mild fluctuations), while for others anticyclical financial policies are the vehicle and occasion for the attainment of more far-reaching goals—stimulating growth, changing the income distribution, expanding the public sector of the economy, etc.

These disagreements and differences concerning policy objectives and the comparative effectiveness of different policy tools, important though they are, do not alter the fact that implicit in these discussions and common to all participants, despite their disagreements, is the rejection of the Marxist theory of the inevitability of the breakdown of capitalism due to the inherent tendency of endogenous cyclical depressions to become more and more severe.

Concluding Remarks

In 1896 Böhm-Bawerk concluded his appraisal of the Marxist system with these words:

What will be the final judgment of the world? Of that I have no manner of doubt. The Marxian system has a past and a present, but no abiding future ... A clever dialectic may make a temporary impression on the human mind, but cannot make a lasting one ... In the very young social sciences it was able to attain influence, great influence, and it will probably only lose it very slowly, and that because it has its most powerful support not in the convinced intellect of its disciples, but in their hearts, their wishes, and their desires.

He added:

But even when this will have happened socialism will certainly not be overthrown with the Marxian system,—neither practical nor theoretical socialism.

And:

Marx will maintain a permanent place in the history of the social sciences ... [His] theoretical work ... was a most ingeniously conceived structure, built up by a fabulous power of combination, of innumerable storeys of thought, held together by a marvelous grasp, but—a house of cards.

Was Böhm-Bawerk's judgment entirely wrong? He did not, of course, foresee that Marxist communism would be triumphant in large parts of the world. But what does that prove if we distinguish, as we must, between Marxist economics and Marxism as a revolutionary movement? True, Soviet writers still pay lip service to Marx. But it is also true that in their economic discussions they are clearly moving away from the Marxist dogmas. There is a story going around that a well-known American Marxist returned from a visit to Russia greatly disillusioned because "the Soviets are no real Marxists any more." If it has not actually happened it has been truthfully invented! Marx's own German Social Democratic Party, which despite some revisionism has traditionally been doctrinaire Marxist (although the truly revolutionary spirit left the party a long time ago), has formally foresworn the Marxist faith.

It is also a fact that many of the new führers and dictators in under-developed countries in Asia and Africa proudly call themselves Marxists. But it is safe to assume that none of them has ever read anything by Marx. If they read the Communist Manifesto and under-stood it, they would not like it. For nowhere has the power of capitalism, of the bourgeoisie as the Manifesto calls it, to develop backward areas been described in more glowing language than in the Communist Manifesto:

> ... It [the bourgeoisie] has been the first to show what man's activity can bring about. It has accomplished wonders far surpassing Egyptian pyramids, Roman aqueducts, and Gothic cathedrals; it has conducted expeditions that put in the shade all former migrations of nations and crusades.
> ... All old-fashioned national industries have been destroyed or are daily being destroyed. They are dislodged by new industries, whose introduction becomes a life and death question for all civilized nations, by industries that no longer work up indigenous raw material, but raw material drawn from the remotest zones; industries whose products are consumed, not only at home, but in every quarter of the globe.
> The bourgeoisie, by the rapid improvement of all instruments of produc-tion, by the immensely facilitated means of communication, draws all na-tions, even the most barbarian, into civilization. The cheap prices of its commodities are the heavy artillery with which it batters down all Chinese walls, with which it forces the barbarians' intensely obstinate hatred of foreigners to capitulate. It compels all nations, on pain of extinction, to adopt the bourgeois mode of production; it compels them to introduce what it calls civilization into their midst, i.e., to become bourgeois themselves. In a word, it creates a world after its own image.
> The bourgeoisie, during its rule of scarce one hundred years, has created more massive and more colossal productive forces than have all preceding generations together. Subjection of nature's forces to man, machinery, application of chemistry to industry and agriculture, steam-navigation, rail-ways, electric telegraphs, clearing of whole continents for cultivation, canalization of rivers, whole populations conjured out of the ground—what earlier century had even a presentiment that such productive forces slumbered in the lap of social labour?

I conclude that Böhm-Bawerk's prediction has come true. The Marxist economic system has slowly lost its influence and has no future. But the close of the Marxist system does not mean the end of socialism, and Marxist economics will always maintain a prominent place in the history of the social sciences and the intellectual history of the nine-teenth and twentieth centuries. The historian of economic thought will never cease rummaging in the voluminous writings of Marx and the specialist will find flashes of insight and even genuine analytical discoveries, bits and pieces of usable scrap. People will always marvel as Böhm-Bawerk did, at the boldness of the whole lofty construction, but Marxism as an economic system is closed and will not be reopened.

Yuan-li Wu

Communist Economic Planning vs.
Capitalism as a Model for Development

The basic faults of the capitalist economy, according to Marxists, are its injustice and inefficiency. The capitalist system is said to be unjust because the total output of productive activity, for which labor alone is allegedly responsible, does not accrue entirely to labor. That part of the output which does not accrue to labor is represented as "surplus value," the existence of which is evidence of "exploitation." Simultaneously, capitalism is said to be inefficient on several grounds. First, it fails to allocate resources in a manner that would satisfy what might be described as "merit" and "social" wants to the extent that a segment of the population would wish to see them satisfied. In the second place, capitalism is said to be inefficient because it cannot maintain economic stability and a rate of growth commensurate with the expansion of the labor force and technological improvements which increase labor productivity. The rate of profit on which capitalism depends for a steady flow of investment tends to fall; insufficient effective demand because of an artificially restricted share of the total output going to labor results in under-consumption; lack of overall economic planning precludes the maintenance of proportionality between different sectors of the economy.

An ever-worsening depression forces the capitalists to seek external markets and, via the state apparatus which they control, to extend "exploitation" from the domestic proletariat to less developed countries. In this manner, inefficiency of the capitalist system inexorably leads to an extension of injustice. Since different national states under capitalism undergo the same experience and pursue the same policy, they must inevitably come into conflict with one another. This is, of course, Lenin's thesis of imperialism and war.

The author wishes to express his appreciation to Miss Grace Hsiao and Mr. Lawrence Lau for research assistance in the preparation of this paper.

Such in a nutshell is the Marxist critique of capitalist society. An implication of the criticism is that the Communist system is free from the same strictures. In a separate paper in this volume, Professor Peter Bauer shows that there is really little ground to assert that past exploitation on the part of colonial powers can be invariably associated with lack of economic development in the former colonies; nor is the thesis that political independence necessarily expedites economic development at all convincing. Both the unsupported assertion that the Communist system is free from the alleged evils of capitalism and the Marxist critique of capitalism need to be examined further.

The Thesis of External Exploitation

"Economic exploitation" of one country by another may be broadly defined as using directly or indirectly the resources of the exploited country without, or with insufficient, compensation. Furthermore, such "exploitation" must result from special powers possessed by the exploiting country or deliberate machination on the part of the exploiter. This qualifying condition is frequently difficult to prove, and is therefore often implicitly assumed by those who believe that such exploitation exists.

First, let us examine what we might describe as the "foreign investment and colonization" thesis. In this connection, it may be argued that external exploitation exists if the outflow of profits from the exploited country exceeds the inflow of capital. If the outflow includes the original investment and any net excess is regarded as a sign of exploitation, then every successful foreign investment would fall into this category. If the excess is measured only when the net profit exceeds a certain sum, then "exploitation" would be predicated upon "exorbitant" profit. It is frequently alleged that foreign investors earn exorbitant profit which should rightfully belong to the country where the investment is made. Unfortunately, what is exorbitant can only be determined on the basis of political, emotional, and perhaps moral values. It is not unnatural for the economist to seek a more objective criterion. We need therefore to compare the rate and pattern of economic development aided by foreign investment with what they might have been in the absence of foreign investment.

Those who maintain such an "exploitation" thesis would argue that foreign capital gives rise to the emergence of a foreign enclave on native soil, that the externally directed investment activities may be concentrated in specialized export sectors, and that such specialization may divert the limited domestic investment potential and entrepreneurial ability to areas which do not strengthen the basic structure of the domestic economy.[1] Foreign capital may even tend to "freeze" the pattern of production, making broad-gauged industrialization more difficult to achieve in the future. Yet without foreign investment domestic capital and entrepreneurial ability would not necessarily develop what might at some uncertain future date eventually be considered the more productive industries. It is also entirely possible that industries developed by foreign investors would be developed anyway, though perhaps on different scales, because of inherent comparative advantages of the underdeveloped country. Furthermore, if they are not developed sooner in the absence of foreign investment, this may simply be due to lack of markets which foreign investors would have brought. Nor are exports necessarily restrictive in the sense of reducing the number of alternatives or options for further development. Export earnings may in fact loosen the balance of payments constraint which effectively limits investment in many less developed countries. A basic difficulty facing such countries is their limited ability to shift resources out of one industry into another, be it native or foreign owned. The fault does not lie with foreign capital; it is a structural problem of underdevelopment, technological inadequacy, and institutional rigidities. To compare what is with what might have been is, of course, as Singer admits, pure speculation, "a tantalizingly inconclusive business."[2]

As foreign capital cannot always be blamed for inadequate or distorted economic development, so the loss of colonies has not prevented some of the erstwhile colonial powers from maintaining a high rate of economic growth. The United Kingdom, France, the Netherlands, and Japan are good recent examples. One might even maintain that the development of these countries after World War II has been facilitated by the liquidation of their empires. Incidentally, the postwar development of these countries was greatly assisted by U.S. capital which, contrary to Marxist doctrine, did not seek to take over the former colonial markets of Europe by establishing an American empire. Besides, colonies have never been important to the development of many capitalist economies, including those of the United States, Switzerland, and Germany.

On the other hand, as Professor Bauer shows elsewhere, the rates of economic growth of a number of countries have not risen with independence. The national income of Indonesia has actually declined with respect to its growth rate. Nor has Egypt improved very much since the departure of the British. And in spite of aid from both the

United States and the U.S.S.R., India has exhibited an average annual growth of 2.9 percent in national income, only slightly higher than the pre-1949 rates.[3]

Secondly, let us consider the terms of trade arguments as another form of "exploitation" that may allegedly take place through international trade. Many non-Marxist economists believe that the terms of trade have shown a secular tendency to deteriorate for the less developed countries. (We abstract for the moment from the condition that direct machination should really be demonstrated.) And most economists view the proposition that the terms of trade have turned against the countries producing primary goods as identical with the proposition that they have become more favorable to the manufacturing countries. Kindleberger,[4] however, found that his data would support the second thesis, but not the first.

Among the various explanations offered for the alleged secular trend is a generalization based on Engel's Law which states that the smaller the family income the greater the proportion spent on food.[5] If demand is inelastic when production rises, then prices tend to fall. This then is generalized and applied to all primary commodities, including industrial raw materials as well as agricultural products. A second explanation relies upon differential degrees of monopoly in both the factors and goods markets. Raul Prebisch, for instance, maintains that "the characteristic lack of organization among the workers employed in primary production prevents them from obtaining wage increases (in the boom) comparable to those of the industrial countries and from maintaining the increases to the same extent (in the depression)."[6] Singer apparently subscribes to a similar "unionization argument." Yet as Haberler points out, while unionization may lead to high or low absolute prices, it does not affect relative prices or comparative cost.[7] Others have stressed a relative monopoly in the goods market.[8] Developed countries possess greater monopoly power as large consumers on primary commodities, and their manufacturing industries also have a higher degree of monopoly, which would enable them to set higher prices. Note should, however, be taken that this comparative monopoly relationship is supposed to hold between the developed countries on the one hand and the less developed countries on the other; it is not meant to apply to capitalist countries only vis-à-vis the less developed countries unless it is further assumed that communist countries do not exercise monopoly power.

Reasons can also be advanced to explain why the terms of trade should turn the other way. Exhaustion of certain raw materials in developed economies, such as coal in the United Kingdom, may require large-scale imports. At the same time, the factors in agriculture and the extractive industries may be fixed in supply, thus leading to diminishing returns, while the same is not true of manufacturing: "Hence the terms of trade must inexorably turn against the manufacturing industries and industrial countries." [9]

Prebisch also claims that the benefits of technical progress have gone mainly to the industrial countries and even that some benefits have been withheld from the primary goods producing countries. But this and the preceding arguments are, to say the least, inconclusive. Empirical evidence should be decisive,[10] but is the evidence advanced unassailable? Does it really constitute what Singer terms "the legitimate germ of truth" in the charge that foreign investment of the traditional type formed part of a system of "economic imperialism" and of "exploitation"? [11]

Long-run comparisons of terms of trade are particularly hazardous because of changes in quality, productivity, and transportation costs. All these factors, however, are generally disregarded in studies on the terms of trade. The quality of manufactured products has improved tremendously over the last few decades whereas that of primary commodities has changed little if at all. The terms of trade may therefore appear to turn in favor of the developed countries when in fact price increases are offset by better quality. Furthermore, agricultural productivity has improved considerably in some areas, at a rate perhaps keeping pace with or even surpassing the growth of productivity in manufacturing. Failure to correct for such changes in productivity, that is, to use the "single" or "double factoral terms of trade," would also produce an upward bias in favor of manufacturing. Lastly, reduction in transport costs in recent years has revolutionized the pattern and composition of world trade. Import prices should decline on the strength of reduced transport costs alone. If the terms of trade are computed as a ratio of c.i.f. import prices to f.o.b. export prices, a reduction of transport cost would show an improvement in the terms of trade independently of any change in quality or productivity. It can also be easily demonstrated that a decrease in transport cost can improve the terms of trade simultaneously for both trading partners. Using the terms of trade index of developed countries as an inverse indicator of the terms of trade of their trading partners—the less developed countries in this case—neglects transport cost as well as local supply and demand conditions.

Other statistical practices raise serious doubt about the proper interpretation of empirical findings. In computing the terms of trade, for instance, unit-value indices of machinery usually represent the declared value divided by weight! [12] Since reduction in bulk and lighter metals and materials are a part of quality improvement in modern machines, the unit-value index thus calculated is of dubious value.

A second consideration is that British trade statistics are most commonly used. From them Prebisch, the United Nations, and others have concluded that there has been a secular deterioration in the terms of trade for the primary goods producing countries since 1870. [13] The year 1876, however, saw the peak of the terms of trade index between primary goods and manufactured products in the United Kingdom's trade for the last two centuries. If the data were traced back to 1800, there would be no evidence of any deterioration. In fact, there were wide fluctuations with peaks at 1876 and 1918. Thus, depending upon the time span chosen, one can come to any desired conclusion concerning the secular trend of the terms of trade. Theodore Morgan has concluded in his essay on "The Long Run Terms of Trade between Agriculture and Manufacturing" [14] that the British data are unreliable as a measure of long-run prices and of the relative position of primary goods producing countries *vis-à-vis* the manufacturing countries. Kindleberger also criticizes these data extensively; he concludes that "in the European context" the terms of trade favor the developed countries. The important qualification seems to be the phrase "in the European context." For it is possible to accept Kindleberger's analysis of the European experience and at the same time reject a broader generalization for the rest of the world. Kindleberger also maintains in the same book [15] that there is no long-run tendency for the terms of trade to move against primary products in favor of manufacturing and that they may have turned against manufacturing if sufficient allowance is made for quality improvements. Furthermore, in the American experience, according to Morgan, primary production has gained considerably *vis-à-vis* manufacturing and the result is a drastic shift of relative prices in favor of the former.

Foreign investment is not necessarily exploitative; the thesis of deteriorating terms of trade for the less developed countries is inconclusive in theory and evidence; developments unfavorable to the less developed countries may be inherent in the economic structure of underdevelopment; export of capital is not necessarily associated with political imperialism. Nevertheless, we have many historical examples of economic exploitation of one country by another through discriminatory trade policy, direct transfer of colonial surpluses without *quid pro quo,* etc. Japanese activities in Korea and certain European commercial activities in African colonies may be cited. But such exploitation is even easier for Communist powers which are simultaneously imperialist.

The Soviet Union has not hesitated to exploit any advantage conferred by preponderant military power *vis-à-vis* her neighbors. Through arbitrary reparation payments, removal of industrial installations, seizure of property, formation of joint companies, and a variety of other techniques, the Soviet Union, according to some estimates, extracted upward of U.S. $20 billion from the Eastern European satellites. Hungary, Rumania, and Bulgaria, according to Spulber, were in debt to Russia for at least twelve years (1944–1956).[16] Until recently the Soviet Union has also dictated and distorted the pattern of production in the satellite countries. For instance, Rumania is supposed to concentrate on agriculture in order to serve the communist bloc as a food supplier.

According to the Pauley report on Japanese reparations at the end of World War II Soviet authorities removed industrial installations from Manchuria worth an estimated $2 billion at the then prevailing reinvestment cost. In the strategic energy-supply and steel-making industries, recent studies on key sectors of the Communist Chinese economy have shown that the pre-Communist level of capacity was not attained again until about 1956 when the Chinese first five-year plan had virtually run its course. The capital goods and technical asistance imported from the Soviet Union by Communist China, which were paid for, merely offset the initial damage the Soviet Union had inflicted. Parenthetically, one might note that the initial devastation of Manchuria was probably designed by the Soviet Union with a dual purpose, to retard the economic recovery of China if the Nationalist government had remained in power, and to make a communist regime economically dependent upon the Soviet Union should the Communist Party of China succeed in seizing power, as it later did. The subsequent repatriation of Soviet capital made sure that Soviet investment would be returned in full. Even without the joint Soviet-Chinese enterprises which operated in Manchuria and Sinkiang until 1954, replicas of similar Nazi and later Soviet devices in Eastern and Central Europe, one can point to Soviet economic practices as examples of exploitation *par excellence.* In many cases the Soviet Government secured large "returns" without any real investment. A number of these comments are confirmed in editorials in the *Hung-Chi,* as well as the *People's Daily,* published in the course of the Sino-Soviet dispute in early 1964.

By offering some of the less developed countries with which they trade long-term purchase contracts for primary products, both the Soviet Union and Communist China have also exerted influence on the pattern of economic development of these countries, including possibly a weakening of the sense of urgency felt to diversify the economy. In dealings with Burma and other Asian countries, Communist China is known to have employed such techniques as delayed shipment, the presentation of a limited shopping list, insistence on package deals, etc., which invariably alter the real terms of trade in her favor. The same techniques have been employed by the Soviet Union in dealing with other countries, including her own satellites. When external trade is consciously developed as a part of economic warfare in a broad sense, then the criterion of deliberate intent in defining "exploitation" is fully satisfied.

The Thesis of Domestic Exploitation

Turning next to the Marxist argument of domestic exploitation, the "rate of exploitation," otherwise known as the "rate of surplus value," is represented by the ratio of "surplus value" to "variable capital." This value, it is said, is extremely high in capitalist countries and tends to become higher. The "rate of exploitation" is so defined because, according to the Marxists, all production must be attributed to labor and what does not accrue to labor must necessarily result from exploitation. Of course, what is not paid out in wages is consumed by non-wage earners or reinvested, or absorbed in collective consumption. Some of the profits consumed are still genuine payments for services rendered, for even managers are workers and must earn a labor income. And the part which represents collective consumption accrues indirectly to the workers.

Leaving aside theoretical criticism of the labor theory of value which has long been abandoned by economists outside Communist countries, we can nevertheless look at some empirical evidence. The following tabulation,[17] the ratio of non-wage factor income to the wage bill, shows the "rate of exploitation" in selected years for the Soviet Union, the United Kingdom, the United States, and Yugoslavia. Because of limitation of data, the Soviet ratio is calculated for industrial production only. The ratio was higher in the Soviet Union and Yugoslavia than in the United Kingdom and the United States in every one of the five years between 1954 and 1958. In the case of the Soviet Union, the "rate of exploitation" within the industrial sector has, moreover, become increasingly severe. In Communist China, profits from state enterprises constitute a multiple of the wage bill, and this ratio has tended to increase over the years. For the steel industry, profits were 60 percent of wages in 1952 and rose to 1,150 percent in 1956.[18] In comparison, employment costs averaged nearly 65 percent of total value added in the American steel industry in 1946–61.

	1954	1955	1956	1957	1958
U.K.	0.42	0.37	0.37	0.37	0.37
U.S.A.	0.44	0.46	0.43	0.42	0.41
U.S.S.R.	0.82	1.07	1.29	1.35	1.59
Yugoslavia	1.47	1.36	1.34	1.36	1.27

The Marxist "rate of exploitation" does not reflect the welfare of the citizens. A better indicator may be found in the ratio of consumption to gross national product. In the Soviet Union and Communist China, however, high "rates of exploitation" coincide with the policies of high investment and low consumption. In most planned economies, the part of the national product reserved for capital formation is usually increased, rather than reduced, by the public ownership of capital. State ownership deprives the capitalists of the "surplus value" but does not guarantee its distribution to the workers. In fact, public owner-ship is often introduced in less developed countries precisely for the purpose of increasing capital formation and reducing current con-sumption. That a planned economy may be able to accomplish this has indeed often been advanced as a strong argument in its favor. Thus the communist system is exploitative in the Marxist sense even though the Marxist concept may be nonsensical.

The Thesis of Inefficiency in Avoiding Fluctuations and in Promoting Economic Growth

According to the Marxists, capitalist economies are unable to main-tain a steady growth of income and employment. Although not as-serting that the capitalist system has found the way to eliminate all fluctuations, most non-Marxist economists would probably agree that governments in capitalist countries now know much more about the ways and means of controlling the amplitude of such fluctuations. Our interest, however, lies in the implied Marxist thesis that Com-munist planning eliminates all fluctuations. The record shows other-wise.

A recent survey by Staller of economic fluctuations in planned and free-market economies in 1950–60 shows that the mean fluctuations of total outputs in agriculture, industry, and construction, were uniformly higher in eight Communist countries (Bulgaria, Czechoslovakia, East Germany, Hungary, Poland, Rumania, the Soviet Union, and Yugoslavia) than in the eighteen OECD countries (Austria, Belgium, Canada, Denmark, France, West Germany, Greece, Iceland, Ireland, Italy, Luxembourg, the Netherlands, Norway, Portugal, Sweden, Turkey, the United Kingdom, and the United States). During the period the free market economies "had fewer interruptions in positive growth of total output and, by a slight margin, of agriculture, while planned economies showed fewer lapses of positive growth in industry and construction." [19] Industry and construction have in general occupied the attention of Communist planned societies above all else, and it is precisely in these sectors, as we shall see presently, that mal-allocation of resources through over-development may result.[20] During 1952–62, fluctuations in total and industrial output were considerably higher in Communist China than the mean fluctuations Staller has computed for the other planned economies. Only in agriculture was the fluctuation less according to our estimates. Fluctuation in the output of modern industry would be very much higher than in other planned economies even if the official Communist Chinese data for 1951–57 were used, i.e., ignoring the violent changes since 1958. (Fluctuations would be below the mean values for the other planned economies in total output and agricultural production, however, if only the official figures for 1951–57 were employed.) [21]

Except in agriculture, therefore, inclusion of Chinese data for the period of 1952–62 in computing the mean fluctuations for all planned economies would make comparisons with free-market economies even more unfavorable than Staller's data would indicate.

Space does not permit any elaborate discussion here,[22] but two points deserve mention. The agricultural sector, which showed least fluctuation in Communist China, was also the sector in which development under the present regime was least. Secondly, industrialization by forced draft, especially during the period of the "Great Leap," would seem to invite sharp fluctuations. Thus, according to the Chinese model, absence of large fluctuations in a sector is not necessarily a merit, while, on the other hand, the presence of large fluctuations in a sector does not necessarily mean a greater rate of growth over the long run, especially if the fluctuations occasionally include large absolute declines.

In the case of Communist China, fluctuations during 1952–62 may be explained in cyclic terms: Investment plans can be delayed and production may fall behind schedule. Unexpected contingencies can always disrupt production. If the original planning is based on an exaggerated notion of what is feasible, the likelihood of plan failures is increased. Adjustments to fulfill the plan may take place in several ways—importation, withdrawal from inventory, or curtailment of supplies for less important sectors which may be outside of the plan altogether. There are, however, certain limitations to these alternatives. Foreign exchange reserve may be limited. Some supplies, by their very nature, cannot be stock-piled. Stocks available on paper may be nonexistent due to faulty statistics. Supplies in the production pipe-line are usually kept at a minimum in underdeveloped countries intent on maintaining a high rate of production. Even if available, the enterprise managers in control of such surplus may be reluctant to let them go because of their concern to fulfill their own production quotas. The same applies to equipment held in reserve. Thus the chief, if not only, adjustment to a shortfall in production in one or more sectors is often an attempt to shift the shortage to the less important sectors of the economy. The least important sector in Communist priorities is personal consumption. When the latter is at a bare mini-mum level, however, it may bear a direct relationship to labor pro-ductivity. Any reduction of consumption below the minimum or even the failure of an anticipated increase may therefore reduce total output.

Such a downswing can become cumulative until a downward ad-justment of the planned rate of growth toward the actual rate is made, but overcorrection cannot be ruled out. When the realized rate of growth falls below the planned rate, depending upon the experience of the planners in the immediate past, the result may actually be an increase in the planned rate in order to make up lost time. If over-correction occurs, a reversal of the decline may soon follow once the initial and secondary difficulties have been resolved; but the resulting fulfillment or overfulfillment of the plan may be the beginning of a new cycle.

In his study of Soviet industrial production, Nutter has found from a time series analysis of the output of several commodities that during each of the four peacetime five year plans (1927–32, 1933–37, 1945–50, and 1950–55), most industries achieved their maximum rates of growth in the second year of the plan. This he attributes to the plan itself. As we have seen above, the fluctuations are even wilder in Communist China. In developing its economic critique of capitalism, Marxism has overlooked the possibility that the planned system may be susceptible to fluctuations of its own. Only recently have Western scholars come to suspect as much.

Some Marxists, notably Mao Tse-tung, admit the possibility of fluctuations, but claim that they will make for a higher average rate of growth. This immediately begs the question of measurement of growth rates. If one measures from trough to peak, the growth rate will obviously be larger. Yet, if one takes the long-run average, or measures from one peak to the next, it is not necessarily true that larger fluctuations bring higher growth rates.

A related point concerns pricing. Official Communist statistics are not reliable, often not even meaningful. Fake reporting to escape punishment, unintentional double counting, and an upward bias in the valuation of new products constitute some of the pitfalls. But a more fundamental question relates to the pricing of goods without reference to demand and changes in demand. If useless and unwanted goods are produced in large quantities and valued at prices which they could not command on a free market—not to mention the production of goods of deficient quality—a high growth rate merely reflects error in the allocation of resources. When the principle of consumer sovereignty is violated, output does not relate in any meaningful sense to the welfare of the citizens. Thus comparisons between a planned and a free market economy are devoid of significance unless the degree of mis-allocation can somehow be estimated. Not too long ago Khrushchev spoke of the "steel blinkers" worn by Soviet planners which had resulted in greater production of steel which was in excess supply relative to other materials. The same stricture is even more applicable to Communist China's economy during the "Great Leap."

The Thesis of Inefficiency in Resource Allocation

One may ask whether the same kind of distortion can arise in a capitalist system—whether unsalable goods can continue to be produced in ever increasing quantities. Normally this cannot happen, because enterprises which persist in such production would disappear. When such a situation does exist, it is usually a result of the suspension of the market mechanism in resource allocation as, for instance, in certain sectors of American agriculture. Yet under Communist economic planning, this situation is common and reflects a general lack of reliable criteria for allocating resources.

Some of the knowledgeable critics of communist economic planning can be quoted to illustrate the problem. According to Liberman,

Profits may successfully be used as the general (though by no means only) indicator of the effectiveness of production. ... Discussion should focus ... not on the absolute total of profits, since the larger the enterprise, the greater

—all other conditions being equal—will be its profits. This means that to evaluate effectiveness, profits must be related to some base that characterizes the enterprise's productive capital. Then the evaluation will be made according to the profitability of production understood as the ratio of profits to the value of productive capital.[23]

Or, as Fan Jo-i has pointed out in Communist China, wide discrepancies existed between the rates of "profit" over cost (which excludes interest cost on fixed capital) and the rates of return over investment (which would include both interest cost and profit) in many industries in China. Fan also noted the inefficient employment of scarce capital in Communist China in giving too much precedence to the development of large enterprises, remote geographical regions, and heavy investment in fixed plants.[24] Both Liberman and Fan, as well as others, have complained about the unnecessary rigidity of planned prices in the Soviet and Chinese economies.

The ferment of self-criticism in both Communist countries has been occasioned by dissatisfaction with the performance of the economic system. What has not been admitted is that this is precisely the kind of criticism that Marxists have levelled against the capitalist system. If the market economy does not always give sufficient weight to the wishes of certain segments of the population, including social reformers, persons with more "cultured tastes," and persons with no effective demand, the communist system functions without giving due weight to the preferences of the consumers in general. The profit motive and the price mechanism in the market economy may not always work satisfactorily in allocating resources, but an equally satisfactory device to serve communist economic planning has yet to be found. Marxist economics might work more efficiently in a primitive society using little capital; it cannot work efficiently in advanced economies unless certain ideological taboos are removed and new incentive systems are devised.

The recent discussion on the role of profit in the Soviet Union relates profit to worker incentive through a bonus system which would vary with the profit rate of the enterprise. According to Professor Liberman, this is not a return to capitalism. Yet if decentralized planning and the profit motive give a better material life, can we be sure that people will not ask for more? It is a common criticism of Western democracies to say that political and personal liberties are meaningless in the absence of a modicum of economic well-being. Is it not possible that more leisure and greater material welfare would sooner or later foster discontent with lack of personal and political liberty? It is not our intention to advance a dynamic theory of transformation for Communist societies which will march inexorably toward capitalism and their own metamorphosis. To do so would be to fall into the Marxists' error of determinism. Yet the prospect of communism remains tantalizingly uncertain.

Peter T. Bauer

Marxism and the
Underdeveloped Countries

I

The founding fathers of Marxism [1] did not concern themselves much
with what is now called the underdeveloped world [2] and their remarks
on the subject are ambivalent. Thus while Marx accused the metropolitan countries of plundering the colonies, he also regarded them
as a progressive force in promoting modernization. In later Marxist
literature the underdeveloped countries are prominently discussed as
victims of exploitation and imperialism, and as natural allies of Communist countries. The subject was a major concern of Lenin's and it
was largely through his writings that Marxist ideas were transmitted
to the underdeveloped world. His writings reveal little of the intellectual insights of Marx and Engels. As his principal ideas on this
subject are familiar and also readily accessible in one small book,
Imperialism: The Last Stage of Capitalism, I need not summarize
them. In spite of its glaring defects, and indeed utter intellectual inadequacy, the Leninist extension of the Marxist analysis has gained
enormous influence not only in the underdeveloped countries, but also
over much of the discussion of their economies. I shall now list some
prominent features of current discussion which, whatever their intellectual origins, reflect the Marxist-Leninist analysis.

In Marxism-Leninism, ownership of the means of production by a
Communist government is necessary for freedom and material progress.
This general idea, applicable to both developed and underdeveloped
countries, is familiar. I shall not discuss it, but confine myself to some
major ideas of Marxism-Leninism specifically applied or addressed to
the underdeveloped world.

First, the underdeveloped world is not only desperately poor but
also stagnant or actually retrogressing; this is the current version of the
doctrine of the ever increasing misery of the proletariat. Second, the

exploitation of underdeveloped by developed countries is a major cause of the poverty of the former; this is the current version of the doctrine of the exploitation of the proletariat. Third, political independence or freedom is meaningless without economic independence; this is an application, or extension, of the suggestion that political freedom and representative government are meaningless under capitalism.

Fourth, comprehensive development planning is indispensable for economic advance in underdeveloped countries, and especially for the industrialization required for material progress. This last point, though less directly reflective of Marxism-Leninism, nevertheless owes much to the recognition of the political possibilities of economic planning (as reflected in Soviet experience), and also to the emphasis on the industrial proletariat in Communist literature and strategy. Advocacy of the key role of industrialization antedates Marxism-Leninism, but this ideology has powerfully reinforced it, especially in the context of underdeveloped countries, and it has also allied its attainment with the distinctive methods and policies of Marxism-Leninism.

II

The late Paul A. Baran, Professor of Economics at Stanford, was a well-known exponent of Marxism-Leninism. According to him, capitalism was responsible for the misery and stagnation of the underdeveloped world.

It is in the underdeveloped world that the central, overriding fact of our epoch becomes manifest to the naked eye: the capitalist system, once a mighty engine of economic development, has turned into a no less formidable hurdle to human advancement ... there [in the underdeveloped world] the difference is between abysmal squalor and decent existence, between the misery of hopelessness and the exhilaration of progress, between life and death for hundreds of millions of people ... A socialist transformation of the advanced West would not only open to its own peoples the road to unprecedented economic, social and cultural progress, it would at the same time enable the peoples of the underdeveloped countries to overcome rapidly their present condition of poverty and stagnation.[3]

In fact there has been substantial material progress in most of the underdeveloped world since the end of the nineteenth century; much of this advance, though by no means all of it, has been taken out in the form of larger populations. In many areas material advance has been extremely rapid. Indeed it has been the rapidity of the change which has created most acute problems; and as I shall argue later, it has also helped to prepare the ground for the support of ideas, notably

Marxism-Leninism, which paradoxically deny the presence of economic growth.

There is ample evidence of this progress from sporadic national income figures and, more relevant and revealing, from statistics of population growth, foreign trade, government revenues, literacy, health, infant mortality, and so on. Ghana (the Gold Coast until 1957) is among the underdeveloped countries which have progressed extremely rapidly since the end of the nineteenth century; this is reflected in statistics which are unusually reliable and meaningful by African standards. The gross domestic product per head is at present about 70 pounds ($200) a year, which is of course low by Western standards but which in real terms has about quadrupled since 1890 and about doubled since 1910.[4] The total population approximately quadrupled between 1890 and 1960, from about 1.6 million to about 6.5 million.

Statistics of foreign trade are of particular interest because well over 99.5 percent of the population is African; all agricultural exports (the bulk of all exports) are produced by them and practically all imports are destined for their use. Until recently there was either no or only negligible local production of the commodities imported, so that imports measure the total use of these products.[5] In 1890 there were no exports (or production) of cocoa; by the mid-1930's about 300,000 tons were exported annually and by now over 400,000 tons, all from farms established, owned and operated by Africans; there are no foreign-owned cocoa farms. In 1890 combined imports and exports were less than a million pounds sterling, by the 1930's they were in tens of millions, and by the mid-1950's in hundreds of millions. Over this period there has been a spectacular increase in imports of both consumer and capital goods. In 1890 there were no imports, or negligible imports, of flour, sugar, cement, petroleum products, or iron and steel. For decades now these have been on a massive scale. In the early 1890's there were about 3,000 children at school; by the mid-1950's over half a million. In the 1890's there were neither railways nor roads, but only a few jungle paths, and transport of goods was entirely by human porterage and by canoe. By the 1930's there was a substantial railway mileage and a good road system; by then journeys by road required fewer hours than they had required days in 1890. Statistical information of this sort can be both multiplied and interpreted easily, but it is hard to convey the far-reaching and pervasive changes which have transformed life there, as elsewhere in West Africa.

The experience of the Gold Coast-Ghana is among the more striking of similar developments elsewhere in Africa, where there has been rapid advance in many areas, generally from primitive and indeed savage conditions. By Western standards, sub-Saharan Africa was materially almost unimaginably backward in the third quarter of the nineteenth century. For instance, there were no schools and no man-made communications in the interior (aside from a few primitive paths chiefly cut by slave-traders or raiders). Apart from slave-trading and raiding, there was practically no contact between the interior of Africa and the outside world, nor indeed between different parts of Africa, even between neighboring areas, because of the absence of communication facilities which have since been developed in many parts of the continent.

Altogether many areas of Latin America, Africa and Asia have developed very rapidly since the nineteenth century; and there has been considerable material advance throughout the underdeveloped world in contact with the advanced countries.

Of course, even in those underdeveloped countries which have progressed rapidly in recent decades, income per head is still low (although not as low as usually suggested). Poverty is compatible even with rapid advance, if the latter is of relatively recent origin and from a very low level. And substantial groups and large areas in the underdeveloped world have progressed little in recent times: the aborigines in many parts of the world, the desert peoples of the Sahara and elsewhere, and the tribal populations of Central and East Africa. And over large areas of South and East Asia (including large parts of rural India, Pakistan and China), progress has been comparatively slow, and much of it absorbed in the form of increased populations. These are areas largely of subsistence agriculture with few external contacts. Their poverty and stagnation are obviously unrelated to capitalism, market forces, or exploitation by richer countries; [6] as they are clearly outside the orbit of these. Their poverty derives from poor climate and natural resources, and from qualities, attitudes, customs, and institutions uncongenial to material progress. Some of these attitudes and customs particularly uncongenial to material progress, such as the reluctance to take animal life, or to breed, keep or slaughter animals for food, go back for centuries and millennia. Some have even increased in importance in recent years. For example, over most of India the slaughter of cattle has come to be prohibited by legislation covering both Hindus and non-Hindus.

III

Underdeveloped countries which have progressed rapidly in recent decades have generally advanced from a materially low level primarily as a result of contact, often established in dramatically short periods, with an economically far more advanced world, where attitudes and institutions have over centuries been adapted to a money economy. Sudden exposure to a vastly different and materially successful economic system has set up extreme problems of adjustment of values, attitudes, customs and institutions in these societies, many of which had undergone little change for centuries. This is highly relevant both to the situation in the underdeveloped world and to the influence of Marxism-Leninism. While both the specifically Marxist-Leninist literature, and the standard current ideology on underdeveloped countries, are almost wholly in terms of stagnation, starvation, retrogression and so forth, there exists a substantial and authoritative body of writings, chiefly by anthropologists, historians, administrators, and even some economists, which discusses the rapid changes in these countries since the end of the nineteenth century and the problems associated with them. These problems and dilemmas include the difficulties of adapting institutions and attitudes to fast-changing conditions, the transition from communal to individual tenure of land, the detribalization and disintegration of communal life and values, and rapid urbanization. I shall quote a few typical passages from this interesting literature, much of which is relatively little known and none of which is widely publicized.

Dr. A. MacPhee, in *The Economic Revolution in British West Africa*,[7] written long before the underdeveloped countries became an internationally discussed issue, reviewed the pervasive change in West Africa since the 1890's.

In fact, the process since the 'Nineties of last century has been the superimposition of the twentieth century after Christ on the twentieth century before Christ, and a large part of the problem of native policy is concerned with the clash of such widely different cultures and with the protection of the natives during the difficulties of transition. The transition has been from the growth of subsistence crops and the collection of sylvan produce to the cultivation of exchange crops, with the necessary implication of a transition from a "Natural" economy to a "Monetary" economy, and the innumerable important reactions from the latter phase.

These various problems were also discussed at length by Sir Keith Hancock, critical and judicious historian of African development, who considered these matters chiefly in his *Survey of British Commonwealth Affairs*.[8] Here are some of his observations on developments in West Africa between the 1880's and 1930's:

In some periods of European history—in our own day, for example, or in the day of the first steam-engines and power mills—the European world has seemed to be transformed. Europe nevertheless has remained the same world, spinning very much faster. But in Africa change means more than acceleration. Europe's commerce and its money-measurements really have brought the African into a new world. Its economics are different from his "primitive economics"; its personal relationships have nothing to do with his relationships of matrilineal families and tribal kinship. His religion does not in any way reinforce or govern the capitalism into which he has been swept.

Nor is this literature confined to Africa. The problems and strains of rapid advance are a major theme of J. S. Furnivall's *Colonial Policy and Practice*,[9] which deals extensively with the experience of Burma.

> The dissolution of the political structure is only the first stage in social dissolution, and it is completed by the second, or economic stage, breaking up the village into individuals. In this process two factors are operative: economic forces are released; and the checks controlling their action are relaxed ... In such circumstances there remains no embodiment of social will or representative of public welfare to control the economic forces which the impact of the West released.

These writers were not simple sentimentalists deploring the passing of the good old days; they noted the very rapid changes and the problems created by them.

IV

In Marxist-Leninist literature the poverty of the underdeveloped countries is attributed largely to exploitation by more advanced countries, especially, but not only, the metropolitan colonial powers; this is the extension of the doctrine of the proletariat. President Nkrumah, an avowed and explicit Marxist-Leninist, writes in a very recent book:

> Thus all the imperialists, without exception, evolved the means, their colonial policies, to satisfy the ends, the exploitation of the subject territories, for the aggrandisement of the metropolitan countries. They were all rapacious; they all subserved the needs of the subject lands to their own demands; they all circumscribed human rights and liberties; they all repressed and despoiled, degraded and oppressed. They took our lands, our lives, our resources and our dignity. Without exception, they left us nothing but our resentment ... It was when they had gone and we were faced with the stark realities, as in Ghana on the morrow of our independence, that the destitution of the land after long years of colonial rule was brought sharply home to us. There were slums and squalor in our towns, superstitions and ancient rites in our villages. All over the country, great tracts of open land lay untilled and uninhabited, while nutritional diseases were rife among our people, our roads were meagre, our railways short. There was much ignorance and few skills.[10]

Nor is this only the past. President Nkrumah goes on:

Our problems are made more vexed by the devices of the neo-colonialists
... The greatest danger at present facing Africa is neo-colonialism, and its
major instrument, balkanization. The latter term is particularly appropriate
to describe the breaking up of Africa into small weak states ... many of
them have deliberately been made so weak economically by being carved
up into many separate countries that they are not able to sustain out of their
own resources the machinery of independent government.[11]

In fact there were, as already noted, practically no man-made communications in nineteenth-century Africa before the advent of the Europeans,
and very little peaceful contact between different tribes; to date Africans are largely dependent on communications constructed by others;
and the division into many small states reflects demands for self-
determination.

Whatever the wider results of political colonialism, a system of
political dependence under which the local government must accept
directives from the metropolitan country, it has not retarded the
material progress of the contemporary underdeveloped world. The
countries in Africa and Asia which have been independent longest
are usually among the materially most backward, usually much more
so than the neighboring ex-colonies. Liberia and Ethiopia, China
and Afghanistan are examples.[12] The habitual references to underdeveloped countries as colonial, semi-colonial or neo-colonial equate
poverty with colonialism, and thereby empty the latter term of all
meaning.

The primary reason for the wide appeal of such terms as colonialism,
economic imperialism, economic colonialism, and neo-colonialism is
obvious: the allegation that external rather than internal or local factors
are responsible for the poverty of the underdeveloped world. On a
world-wide level it confers "the desired status of victim" (an expression
of Jacques Barzun); it extends on the widest possible scale the Marxist-
Leninist idea that poverty is a result of exploitation by others. There
are several special factors reinforcing this obvious general appeal.

Throughout the underdeveloped world, particularly but not only in
the former colonies, great expectations were aroused after the Second
World War about the great material improvements which would result
from political independence, or from development planning, or industrialization. External factors are most conveniently blamed for the
inevitable disappointment. This is particularly significant where the
political, and possibly even the physical, survival of the ruling politicians
may depend on their ability to blame external forces for the continued
poverty of their countries, particularly for the lack of lucrative em-

ployment for the younger generation of often Soviet-oriented or trained politicians and intellectuals, who stand ready to succeed the present leaders. The relatively high incomes, compared with those of the local population, earned by foreigners residing in these countries or trading with them, enhance the superficial plausibility of the evil results of economic dependence and foreign exploitation, particularly at a time when people are freely told that all men are created equal so that the difference in prosperity must be the result of evil influences emanating from abroad.

V

The suggestion, now widely accepted, that political independence is meaningless without economic independence reflects the Marxist idea that outside communism neither freedom nor democracy is real. At times the emphasis on economic independence serves obvious political purposes: the promotion of a closed and therefore more readily controllable economy, the orientation of external contacts toward Communist countries, or the diversion of attention from domestic problems. Moreover, in orthodox Marxism-Leninism any return on capital connotes exploitation, and service industries are regarded as unproductive; thus if foreign capital in poor countries earns a positive return, or foreigners in service industries, including traders, earn incomes from these unproductive activities, the local population by definition is exploited, which would not be tolerated in truly independent countries.

A few passages from Academician I. Potekhin's *Problems of Economic Independence of African Countries*[13] illustrate the approach:

The economic essence of colonialism, whatever form it takes, consists in exporting a part of a colony's national income to the metropolitan country without return imports of an equivalent value. This explains why metropolitan countries made such big strides in their economic development during the last century while colonies lagged behind ... Why is there little capital in Africa? The reply is evident. A considerable part of the national income which is supposed to make up the accumulation fund and to serve as the material basis of progress is exported outside Africa without any equivalent.

Unlike political independence, which means that the government does not have to accept orders from abroad, economic independence has no unambiguous meaning. An obvious interpretation would be the absence of external economic contacts. This is most completely satisfied by subsistence production. On a slightly more sophisticated level, it is a condition under which the fortunes of a country are least likely to be diminished by adverse developments abroad; this is most likely to be true of rich countries with a wide range of domestic resources.

In current Marxist-Leninist literature, economic independence seems to refer especially to underdeveloped economies whose external economic relations are oriented to the Communist world, and whose external economic contacts (or even their domestic economies as well) are closely controlled by a government acting on behalf of the people, that is, a Communist (often termed socialist) government. At times only countries with Communist governments engaged in comprehensive development planning are deemed genuinely independent.[14] The usual interpreation of the term economic colonialism in Marxist-Leninist and related literature has certain very definite and specific political implications. Any country in which foreign private capital earns a positive return or where foreigners are engaged in service industries is an economic colony; and conversely any country whose citizens have investments abroad, or who perform services there, is economic imperialist or neo-colonist.

Afro-Asian spokesmen constantly state that the independence of their countries is not secure while colonialism in any form survives. While this is often only a convenient slogan to divert attention from domestic difficulties, notably continued poverty, it is also a reflection of the messianic nature of Marxism-Leninism and anti-colonialism. A messianic creed is never victorious until it has conquered all internal and external enemies within sight; the history of the French Revolution is a familiar example. If the current interpretation of economic or neo-colonialism prevails, then decolonization is not complete until all foreign private capital in poor countries has been liquidated and all foreign enterprises and activities terminated. Moreover, as the people are not deemed really free and truly independent except under a Communist government, complete decolonization requires the establishment of such governments throughout the underdeveloped world.

VI

Until such time as the means of production are owned by the Communist state, Marxism-Leninism regards comprehensive development planning, that is, government determination of the composition and direction of economic activity outside subsistence production, as essential for development. Baran writes (p. 261): "The establishment of a socialist planned economy is an essential, indeed indispensable, condition for the attainment of economic and social progress in underdeveloped countries." In this literature, comprehensive development planning is deemed necessary for economic advance generally and in particular for the promotion of manufacturing, especially the production of capital goods, which in turn are required for economic progress and independence. For instance, according to the late Academician Potekhin (p. 10): "To develop mining and consumer goods industries machine-tools and equipment are required. Who is to supply them? The industrially developed Western countries would like to reserve the monopoly in delivering machinery to African countries... 'Balanced industrialization' entails the setting up of an industry putting out the means of production." [15]

I shall not discuss these contentions in detail but simply note a few relevant points. Neither the level of prosperity, nor the rate of development, nor the rate of capital formation, nor the subsequent development of manufacturing, depends on the prior establishment of a national or local capital-goods industry. Nor is the development of manufacturing industry generally a necessary condition either of prosperity or of economic development. The richer countries are usually, but by no means invariably, the more industrialized ones largely because the higher rate of development and the presence of manufacturing industries reflect their possession of valuable resources (including capital, skill, attitudes, and experience); the presence of manufacturing is not simply the cause of the prosperity. Again, there are many highly developed and rich agricultural regions in the world, and conversely, relatively poor industrial areas. And the rich, industrially advanced countries were already relatively prosperous while still predominantly agricultural, far richer than many of the present poor countries.

In the planning literature, comprehensive planning is regarded as a condition of economic advance, of industrialization, and usually also of economic independence. And economic advance is usually defined without reference to general living standards but primarily in terms of industrial development, notably of capital goods industries, or in terms of the performance of some other particular sector. The advocates of large-scale industrialization, and especially of the massive development of heavy industries, hardly ever refer to prices, incomes, costs, demand, or standard of living. They are not mentioned in the passages already quoted.

There are obvious political motives behind the insistence on comprehensive planning: The establishment of a socialist or Communist government is much easier once close and comprehensive economic controls have been established. And such governments are more likely to support other Communist governments. Marxist-Leninist literature has traditionally regarded the industrial proletariat as the vanguard of the revolution and the recruiting ground for the most active, reliable and effective party members; and it has also regarded the industrial sector as most readily subject to effective political control. Its emphasis on industrialization seems to derive largely from such political motives; this is suggested by the absence from the literature of the sophisticated or popular arguments for industrialization found in the economic text-books or the popular non-Marxist literature.

More recently Marxist-Leninist literature on underdeveloped countries has shown much greater interest in the development of agriculture as long as this is part of development planning. This seems to derive in part from the realization that in many underdeveloped areas, notably Africa and much of Asia, the industrial proletariat is, and will remain for many years, negligible, and also from the realization that without a sizable agricultural surplus, not yet available in many poor countries, industrialization would be politically inexpedient. Moreover the possibility of close control over agricultural producers through government-organized cooperative societies, state trading companies, and government export monopolies, has come to be recognized. By these and similar devices it is possible even with rudimentary administrative machinery to control closely the pattern of agricultural production for sale, the prices and incomes received by the producers, and the use of the agricultural surplus; and it is possible also to prevent the emergence of prosperous or independent peasant population, or of a trading class or a bourgeoisie. In Communist literature on agricultural development the adoption of one or more of these devices (as well as the expropriation of landlords whenever possible) is prominent; without such measures agricultural development is regarded as a colonial-type development incompatible with economic independence.

VII

The views about underdeveloped countries and the policy prescriptions for their progress which I have been describing as Marxist-Leninist have in fact become the current orthodoxy in this field. Whatever the exact process of their intellectual derivation, these views are widely and frequently expounded by prominent writers who are not regarded as Marxist-Leninists. The current non-Marxist literature on this subject emphasizes the ever widening discrepancy of incomes and living standards between rich and poor countries and the starvation or near-starvation in the latter in much the same way as orthodox Marxism stresses the gulf between oppressor and oppressed and the ever increasing misery of the proletariat, and as Marxism-

Leninism stresses by extension the ever widening gap between rich and poor countries.

For instance, Professor Gunnar Myrdal has frequently emphasized the ever widening international inequality and has often referred to Western Europe, North America and Australasia as the upper class of countries, and to the rest of the world as underprivileged:

The trend is actually towards greater world inequality. It is, in fact, the richer countries that are advancing while the poorer ones, with the large populations, are stagnating or progressing much more slowly ... For mankind as a whole there has actually been no progress at all [*sic*]. I have chosen to focus attention on one particular aspect of the international situation, namely the very large and steadily increasing economic inequalities as between developed and underdeveloped countries ... These inequalities and their tendency to grow are flagrant realities.[16]

The policy prescription for this description or diagnosis also echoes Marxist-Leninist ideas, or indeed the practice in the Soviet Union. Professor Myrdal writes again:

It is now commonly agreed that an under-developed country should have a national economic development policy. Indeed, it should have an overall, integrated national plan, as is also urged by everybody ... It is assumed by all that it is the national state which must be responsible for the overall plan and, indeed, for its initiation and pursuance. From one point of view, the plan is a program for the strategy of a national government in applying a system of state interferences in the play of the forces in the markets, thereby conditioning them and giving a push upwards to the social process which had settled down in a vicious circle of inequality and economic regression, stagnation or a too slow development ... What we witness is how this much more than half of mankind living in poverty and distress is not only accepting for itself the pursuance on a grand scale of a policy line which we are accustomed to call "socialistic", but that positive and urgent advice to do so is given to them by all scholars and statesmen in the advanced countries and by their governments when participating in solemn resolutions of all the inter-governmental organizations.[17]

The pervasive influence of Marxism-Leninism, even on professed critics of communism, is neatly illustrated in a book entitled *Africa and the Communist World:*

The "demonstration effect" of Soviet economic growth most certainly had a profound impact on the thinking of the leaders of nationalist movements in backward areas. But to be impressed [by Soviet growth] does not necessarily mean to be converted. Obviously, one need not be a very orthodox "Marxist-Leninist" or a particularly heterodox "bourgeois economist" in order to agree with the following baldly stated propositions: (1) a rapid increase in the rate of economic growth in backward countries, which is indispensable in order to break out of the vicious circle of near stagnation, calls for a marked increase in the saving-investment effort; (2) economic development is bound to involve industrialization at a rather early stage, and also, before long, a relatively rapid growth of domestic capital-goods industries coming both in response to and as an added stimulant of the accelerated pace of overall expansion; (3) the availability of a sufficiently large volume of foreign investment and sufficiently extensive foreign trade connections cannot always be taken for granted; (4) since superior productive technology in developed countries represents both a challenge and a threat, the new state would have to intervene more actively to promote and protect economic development than was necessary in older industrialized countries during comparable periods of their history.[18]

In this passage, items (1) and (2) are demonstrably and obviously untrue; (3) is irrelevant, and (4) is an obvious *non sequitur*. It would seem that, contrary to what they say, these writers have been both impressed and converted.

VIII

How can we account for this pervasive influence of Marxism-Leninism? Marxism-Leninism is an intellectual structure comprising method, analysis and empirical observation, which claims to explain the operation and prospects of society; and it is also a secular messianic faith or creed which promises salvation here but not now. The intellectual structure exhibits major internal inconsistencies, and its most specific and explicit predictions have been refuted by events. The attempts to rationalize these intellectual contradictions are unconvincing and at times unedifying. On the other hand, Marx and Engels revealed some exceptional insights over a wide and diverse area. These include, for instance, the explicit recognition (by Engels in *Anti-Dühring*) of the massive technical progress of Europe in the fourteenth and fifteenth centuries; the habitual treatment of phenomena as part of a process; the assessment of developments and policies in terms of their effects on the total situation, and the interest in both micro and macro-economics (individual or particular sectors and totals or aggregates).

However, the main reason for the appeal of Marxism-Leninism derives from the creed, and also from the political successes of Marxist parties and governments. The attraction of a messianic, all-embracing secular religion promising salvation on earth, but in the future, i.e., here but not now, is obvious at times of rapid erosion of traditional values and beliefs. The attraction of the emphasis on the future derives in part from the fact that promises cannot be checked against performance, but also from the appeal to selflessness, that is, from the concern with the future against the present. The adherents also feel that they belong to a movement which is destined to achieve victory, that they are active participants in the march of history; the faith successfully combines a suggestion of freedom with predestination— freedom is the recognition of necessity. The doctrine of exploitation has obvious appeal with its suggestion that poverty is the result of oppression by others and is removable by human action. Then there is a quasi-scientific appeal in a system working with a few apparently clearly defined variables and establishing grand functional relationships. The Marxist faith also helps to integrate the intellectuals and the masses, bridging the void which has arisen with the decay of religion and the remoteness of philosophy and art from the great majority of people. The presence of a logical structure, however defective, has enhanced the attractiveness of Marxism as a Messianic faith to the intellectuals by making its acceptance intellectually more respectable than that of other types of Messianism.

And the fact that Marxist parties have gained control in several countries, including two of the most powerful, also has evident appeal. *On ne juge pas les vainqueurs.* This applies notably in the social sciences, especially economics, where there has always been an ambivalence between the advancement of knowledge and the promotion of policy. Marxism-Leninism has been politically successful, and those who do not distinguish between political results and scientific achievement are particularly prone to accept its intellectual claims.

IX

Throughout the underdeveloped world public opinion on economic matters is pervaded by Marxism-Leninism. This is a result of the operation and interaction of various influences: the operation, often in an enhanced form, of the same factors responsible for its appeal to the West, which I have just noted; the implicit or explicit suggestion that external forces account for the poverty of the underdeveloped world; the political and military successes of Marxist parties and governments, and the demonstration effect of Soviet experience; the left-wing influence in the international flow of ideas and information; and the impact of sudden change brought about by greatly extended contacts with advanced economies. I shall deal briefly with the more obvious and familiar of these factors and at greater length with others.

As I have just noted, the doctrine of exploitation has always been a major factor in the appeal of Marxism. Leninism has helped to extend this on a world scale, with obvious appeal to the political and intellectual leaders in underdeveloped countries. Because this factor is so obvious I need not enlarge on what I have said on this in the context of the allegations of colonialism and neo-colonialism. The military and political successes of Marxist governments have clearly contributed to its appeal. So has the pursuit of comprehensive economic planning in the Soviet Union, particularly the large-scale development of capital-goods industries.

Although it may be said to be implicit in state ownership of the means of production under the dictatorship of the proletariat, economic planning as such does not figure in pre-1917 Marxist-Leninist literature. For various reasons, however, it has become an integral part of Com-munist economic policy. Its influence and appeal again derive from a number of interrelated factors: the Soviet experience (as usually interpreted), notably the political and military success of the Soviet Union, often identified with economic development and attributed to economic planning; the widespread belief in the efficacy of conscious organization or engineering in social affairs,[19] and the support from businessmen to whom a closely controlled economy often secures handsome profits shielded from competition. Perhaps most important, it has a most powerful appeal to politicians and intellectuals, since it implies massive concentration of power in the hands of the govern-ment. These groups believe that they can and should closely control the rest of society, a belief even stronger in underdeveloped countries than elsewhere, because there these groups feel so much superior to the rest of the community.

Once comprehensive development planning is accepted axiomatically as a condition of economic advance, then its extension can always be plausibly advocated. Either a rapid or a slow rate of material progress (or any other criterion) can be invoked in support of its extension: success as evidence of its efficacy, failure as evidence that it has not been adopted on a sufficient scale. And a closely controlled economy presents a ready-made framework for the establishment of a totalitarian govern-ment. Moreover, such a situation also greatly increases the prizes of political power and therefore the intensity of the struggle for them. Close and intensive government control of much of economic and social life promotes political polarization, and in this way presents distinct opportunities and advantages for a revolutionary ideology and party.

These opportunities are greatest where the mass of the people are traditionally unconcerned with politics, at least beyond the village level. Practically throughout the underdeveloped world the vast majority have never known elected government or majority rule, and in fact have not participated in politics but have concerned themselves only with the tasks of their daily lives. On the other hand, the rulers or governments, while not elective, usually have had little impact on the lives of the great majority of people. A well-organized, vocal, articulate and often well-armed movement, even if numerically small, can readily exploit such a situation, and establish a totalitarian society relatively easily. Both Communist ideology and practice ensure that the Communist Party should benefit most from the potentialities of such a situation.

Much of the appeal of the Soviet experience derives from its interpretation to the underdeveloped world by both Soviet and Western writers. These interpretations simply emphasize the growth of industrial capacity and military power without reference to consumer demand, cost, or welfare either in terms of human lives (including the mass famines of the 1930's), standard of living, or political arrangements; and without reference either to such relevant matters as the comparatively advanced nature of pre-revolutionary Russia (as reflected in a sizable agricultural surplus and a relatively high literacy rate compared to the underdeveloped world), or the country's rapid industrialization before 1914, or to the development of many underdeveloped countries such as Japan, Malaya, Hong Kong, Gold Coast-Ghana and various Latin American countries, which have progressed rapidly without massive government coercion. Nor do these interpretations usually examine the meaning or limitations of Soviet statistics.

The interpretation of Soviet experience in turn reflects the strong left-wing influence in the media of mass communications; this influence is particularly strong in international communication, and especially in intellectual contacts between the West and the underdeveloped countries, which are practically confined to anti-capitalist views.[20] The guilt-feeling of the West is often said to be a factor in the appeal of Marxism-Leninism in the approach to underdeveloped countries. There is an association here. But it is more likely an effect or a symptom rather than a cause. It already reflects acceptance of the view that a return on capital investment or the poverty of underdeveloped countries implies exploitation.

Many parts of the underdeveloped world have experienced sudden and uneven changes (uneven in that it affects some aspects of life more than others) in recent decades, largely through contact with more advanced economies. The resulting strains and problems of adjustment are particularly acute for the intellectuals who have to face not only the sudden erosion or disappearance of traditional beliefs and values, but often a conflict of loyalties and an alienation from the rest of the community.[21] Throughout the underdeveloped world the Western-educated or semi-educated intellectuals feel much superior to the rest of the community and yet are desperately anxious to belong to it. The gap is perhaps widest in the African tribal communities, but it is also wide and deep throughout Asia. The strains are much enhanced by the clashes of loyalties which such people often experience when traditional and tribal custom or family ties conflict with obligations imposed by modern legal systems. The attractions of an all-embracing, pervasive, secular materialistic faith are readily understandable in such conditions. It offers a haven to people who have lost their moorings and, perhaps even more important, a reunification for intellectuals with the rest of the community.[22]

Other consequences of sudden change are relevant here. Such changes invariably result in appreciable shifts in the relative economic and social position of individuals and groups. Price changes always affect adversely some groups in the community; the advance of the market economy undermines the position and authority of traditional leaders; so do various political developments resulting from external contacts. Such changes present ample opportunity for grievances, particularly, but not only, when their causes are man-made but at the same time not clearly understood. For these reasons the hazards of an exchange economy, although far less acute than those of a subsistence economy, are much less readily accepted, particularly when the impact of a money economy has been rather sudden. Such developments present excellent opportunities to a party ready and resolved to exploit all grievances.[23] The breach of continuity with the past is pronounced even when the rapid advance is by the production of cash crops, as this is relatively closely related to people's traditional activities and pursuits. It is stronger under rapid industrialization and urbanization, which may be an additional reason for Communist pressure in this direction.

I refer to one more factor in the success of Marxist-Leninist ideology in underdeveloped countries. This is the advantage the ideology derives from the debasement of the language, to which it has powerfully contributed. In recent decades this debasement, or even debauchment, of the language has been perceptively discussed by George Orwell, Jacques Barzun, Richard M. Weaver and others.[24] Marxist-Leninist literature has both promoted and exploited this debasement by systematic reliance on vague general terms whose interpretation can be varied in different circumstances and adapted to the promotion of specific political goals, by the use of terms in a manner divorced from their accepted meaning, and by ceaseless repetition of demonstrably untrue statements. This debauchment of the language is particularly effective in underdeveloped countries where a critical approach to the printed word or to political discussion is even less developed than in the West.

This debauchment of the language has gone to such lengths in both popular and academic writing in this field that words have lost their meaning. Only then can it be seriously stated that underdeveloped countries stagnate because they are caught in a vicious circle of poverty or are exploited by the advanced countries. And only then is it possible for Baran to write thus (p. 177): "To the dead weight of stagnation characteristic of pre-industrial society was added the entire restrictive impact of monopoly capitalism. The economic surplus appropriated in lavish amounts by monopolistic concerns in backward countries is not employed for productive purposes. It is neither plowed back into their own enterprises, nor does it serve to develop others." [25]

Systematic discussion becomes impossible if widely different meanings are attributed to the same expression. Marxism-Leninism accepts any debauchment of the language if this contributes to the ultimate political goal, since then it is deemed to be objectively true even if it is subjectively empty or untrue. It has thereby powerfully contributed to the difficulties of serious study or discussion of underdeveloped countries. Collingwood wrote that the prime task of historical scholarship was "to reveal the less obvious features hidden from a careless eye in the present situation." In discussions on underdeveloped countries Marxism-Leninism aims at, and often achieves, the exact opposite.

Notes

Notes

Marxism in the Western World: From "Scientific Socialism" to Mythology

1. Herbert Butterfield, *Christianity and History* (Cambridge and New York, 1950), p. 60.
2. See the critique of J. Bernal, J. B. S. Haldane, Hyman Levy, *et al.* in my *Reason, Social Myths and Democracy* (New York, 1940), pp. 220 ff.
3. New York, 1962.
4. Mills, *The Marxists,* pp. 96 ff.
5. *Ibid.,* p. 115; italics in the text.
6. *Ibid.,* p. 112.
7. *Ibid.,* p. 129.
8. Karl Korsch, *Karl Marx* (New York, 1938).
9. *The Marxists,* p. 21.
10. Cf. his *World Socialism Restated* (London, 1957), *passim,* and more particularly in *The New Statesman and Nation,* January 12 and April 20, 1957. Also my "Moral Judgment and Historical Ambiguity," *Problems of Communism,* VI (July–August 1957), 47 ff.
11. Paris, 1960.   12. Sartre, *Critique,* p. 30.
13. *Ibid.,* p. 87.   14. *Ibid.,* p. 118.
15. Sainte-Beuve, *Nouveaux Lundis,* VIII (1864).
16. *Critique,* p. 630.
17. Lional Abel, *Dissent,* spring 1961, pp. 137 ff.
18. Martin Heidegger, *Platons Lehre von der Wahrheit* (Bern, 1947), p. 87.
19. *Ibid.,* p. 87: "Homelessness has become a world fate. That is why it is necessary to think this Fate through the history of being. What Marx in an essential and significant sense had recognized in Hegel as the alienation [*Entfremdung*] of man reaches back with its roots into the homelessness of contemporary man. This is called forth from the fate of being in the form of metaphysics, is strengthened by it, and at the same time concealed from it as homelessness. Because Marx experiences alienation as reaching into an essential dimension of history, the Marxist conception of history is superior to all others. Since neither Husserl nor, as far as I can see, Sartre recognizes the essentiality of the historical in being neither phenomenology nor existentialism enters into that dimension within which a fruitful dialogue with Marxism is possible."

20. *Humanisme et terreur* (Paris, 1947), p. 57.

21. *Ibid.*, p. 132.

22. Jean Yves Calvez, *La Pensée de Karl Marx* (Paris, 1956), p. 39.

23. Erich Fromm, *Marx's Concept of Man* (New York, 1961), p. 79.

24. I have developed this point in the new Introduction to the second edition of my *From Hegel to Marx* (Ann Arbor, Michigan, 1962), p. 4: "To seek what was distinctive and characteristic about Marx in a period when he was still in Hegelian swaddling-clothes, or when he was still more or less a Feuerbachian before he had fought his way clear of every variety of seductive idealism and reductive materialism, is to violate accepted and tested canons of historical scholarship. A period of intellectual maturation, surveyed and evaluated from the perspective at which a thinker has subsequently arrived, is significant more for the doctrines and attitudes which have been *abandoned* than for those which have been retained. Otherwise there is no explanation of the process of *development* and we should have to conclude that Marx was born a Marxist."

25. Adam Schaff, *History and Theory,* vol. II, no. 3 (1963), p. 316.

26. *Marx-Engels Gesamtausgabe* (Berlin, 1932), Erste Abteilung, Bd. 3, pp. 33–172.

27. *Ibid.*, p. 86.   28. *Ibid.*, pp. 83–84.

29. *Ibid.*, pp. 89–90.   30. *Ibid.*, pp. 89–90.

31. *Ibid.*, p. 117.   32. *Ibid.*, p. 144.

33. Robert Tucker, *Philosophy and Myth in Karl Marx* (London and New York, 1961), p. 238.

34. *Slavic Review,* March 1963, p. 188.

35. *Gesamtausgabe*, p. 235.   36. Tucker, p. 235.

37. Cf. my *Reason, Social Myths and Democracy;* also *The Ambiguous Legacy, Marx and the Marxists* (New York, 1955).

38. Henry Aiken, "The Revolution Against Ideology," *Commentary,* April 1964, pp. 29–39.

39. John Dewey, *Liberalism and Social Action* (New York, 1935) and *Freedom and Culture* (New York, 1939).

40. *The Rebel, an Essay on Man in Revolt* (New York, 1954), p. 195.

Alienation: The Marxism of Contemporary Student Movements

---

1. Cf. Lewis S. Feuer, "A Neo-Marxist Conception of Social Science," *Ethics,* vol. LXX (1960), p. 239.

2. Karl Marx and Friedrich Engels, *Historisch-Kritische Gesamtausgabe* (Berlin, 1932), Erste Abteilung, Band 4, p. 341.

3. Martin Buber, *Paths in Utopia,* tr. R. F. C. Hull (Boston, 1958), pp. 14, 140–141.

4. Karl Marx and Friedrich Engels, *Basic Writings on Politics and Philosophy,* ed. Lewis S. Feuer (New York, 1959), p. 238.

5. Karl Marx, *Early Writings,* tr. T. B. Bottomore (London, 1963), p. 52.

6. Lewis S. Feuer, "Marxisms—How Many?," *Problems of Communism,* XIII, no. 2 (1964), p. 56.

7. C. Wright Mills, "On the New Left," *Studies on the Left,* vol. 1, no. 4 (1961), p. 70.

8. Georg Lukacs believed quite frankly that Marxism was the ideology of irrational men who nonetheless were elected to make history: "We Marxists do not only believe therefore that social progress is led by the frequently disturbed 'mentality' but we also know that it is only in Marx's teachings where this 'mentality' has come to self-awareness and is destined for leadership." Cf. Victor Zitta, *Georg Lukacs' Marxism, Alienation, Dialectics, Revolution: A Study in Utopia and Ideology* (The Hague, 1964), p. 181.

9. Mario Savio, "The Future of the Student Movement," Speech at Symposium of Young Socialist Alliance, Westminster Hall, Berkeley, Nov. 20, 1964. Also, cf. T. Walter Herbert, Jr., "To Whom It May Concern," *Daily Californian*, Nov. 19, 1964, p. 9.

10. Interview, Aug. 3, 1962, Tokyo, Japan. "Zengakuren" is the abbreviated form in Japanese for *Zen Nippon Gakusei Jichikai Sorengo*.

11. Interview with Shigeo Shima, July 29, 1962.

12. Interview with Shigeo Shima, Hiroko Shima, Mitsvo Nakamura, Tokyo, August 17, 1962. Also, cf. Lewis S. Feuer, "Currents in Japanese Socialist Thought," *New Politics*, vol. I, no. 2 (1962), p. 119; Lewis S. Feuer, "A Talk with the Zengakuren," *The New Leader*, vol. XLIV, no. 18 (May 1, 1961), p. 20.

13. Pyata P. Gaidenko, "Existentialism and the Individual," *The Soviet Review*, vol. 3 (1962), p. 18. Translated from *Vestnik Istorii Mirovoi Kul'tury*, 1961, no. 5.

14. Yuri Davydov, *Trud i Svoboda* (Moscow, 1962), pp. 55, 58.

15. Leaflet of Independent Student Association, December 1, 1964.

16. Cf. Lewis S. Feuer, "Youth in the '60's," *The New Leader*, vol. XLIV, no. 10 (March 6, 1961), p. 18.

17. A student publication in 1961 said: "We call the basis upon which we work together the 'lowest significant common denominator' and we link this concept to the idea of 'issues orientation.' It is not our purpose to develop an ideology." *About Slate*, pamphlet, Berkeley, 1961–62, p. 7.

18. Square—Conformist, Organization Man, solid citizen, anyone who doesn't swing and isn't with it. Also called Creep and Cornball. Man, if you still don't dig me, you'll never be anything but—." Lawrence Lipton, *The Holy Barbarians* (New York, 1962), p. 318.

19. *Ibid.*, Preface.

20. *International Correspondence of RMF-JRCL* (Revolutionary Marxist Faction of Japan Revolutionary Communist League), Tokyo, Dec. 1, 1964, no. 1, p. 5. Remarks of Theodore Draper, Conference on One Hundred Years of Revolutionary Internationals, Hoover Institution, Stanford University, Oct. 7, 1964.

21. Louis I. Dublin and Bessie Bunzel, *To Be or Not to Be: A Study of Suicide* (New York, 1933), pp. 409–10.

22. George A. DeVos, "Deviancy and Social Change: A Psychocultural Evaluation of Trends in Japanese Delinquency and Suicide," in Robert J. Smith and Richard K. Beardsley, eds., *Japanese Culture: Its Development and Characteristics*, (Chicago, 1962), p. 162. George A. DeVos, *Role Narcissism and the Etiology of Japanese Suicide* (mimeographed) (Berkeley, 1964), pp. 6–7.

23. Alexander Kornilov, *Modern Russian History*, tr. Alexander S. Kaun (New York, 1917), II, 332.

24. N. K. Krupskaia, "Samoubiistva Sredi Uchashchiksia i svobodnaia trudovaia shkola," *Pedagogicheskie Sochineniia* (Moscow) I, 1957, 139. Originally in *Svobodnoe Vospitanie* 1910–11, no. 11.

164

25. Nicolas Hans, *History of Russian Educational Policy (1701–1917)* (London, 1931), p. 238. *Letters from Mississippi,* ed., Elizabeth Sutherland (New York, 1965), p. 35. John Herbert, "600 Students Join Mississippi Drive," *The New York Times,* May 17, 1964.

26. Cf. *The Daily Californian,* December 17, 1964. *The San Francisco Chronicle,* May 17, 1965.

27. Avrahm Yarmolinsky, *Turgenev: The Man, His Art, and His Age* (New York, 1961), p. 201.

28. Karl Marx, *Economic and Philosophic Manuscripts of 1844,* Moscow, tr. Martin Milligan, p. 158.

29. E. Dupont, F. Engels, Leo Frankel, C. LeMoussu, Karl Marx, Aug. Serrailler, *L'Alliance de la Démocratie Socialiste et L'Association Internationale des Travailleurs* (London, 1878), pp. 60, 74. On the authorship of the "Alliance Pamphlet," cf. Franz Mehring, *Karl Marx: The Story of His Life,* tr. Edward Fitzgerald (New York, 1935), p. 504. Gustav Mayer, *Friedrich Engels: A Biography,* tr. Gilbert and Helen Highet (New York, 1936), p. 226.

30. Friedrich Engels, *Germany: Revolution and Counter-Revolution* (New York, 1933), p. 103. Friedrich Engels, Paul and Laura Lafargue, *Correspondence* (Moscow, 1960), II, 386. Lewis S. Feuer, "Marx and the Intellectuals," *Survey,* no. 49 (1963), p. 103.

31. The first use of the metaphor "best barometer of society" has been traced to N. I. Pirogov. Cf. J. M. Meijer, *Knowledge and Revolution: The Russian Colony in Zuerich (1870–1873)* (Assen, Van Gorcum, 1955), pp. 16, 170; Nicholas Hans, *The Russian Tradition in Education* (London, 1963), p. 60.

32. Avrahm Yarmolinsky, *Road to Revolution: A Century of Russian Radicalism* (New York, 1959), p. 10.

33. V. I. Lenin, "The Tasks of Revolutionary Youth," a mimeographed pamphlet printed in 1903, *Collected Works* (Moscow, 1961), vol. 7, p. 44; "The Signs of Bankruptcy," *Iskra,* Feb. 15, 1902, *Collected Works* (Moscow, 1961), vol. 6, p. 81.

34. Lenin, *Collected Works,* vol. 7, p. 53.

35. V. I. Lenin, *One Step Forward Two Steps Back,* 1904 (Moscow, 1947), pp. 92, 93, 81.

36. V. I. Lenin, *What Is to Be Done?* (New York, 1932), pp. 95, 36.

37. V. I. Lenin, "The Student Movement and the Present Political Situation," *Proletarii,* No. 36, 16 (3), October, 1908, reprinted in V. I. Lenin, *Sochineniia* (Moscow, 1931), Tom. XII, pp. 336–341, translated in V. I. Lenin, *The Young Generation,* New York, 1940, pp. 14, 19, 20.

38. Leon Trotsky, *The History of the Russian Revolution,* tr. Max Eastman (New York, 1933), III, 191. Also, cf. M. N. Pokrovsky, *Brief History of Russia,* tr. D. S. Mirsky (London, 1933), II, 47; N. K. Krupskaia, *Reminiscences of Lenin,* tr. Bernard Isaacs (Moscow, 1959), pp. 352, 151; Oliver H. Radkey, *The Agrarian Foes of Bolshevism* (New York, 1958), p. 61.

39. J. V. Stalin, "The Russian Social-Democratic Party and Its Immediate Tasks," Nov.–Dec., 1901, *Works* (Moscow, 1952), I, 22. Georgia did not have a regular university until 1918. Its revolutionary students, such as Noe Zhordania and Joseph Stalin, came from the Tbilis Theological Seminary. Cf. David Marshall Lang, *A Modern History of Georgia* (London, 1962), pp. 122, 211.

40. *Ibid.,* pp. 24–26.

41. Raphael R. Abramovitch, *The Soviet Revolution 1917–1939* (New York, 1962), p. 285; see also Edward Hallett Carr, *A History of Soviet Russia: The Interregnum, 1923–1924* (New York, 1954), pp. 325–27.

42. Karl Marx and Friedrich Engels, *Selected Correspondence* (Moscow, 1953), pp. 409, 435.

43. E. Roy Lankester, "Degeneration: A Chapter in Darwinism," in *The Advancement of Science* (London, 1890), pp. 47–48.

44. Benjamin I. Schwartz, *Chinese Communism and the Rise of Mao* (Cambridge, Mass., 1952), pp. 10–11.

Marxism in the Communist Countries

---

1. Philosophy is, logically, the foundation of the whole Marxist system, as is said in one of the basic Soviet texts: The "foundation of the whole Marxist-Leninist system is its philosophical doctrine, Dialectical and Historical Materialism"—*Osnovy Marksizma-Leninizma* (Moscow, 1959), p. 15. It must be stressed that the official doctrine does not distinguish between the logical and the epistemic "foundation." Logically, Historical Materialism is supposed to be deduced from Dialectical Materialism, and such doctrines as the theory of morals and aesthetics, and even moral rules themselves, are said to be deduced in turn from Historical Materialism. Whatever the case may be (for it seems certain that one cannot obtain the propositions forming Historical Materialism from those of Dialectical Materialism alone, and far less still such theories as that of the Dictatorship of the Proletariat, etc.), it seems that philosophy is not, at least in its present form, the epistemic foundation of the system, but that it has been constructed as a sort of explanatory generalization of statements belonging to the field of morals, economics, and sociology.

2. The rather complex theoretical problems connected with the situation of a believer in face of the results of science etc., are discussed in some detail by the present author in his *Logic of Religion* (New York, 1965) which deals with a field similar to Communist ideology.

3. Soviet writers and, to a certain extent also, those of other Communist countries regularly use the expression "Marxism-Leninism" and not "Marxism." There are, however, exceptions. Thus, in 1958 an important textbook bearing a semi-official character was published under the title of "Principles of Marxist Philosophy." Also, in some countries other than the Soviet Union, the term "Marxism," "Marxist," etc., are more frequently used. This seems to be, above all, the case in Poland. E.g., in the bibliography of Adam Schaff published by Z. Jordan (*Philosophy and Ideology*, Dordrecht, 1963, pp. 580 ff.) we do not find a single one of the 37 items quoted which contains "Marxist-Leninist" or "Marxism-Leninism" in its title; it is always "Marxist" or "Marxism" ("marksistowski," "marksizm"). In non-Communist countries the terms "Marxist" and "Marxism" are often used for "Marxist-Leninist" and "Marxism-Leninism." This use is incorrect and should be avoided. Between Marx and contemporary Soviet thought lies a long period of development and change; today there are many varieties of Marxism, and contemporary Soviet Philosophy contains many statements which cannot by any extension of the term be called "Marxist."

4. *Proletarskaia revolutsia i renegat Kautsky* (1918). Lenin published two

writings under that title, both of which are reproduced in *Polnoe sobranie sochinenii*, ed. 5 (Moscow 1963); the first (Vol. 37, pp. 101–110) is an article which appeared in *Pravda* in 1918, while the second (Vol. 37, pp. 235–38) is the pamphlet mentioned in the text.

5. S. N. Valentinov, "Tchernychevski et Lénine," *Contrat Social*, I (1957), No. 2, pp. 104 ff. In *Materialism and Empirio-criticism* and the *Philosophical Notebooks*, Chernyshevsky is the third most-quoted author after Hegel and Feuerbach, at least 28 times (there are only 13 quotations from Marx and 12 from Engels).

6. N. Berdiaev, *Wahrheit und Lüge des Kommunismus* (Luzern, 1934); *The Origin of Russian Communism* (London, 1937). There are also many other good books on the subject—one recent instance is E. Lampert: *Sons against Fathers* (London, 1964)—which do not seem to have been read by some of the authors writing on Soviet thought.

7. This is in short the following: by the act of election the individual expresses publicly his allegiance and solidarity with the group. In Western countries elections have been always thought as a device invented in order to solve conflicts between opposed views and groups. No wonder that a Westerner cannot understand what is really meant by Communist "elections."

8. J. Harper, *Lenin als Philosoph* (Amsterdam, 1936).

9. Cf. "On Soviet Studies," *Studies in Soviet Thought*, I (1965), pp. 5 ff.

10. See *Voprosy filosofii*, 1947, No. 1, p. 160a (Baskin) 200b (Tshagin).

11. This is exemplified by what is mentioned below, e.g. on the views concerning logic. But there are similar discussions and divergences of views on other topics. Of these, ontology has been perhaps best studied (H. Fleischer, "On Categories in Soviet Philosophy," *Studies in Soviet Thought*, I (1961), pp. 64 ff.; G. Planty-Bonjour, *Les catégories du matérialisme dialectique* (Paris, 1964). A case which has perhaps received insufficient attention is the position of A. Blauberg ("O kategoriakh tselogo i chasti v marksistkoi filosofii," *Voprosy filosofii*, 1957, No. 4, pp. 40–50) and V. P. Tugarinov (*Sootnoshenie kategorii dialekticheskogo materializma*—Leningrad, 1956) who stress the Aristotelian view of the structure of phenomena, as against the current, more Hegelian view. Soviet philosophers dislike statements affirming the existence of conflicting opinions among them. But whoever has read such philosophers as A. A. Zinov'ev and P. V. Kopnin, or V. P. Tugarinov and E. V. Illyenkov, cannot but state that the differences of views concerning quite *basic* issues in philosophy are sometimes very great indeed.

Different trends should not be confounded with different *levels* of thought and expression. In the Soviet Union, as elsewhere but perhaps to a larger degree, authentic, well-trained thinkers coexist with superficial agitprop types.

12. Yugoslav philosophy is still a practically unexplored field. Yet we know from L. Vrtačić, *Einführung in den jugoslawischen Marxismus-Leninismus* (Dordrecht, 1963) and also from his short report: "Der jugoslawische philosophische Revisionismus im Lichte der sowietischen Kritik," *Studies in Soviet Thought*, II (1964), pp. 104 ff., that there *is* at least a particular and, it seems, rather interesting Yugoslav philosophy. Mr. Vrtačić is at present working on a monograph concerning some aspects of that philosophy.

13. For Poland there exists a full monograph covering the years 1945–62: Z. Jordan, *Philosophy and Ideology* (Dordrecht, 1963).

14. The development of Czech and Slovak Marxist-Leninist philosophy has been described by N. Lobkowicz, *Marxismus-Leninismus in der CSR* (Dordrecht, 1961). On newer developments, see his "Philosophical Revisionism in post-war Czechoslovakia," *Studies in Soviet Thought,* IV (1964), pp. 89 ff. and the review of the highly interesting book of K. Kosik, *Dialektika konkretniho,* in the same issue, pp. 248 ff. What we learn from the latter is truly revolutionary. It is understood that Professor Lobkowicz is working on an English translation of this book. Unfortunately we have to date no studies on the philosophy of other Communist countries in spite of the fact that, e.g., Bulgaria would certainly merit one. E. Laszlo is, however, preparing a monograph on Hungary at the Institute of East-European Studies in Fribourg.

15. As far as we know, the only sort of non-Marxist-Leninist philosophy existing in Yugoslavia is Christian (Catholic) philosophy. In Poland the situation is different, for alongside a rather flourishing Christian philosophy there is a strong non-Leninist and even non-Marxist trend represented by the traditional analytic philosophy of that country. One of its leaders, T. Kotarbinski, was for a long time president of the Academy of Sciences; another, K. Ajdukiewicz, enjoyed high esteem and practically unlimited possibility of expressing himself. There is also "revisionism," of which a word will be said later.

16. Such statements are very numerous, indeed, it would appear that they are more numerous and more categorical now than they were under Stalin. It will suffice to recall: the decision of the Twentieth Party Congress ordering the Central Committee to take care of the purity of Marxism-Leninism as if it were the "pupil of the eye;" the ukase by the same Central Committee introducing Marxism-Leninism in the teaching of the higher institutions of learning in 1956; the many emphatic statements by N. S. Khrushchev (*Za prochnyi mir i mirnoe sosushchestvovanie*—Moscow, 1958—pp. 13, 16, 21, 27, 49, 226 and 242 *i.a.*); the New Party Statutes established at the Twenty-Second Party Congress, where the study of ideology was raised to a higher place, and a new ideological precept introduced (fighting against pro-religious prejudices); and the different statements at the international Party Conferences. One text among many, drawn from the declaration of the twelve ruling Parties at their Congress in Moscow in 1957, will suffice to illustrate the attitude mentioned here:

"The theoretical foundation of Marxism-Leninism is Dialectical Materialism. This view of the world [*mirovozrenie*] reflects the general laws of development of nature, society and human thought. This view of the world is valid for past, present and future. When a Marxist political party does not begin with the analysis of its questions from dialectics and from materialism, this leads necessarily to onesidedness and subjectivism." *Pravda,* Nov. 22, 1957.

It must be admitted that many Western observers tend to overlook these statements or, more frequently, to consider them irrelevant. But they are certainly there in great quantity and unequivocally categorical. According to all Communist leaders Marxism-Leninism is a very important matter.

17. *Friedrich Ueberwegs Grundriss der Geschichte der Philosophie* is the classical reference work in the history of philosophy. There is less than one page (V, 361 f.) entirely devoted to Br. Petroniewics.

18. S. Vrtačić, quoted in footnote 12.

19. *Bibliographie der sowjetischen Philosophie* (I, 1959; III, 1962; IV, 1963; V, 1964). A check of the libraries of Moscow and Leningrad showed that this

168

bibliography (the only existing one, Soviet philosophers not having produced anything of the sort up to now) contains about 80–85 per cent of all titles, and it is probably nearly complete insofar as significant titles are concerned.

20. *Novye knigi* 1959, 14.

21. *Bibliographie der sow. Phil.* Since 1958 the number of copies has diminished, but the magazine now prints twelve issues a year and another philosophical magazine (*Filosofskie nauki*) has been founded. The *Voprosy filosofii* is, both in size and copies distributed, by far the largest magazine of its kind in the world.

22. This was, at least the estimation of A. F. Okulov, as reported by A. P. Ermilov (*Voprosy filosofii*, 1961, No. 7, p. 146) concerning the number of students of philosophy in the Soviet Union, see *Studies in Soviet Thought*, IV (1964), 61; in 1960–61 there were according to *Vysshee obrazovanie v SSSR*, 1961, not less than 1510.

23. Marxism-Leninism contains a peculiar doctrine of absolute truth, which has been often misunderstood. Absolute truth is defined as "that element of knowledge which cannot be refuted [*oprovergnut'*] in the future" (M. M. Rozental' and P. F. Yudin, ed., *Filosofskij slovar'*—Moscow, 1963, p. 56) and at the same time as "full, exhaustive knowledge of reality" (*ibid.*). So-called "relative truth" is opposed to it only in the second aspect, not in the first. Marxism-Leninism holds that there are absolute truths in the field of every science (*Osnovy*, p. 340). Above all, the basic tenets of Marxism-Leninism itself are absolute truths. This has been misunderstood and even doubted, because of the constant talk by the Communists about "dialectics." But dialectics, as they understand it, does not contradict the absolute character of truth. Marxism-Leninism is, indeed, an extremely absolutistic view. This is one aspect of the situation. The other is *partijnost'* (party-mindedness); according to this principle every philosophy is a class philosophy and *should* be such. But being a class philosophy, it should be "the expression and the weapon" of the interests of a class; for the latter being essentially engaged in a struggle with another class or classes, then the moral obligation to hold the tenets of a given philosophy (in our case of Marxism-Leninism) follows quite naturally. About truth see K. Ballestrem: "The Soviet Concept of Truth," *Studies in Soviet Thought*, IV (1964), pp. 1 ff.

The best Soviet statement of the doctrine of *partijnost'* known to the author is still that of M. Z. Selektor: "Princip partijnosti v ideologii," *Voprosy filosofii*, 1957, No. 5, pp. 67–81. Some important distinctions are made by G. M. Shtraks, *Predmet dialekticheskogo materializma* (Moscow, 1960). See also G. E. Glezerman, *Bazis i nadstrojka v sovetskom obshtchestve* (Moscow, 1954); V. Z. Kelle and M. Ya. Koval'zon, *Formy obshtchestvennogo soznania* (Moscow, 1959); G. M. Gak, ed., same title (Moscow, 1960); V. P. Tugarinov, *Sootnoshenie kategorii istoricheskogo materializma* (Leningrad, 1958) and *O tsennostiakh i formakh dukhovnoi deiatel'nosti obshtchestva* (Leningrad, 1961). Some excerpts have been quoted by H. Fleischer in *Studies in Soviet Thought*, IV (1962), 119 ff. On the whole problem see the same author's "The Limits of 'Party-Mindedness,'" *ibid.*, and J. Bochenski, "On Partijnost' in Philosophy," *ibid.*, V, 1–2 (forthcoming).

24. The Lyssenko case illustrates the role of the Party and not that of Marxism-Leninism as a body of doctrines. For it is more than doubtful whether Lyssenko's theories were in agreement with the latter. This problem has been discussed by

G. A. Wetter, *Der dialektische Materialismus* (Vienna, 1960), pp. 524 ff., who also gives bibliographical information. See also my *Der sowjetrussisch dialektische Materialismus* (Bern, 1950) for texts of self-criticisms and bibliography.

25. The leading anti-Einsteinian, a certain A. A. Maksimov, was finally accused of "dogmatism" and removed from the board of editors of *Voprosy filosofii*. The discussion is described in the ample volume of S. Müller-Markus, *Einstein and die Sowjetphilosophie* (Dordrecht, 1960). This is probably the best-known case of "liberalization" in Soviet thought. But it is neither the first nor the most relevant to philosophy. Already in 1950–51, immediately after the statements of Stalin on language (June 20, 1950), a long discussion about logic was published in *Voprosy filosofii* which concluded with a statement by the board of editors of the magazine (the official organ of the Philosophical Institute of the Academy of Sciences of the USSR), granting freedom to formal logic.

26. The theory sketched out here is presented more fully in my article, "The Three Components of Communist Ideology," *Studies in Soviet Thought*, II (1962), 7 ff. At that time it was merely a working hypothesis. But further research and also the fact that it has been found convenient and was accepted by some Sovietologists working in other fields (e.g., professor K. Thalheim) now permits one to consider it as a well-founded explanatory statement. This view has never been explicitly proposed by any Soviet writer, as far as is known. However, since G. E. Glezerman's *Bazis i nadstroika v sotsialisticheskom obshchestve* (Moscow, 1954), at least one distinction is made—between "purely scientific" and philosophical doctrines. The former are considered class free.

27. The expression "declassified doctrines" was suggested by D. D. Comey. The author of the present paper proposed another classification of the elements of Communist ideology in "Toward a Systematic Logic of Communist Ideology," *Studies in Soviet Thought*, IV (1964), pp. 1, 85 ff. According to it, four classes of statements should be distinguished: the *Weltanschauung* proper (corresponding to the basic faith), the political doctrines imposed by the Party, philosophy, and sciences. This division is made from a different point of view than the first, in that it distinguishes the doctrines not according to their relevance to the Party (as the first does) but according to the reason for their acceptance. "Political doctrines" are assumed to be accepted *only* because they are imposed by the Party. At the same time this interpretation should not be oversimplified to admit only *two* sorts of doctrines, those imposed by the Party and those which belong to pure (meaning mostly natural) science. We know of a number of Soviet philosophers who fought some Party decisions, even risking their lives, and who still remained devout Communists. Moreover, it is also certain that many of them hold some doctrines because of a sort of philosophic insight which has little to do with the results of sciences. One instance is the discussion about the basic structure of reality (Aristotelianism vs. Hegelianism) mentioned earlier.

28. A complete study on the dialectical method is still wanting. The best is a series of reviews by Th. J. Blakeley, *Studies in Soviet Thought*, III, 1963, pp. 78–80, 162–69, 214 f., and a chapter in his *Soviet Theory of Knowledge* (Dordrecht, 1964), pp. 29 ff. Systematically speaking, if there is any dialectical logic at all it can be only a sort of methodology or a philosophy of logic. Some confusion has been caused in Soviet philosophy (as often happens in European philosophy) between the three basic parts of logic: formal logic, methodology,

and philosophy of logic. This confusion is often evident in the writings of philosophers who oppose mathematical logic because they feel that it does not contain their methodological or purely philosophical views.

29. This decision was preceded by a long and rather confused discussion published, at least in part, in *Voprosy filosofii*, 1950, No. 2 and 1951, No. 6. A German translation of the discussion was published under the title *Über formale und dialektische Logik* ([East] Berlin, 1952). A complete study of Soviet Logic between 1947 and 1960 (the most interesting period as it seems) is still wanting, but some details have been published by G. A. Wetter, *Der dialektische Materialismus*, pp. 598 ff.; J. Bochenski, "Soviet Logic," *Studies in Soviet Thought*, I (1961), pp. 29 ff.; D. D. Comey, "Two Recent Conferences on Logic," *ibid.*, II (1962), pp. 21 ff. Much material is to be found in H. Dahm, "Renaissance der Formalen Logik," *Ost-Probleme*, VIII (1957), pp. 254 ff.

30. For mathematical logic in the Soviet Union there is an excellent survey by Mrs. S. A. Janovskaya, "Matematicheskaia logika i osnovnaia matematika" in *Matematika v SSSR za sorok let*, 1958. See also G. Küng, "A Bibliography of Soviet Mathematical Logic," *Notre Dame Journal of Formal Logic*, 1963, and the current reviews in the *Journal of Symbolic Logic*. In this context it must be said that Russia has an old and, it would seem, uninterrupted tradition of studies in mathematical logic. However, those studies were conducted until recent years exclusively within the framework of *Mathematics*. Even the most reactionary Soviet philosophers did not dare to deny that it might have some importance for mathematics. A new phenomenon is, however, the impact of such studies on philosophy. In September 1956 a seminar for logic—apparently mathematical logic—was established at the Institute of Philosophy of the Academy of Sciences of the U.S.S.R. Two years later an important discussion took place on contradiction, during which some speakers—such as A. Kol'man and A. A. Zinov'ev—successfully used mathematical logic. Cf., N. Lobkowicz, *Das Widerspruchsprinzip in der neueren sowjetischen Philosophie* (Dordrecht, 1959). This is the new fact, relevant to our problems. One can grasp how different the situation is now by comparing the texts published by Lobkowicz with the humiliating self-criticism Mrs. Janovskaia was obliged to publish in 1950 (*Voprosy filosofii*, 1950, No. 3, pp. 339 ff.).

31. Th. J. Blakeley, *Soviet Scholasticism* (Dordrecht, 1961), especially pp. 13–70.

32. K. S. Bakradze, "K voprosu o sootnoshenii logiki i dialektiki," *Voprosy filosofii*, 1950, No. 2, pp. 198 ff. and "Protiv nenauchnoy i nedobrozhelatel'noy kritiki," *ibid.*, 1956, No. 2, pp. 218 ff. It must be said that the courageous thinker from Tbilisi is rather isolated in Soviet Philosophy. As Professor Blakeley puts it, we have now a sort of "Anti-Bakradze" tendency comparable to the "Anti-Dühring" of Engels.

33. A. A. Zinov'ev, *Filosofskie problemy mnogoznachnoy logiki* (Moscow, 1960).

34. "K itogam obsuzhdeniia voprosov logiki," *Voprosy filosofii*, 1951, No. 6, pp. 143 ff. This is an official statement by the board of editors of the journal.

35. The first clear statement concerning this matter seems to have been that of Glezerman, *Basis i nadstroika*.... But the doctrine was not readily accepted. E.g., the *Osnovy Marksistkoi Filosofii*, published four years later (Moscow, 1958), declares that "the theoretical problems of natural sciences are a battlefield of ideology which reflects in one way or another the struggle of classes" (p. 373).

36. S. Müller-Markus, *Einstein.* . . .

37. S. G. Fisher, *Science and Politics: the New Sociology in the Soviet Union* (Ithaca, N.Y., 1964). The important event is the foundation of a sociological society, under Polish influence it seems (in Poland sociology did not cease after 1945). But the attitude of Soviet philosophers toward sociology is far from being uniform. Some among them still identify it with historical materialism, while others would like to consider it as a separate, autonomous science.

38. This division has been suggested by Th. J. Blakeley, *Soviet Philosophy* (Dordrecht, 1964). Soviet authors themselves divide philosophy into two chapters only, dialectical and historical materialism. However, the first one is subdivided in a way similar to that mentioned here.

39. Soviet theory of knowledge has been studied by J. de Vries, *Die Erkenntnistheorie des dialektischen Materialismus* (Munich, 1958)—a study of the essentials based mostly on translations—and Th. J. Blakeley, *Soviet Theory of Knowledge* —using much Soviet material.

40. E.g., M. N. Rutkevich, *Dialekticheskii materializm* (Moscow, 1958), and S. T. Meliuknin, *O dialektike razvitia neorganicheskoi prirody* (Moscow, 1960). There is a report on such tendencies by H. Fleischer in *Studies in Soviet Thought*, II (1962), pp. 12 ff. and in his forthcoming book, *Die Ontologie des dialektischen Materialismus.* The central concept used is that of "inexhaustibility" (*neischerpaemost'*) of matter (i.e. nature); according to V. V. Orlov, *Dialekticheskii materializm i psikhofisiologicheskaia problema* (Perm, 1960), p. 170, quoted by Fleischer, p. 18, "the lower form of matter contains in itself tremendous [*ogromnye*] possibilities of development, which actualize themselves only under new conditions." See also Fleischer's review of Rutkevich in *Studies in Soviet Thought*, II (1962), pp. 157 ff.

41. There is in the West a widespread opinion that Soviet philosophers deny the existence of mind (consciousness) or that they identify it with matter. They have never maintained this, at least not since the fall of the "mechanists" in 1930. The official position is that mind is not matter; whoever asserts this is called a "vulgar materialist"—see e.g. M. M. Rozental' and P. R. Yudin: *Filosofskii slovar'* (Moscow, 1963), col. 83a. The *Osnovy marksistkoi filosofii* states (p. 160): "Consciousness is not a particular form of matter . . . Consciousness does not have physical properties, as bodies have them."

42. This (Leninist) definition is repeated in every textbook, e.g., in the *Osnovy*, pp. 116 ff.

43. S. L. Rubinshtein, *Osnovy obshchey psikhologii* (Moscow, 1940; revised ed. 1946). About the author, see R. Payne, "Sergej Leonidovič Rubinštejn," *Studies in Soviet Thought*, III (1963), pp. 208 ff., and "Books and Articles by S. L. Rubinštejn," *ibid.*, IV (1964), pp. 78 ff. The same author is preparing a monograph of this leading Soviet psychologist.

44. The stenographic transcript, *Nauchnaia sessiia posviashchennaia problemam fiziologicheskogo ucheniia akademika I. P. Pavlova* (Moscow, 1950).

45. He did it rather late in his article "Uchenie I. P. Pavlova i nekotorye voprosy perestroiki psikhologii," *Voprosy filosofii*, 1952, No. 2, pp. 197–210.

46. This is, for example, emphatically stated in the *Osnovy*, p. 163.

47. Soviet Ethics have been but little studied. There are two books only, by S. Vagovič, *Etica communista* (Rome, 1959) and E. Kamenka, *Ethical Foundations of Marxism* (London, 1962), both unsatisfactory. About the latter, see *Studies in Soviet Thought*, III (1963), pp. 81 ff. R. T. DeGeorge recently pub-

lished two articles on the subject: "The Foundations of Marxist-Leninist Ethics," *ibid.*, pp. 121 ff. and "Soviet Ethics and Soviet Society," *ibid.*, IV (1964), pp. 206 ff. Those articles, together with "A Bibliography of Soviet Ethics," *ibid.*, III (1963), pp. 83–103, by the same author form a good introduction in the field. Professor DeGeorge is preparing a monograph on the subject.

48. *Osnovy*, p. 582.

49. See the statistical introduction in DeGeorge's bibliography.

50. *Osnovy*, p. 581.

51. The outstanding instance is V. P. Tugarinov, *O tsennostiakh zhizni i kul'tury* (Moscow, 1960); cf. H. Fleischer's review in *Studies in Soviet Thought*, II (1962), pp. 72 ff.

52. In the first issue of the *Voprosy filosofii*, 1965, there is an article of A. F. Shishkin, the leading theoretician of Soviet ethics, which even bears "otchuzhdenie" (alienation) in its title. Yet, the way in which Mr. Shishkin is interpreting alienation is not one which would bring Soviet philosophy nearer to an understanding of existential questions. This seems to be one of the fundamental differences between orthodox Marxism-Leninism and so-called "revisionism," which, wherever it appears, seems to manifest some interest in those questions. And this difference is one reason why all those who treat the official Marxism-Leninism of the Soviet Union and other Communist countries as if it were "Marxism," trying to understand it through Marx or even the young Marx, are bound to fail.

53. The field is still largely unexplored. See, however, Th. J. Blakeley, "Scientific Atheism. An Introduction," *Studies in Soviet Thought*, IV (1964), pp. 48 ff., and the bibliography by the same author, "Soviet Writings on Atheism and Religion," *ibid.*, IV (1964), pp. 319 ff. (to be continued). Professor N. Lobkowicz has suggested that here lies another important difference between Karl Marx and contemporary Marxism-Leninism. For while Marx thought that the problem of religion had been definitively solved and did not pay much attention to it, Soviet Marxism-Leninism continuously stresses the vital importance of "fighting" religion on the philosophical level.

54. N. Lobkowicz, "Philosophical Revisionism in Post-War Czechoslovakia," *Studies in Soviet Thought*, IV (1964), pp. 89 ff. This article is important as an analysis of the concept of revisionism and of its various kinds.

55. E. Bloch, *Das Prinzip der Hoffnung* (Leipzig, 1955).

56. We still lack a monograph on this philosopher in any Western language. His revisionist views are hardly treated in Z. Jordan's *Philosophy and Ideology*, the standard book on Polish Marxism-Leninism. There exists a German edition of Kolakowski's selected writings: L. Kolakowski, *Der Mensch ohne Alternative* (München, 1960).

57. V. I. Lenin, "The Tasks of the Youth League" [October 2, 1920], *Selected Works* (New York, 1935), IX, pp. 475 ff.

The "End of Ideology" in the Soviet Union?

1. Reprinted in *Revisionism*, ed. Leopold Labedz (London, 1962), pp. 179–95.

2. Take, as one example, the resolution of the special Central Committee plenum on ideology in June 1963. An unprecedented convocation, which brought

together party officials with leading writers and literary editors, it declared: "Under the flag of anti-communism, the imperialists are . . . trying by every means to carry the war of ideas into the Socialist countries. Under the cover of the slogan of peaceful coexistence of ideologies, they are trying to smuggle into our society the false conceptions of the non-party nature of art, the absolute freedom of creative work, ideological vacuity and aloofness from politics, the conflict of generations, and are trying to corrupt ideologically unstable people." (Text reproduced by "Background Information," Radio Free Europe, Munich, June 24, 1963.)

3. This world outlook, embodied in a number of doctrinal formulations, is presented in the curriculum of the Higher Party Schools within four sets of courses: (1) dialectical materialism—the structure of matter and nature; (2) historical materialism—the movement of history and the laws of the development of society; (3) political economy—the contrasting bases of socialism and capitalism; (4) scientific communism—the world of the future.

4. Emile Durkheim, *On the Division of Labor in Society* (New York, 1933), p. 228. As Durkheim spelled out his view (p. 14): "it is impossible for men to live together . . . without acquiring a sentiment of the whole formed by their union, without attaching themselves to that whole, pre-occupying themselves with its interests and taking account of it in their conduct. . . . This subordination of particular interests to the general interests is, indeed, the source of all moral activity."

5. Max Weber, *The Sociology of Religion* (Boston, 1963). See especially the introduction by Talcott Parsons, specifically pp. xxviii–xxxii.

6. *Ibid.*, p. xxxii.

7. As Edward Shils has put it: "The center or the central zone [of a society] is a symbolic phenomenon. It is the center of the body of symbols which govern the society. It is the source of legitimacy. It is the ultimate and irreducible; and it is felt to be such by many who cannot make a logical analysis of its irreducibility. The central zone partakes of the nature of the sacred. In this sense, every society has an 'official' religion, even when that society or its interpreters and exponents conceive of it as a secular pluralistic and tolerant society. The principle of the Counter Reformation: *Cuius regio, illius religio,* although its rigor has been loosened and its harshness mollified retains a core of permanent truth." "Center and Periphery" in *The Logic of Personal Knowledge: Essays Presented to Michael Polanyi* (London, 1961), p. 117.

8. For Talcott Parsons, who has done more than any other contemporary sociologist to construct a theoretical scheme to understand the integrative systems of a society, *values* stand at the apex of a hierarchy which includes, in descending order, *differentiated norms, collectives,* and *roles,* as the analytical units in the institutionalization of social action. Parsons, however, begins from the viewpoint of *society.* If one starts from the problems of *politics* (or the *State*), then a crucial element in the analysis of social control is lacking. I think that for the analysis of "mobilized societies" one gains considerably by seeing the role of *ideology* as an intervening variable of social control.

For an elaboration of Parsons' argument, see his essay "Authority, Legitimation and Political Action" in his *Structure and Processes in Modern Society* (Glencoe, Illinois, 1960), chapter 5, and his essay "Durkheim's Contribution to the Theory of Integration of Social Systems" in Kurt H. Wolff (ed.), *Essays on Sociology and Philosophy* by Emile Durkheim, *et al.* (New York, 1964) pp. 118–54.

9. "Since there can be no talk of an independent ideology being developed by the masses of the workers themselves in the process of their movement, the only choice is: either the bourgeois or the socialist ideology. There is no middle course (for humanity has not created a 'third' ideology, and, moreover, in a society torn by class antagonisms there can never be a non-class or above-class ideology). Hence to belittle the socialist ideology *in any way, to turn away from it in the slightest degree,* means to strengthen the bourgeois ideology." V. I. Lenin, "What Is To Be Done?" *Selected Works* (Moscow, 1950), I, 242–44. Emphasis in the original.

10. *Structure and Process,* p. 172.

11. The phrase is chosen as a parallel to the characterization of the American value system as one of "instrumental activism," an attitude of active mastery over nature, a commitment to generalized progress, and a pragmatic attitude toward organization and authority. See, Parsons, *Structure and Process,* pp. 172–73.

12. In this section, I have relied substantially on the discussion by Gustave Wetter, *Dialectical Materialism: A Historical and Systematic Survey of Philosophy in the Soviet Union* (London, 1958); the article "Diamat and Einstein" by Siegfried Müller-Markus in *Survey* (London), July–September 1961; and three articles by C. Olgin, "Soviet Dialectical Materialism in Transition," "Physics and Dialectical Materialism," and "Science and Philosophy in the U.S.S.R.," in the *Bulletin of the Institute for the Study of the USSR* (Munich), November 1959, May 1960, and December 1960.

Since completing the first draft, I have had occasion to read the unpublished Ph.D. thesis (Columbia University) of Maxim Mikluk, "Relativity, Theory and Soviet Communist Philosophy, 1922–1960." It is a comprehensive effort to deal with the fate of Einsteinian physics in the Soviet Union, and it argues that Russian physicists, although unable publicly to air their views, were more free than Western observers had supposed to discuss and even accept relativity theory. I have profited considerably from reading Dr. Mikluk's manuscript.

13. In *P. Z. M.* (Pod Znamenem Marksizma), 1932, nos. 1–2, pp. 221–22, cited by Jerome Rosenthal, "On the Soviet Philosophic Front," *Modern Monthly* (New York), December 1936.

14. In the satellite countries, of course, these ideas about the relation of dialectical materialism to physics were repeated ritualistically. For example, in March 1952 the Academy of the Rumanian People's Republic held a special scientific session. Speaking on physics and mathematics, Professor Stefan Vencov, Director of the Polytechnic Institute in Bucharest, said: "here is a hard struggle for the victory of the scientific concept of dialectic materialism. . . . Idealistic concepts in physics are characterized by very abstract mathematical formulae devoid of material foundation. . . . Contemporary idealism in physics denies the objective character of space and time. Quantum mechanics is also faked and faultily interpreted by idealists and agnostics."

Professor Vecan, corroborating Professor Vencov, pointed out that idealistic elements were present in the work of Western physicists such as de Broglies and Heisenberg, and admitted that "in my work, too, a conciliatory attitude toward Einstein's deviations has manifested itself." (Quotations from *Scinteia,* Bucharest, March 25–26, 1952; translations by Radio Free Europe.)

15. Soviet philosophy has shown a striking abhorence of the expression "relativity." In the recent years, this has derived from an effort to defend the notion of an absolute physical universe. But in the early years, the opposition was based on a "vulgar" reading of Lenin. When Lenin wrote his *Materialism and Empirio-Criticism,* there was no indication that he was familiar with Einstein's work or the idea of relativity. He did, however, denounce *philosophical* relativism, as it derived from the work of Ernst Mach and his reinterpretation of modern physics, as rejecting objective knowledge and absolute truth. He never considered *physical* relativism from a philosophical point of view. Later, Soviet Marxists pounced on one of Lenin's sentences about the objective reality of the universe as proof that Lenin unequivocally opposed relativism in both the physical and philosophical sense. (Cf. Mikluk, chapter 1.)

16. In a paper significantly entitled "Cybernetics and Natural Sciences" presented at the October 1958 conference on dialectical materialism, cited by Olgin, Dec. 1960.

17. Cited by A. Bucholz, "Problems of Ideological East-West Conflicts," *Studies in Soviet Thought,* I (1961).

18. "Breaching the Dialectical Curtain," *The Observer* (London), April 8, 1962.

19. Z. A. Jordan, *Philosophy and Ideology: The Development of Philosophy and Marxism-Leninism in Poland Since the Second World War* (Dordrecht, Holland, 1963), p. 302.

20. Mikluk, pp. 323, 308.

21. See, for example, the debate between Hessen and Clark on the "social roots of science": B. Hessen, "The Social and Economic Roots of Newton's *Principia"* in *Science at the Cross-Roads* (London, 1931), and G. N. Clark, *Science and Social Welfare in the Age of Newton* (London and New York, 1949).

22. For an acute analysis of the Marxist schema, see J. H. Hexter, "A New Framework for Social History" in *Reappraisals in History* (New York and London, 1961).

23. See, for example, Weber's discussion of bureaucracy in *The Theory of Social and Economic Organization,* ed. Talcott Parsons (New York, 1947), pp. 329-47. The most comprehensive formulation of the theory of industrial society is contained in the lectures of Raymond Aron at the Sorbonne, published in mimeographed form in Les Cours de Sorbonne. These are: *Le Développement de la Société Industrielle et la Stratification Sociale* (two parts), and *Sociologie des Sociétés Industrielles.* A concise published version is *Dix-Huit Leçons Sur La Société Industrielle* (Paris, 1962).

24. As Raymond Aron has sought to sketch industrial society: "Modern societies are defined first and foremost by their organization of labor, that is their relationship to the external world, their use of machinery, the application of scientific methods, and the social and economic consequences of the rationaliza-tion of production. It is impossible, in an introductory study, to give a definition of the family, the State, and the nature of culture in modern society (because all three can take various forms). But there is no doubt that they are affected by development and that they present certain similarities in all advanced societies: for instance, the extended family will tend to be nuclear; the State will operate through a rationally organized and comparatively centralized bureaucracy, culture

purveyed to millions through the mass media will gradually drive out local cultures or super-impose itself upon them." "The Epoch of Universal Technology," *Encounter Pamphlet* no. II (London, 1964), p. 4. This essay is probably the most succinct statement of Aron's argument.

25. Adam Ulam, "Socialism in Current Soviet Historiography," paper read at the Conference on Contemporary History in the Soviet Mirror, Geneva, July 16–23, 1961. See also Merle Fainsod, "Soviet Russian Historians, or: The Lesson of Burdzhalov," *Encounter* (London), March 1962.

26. In opening the archives to Soviet historians, the Party's explicit wish has been that historians would destroy the Stalinist myths; but with the documents available, it becomes more and more difficult to distort or suppress details that are damaging to Party myths. Despite the setback to Burdzhalov, Soviet historians, by posing "technical" problems in the use of the archives, continue to demand more open inquiry. Thus in the February 1962 issue of *Kommunist,* I. Smirnov wrote a sweeping attack on the "Review of Sources on Party History," published by the Moscow University history faculty, because of its failure to use archival sources carefully. He demands critical use of sources and citations that will permit readers to confirm or refute the author's assertions. ("Scholars cannot but be disturbed by the fact that one still encounters instances of arbitrary handling of the texts of published sources, even instances of 'editing.' ")

In calling for greater respect toward "authentic factual data," Smirnov points out: "In publishing the 'Letter to Comrades on Our Organizational Tasks,' Lenin observed in the notes that this letter had already become completely public property and that 'after my opponents expressed the desire more than once to use this letter as a document, I would consider any changes in it on my part in the course of republication as even—how can one express it more mildly?—embarrassing.' " As Fainsod puts it, "one cannot help wondering whether there might arise in sustained form among the new generation of 'archive rats' the desire to know and to tell the truth."

27. *Pravda,* January 28, 1957.

28. Moscow: Foreign Languages Publishing House, 1960. Glezerman writes in his introduction: "This book derives from a set of lectures and seminars for postgraduates of the Philosophy Faculty of Moscow University and the Philosophy Department of the Academy of Social Sciences of the Central Committee, C.P.S.U."

29. *Ibid.,* p. 259.

30. Mao's theoreticians seem to have the same difficulties as Khrushchev's. A report in the *New York Times* for September 14, 1964, indicates the scope of the problem:

"Ideological documents reaching Hong Kong indicate that Peking is undertaking the most far-reaching repression of intellectuals since its anti-rightist campaign of 1958.

"The most prominent victim of the drive on intellectuals has been Yang Hsien-chen, a member of the party's Central Committee. He has been accused of stating revisionist views in lectures before the Higher Party School between November 1961 and last April. The school is the party's major ideological study institution.

"On the surface, the struggle against 'revisionist' intellectuals has taken the form of a theoretical-sounding philosophical debate over the nature of a dialectical materialism, the Communist view of history as an ideological tug of war.

"Mr. Yang is said to interpret the basic law of social development to mean that things 'Unite, two into one'—that forces merge, rather than clash. Chairman Mao takes the opposing view—that things 'divide one into two.'

"In advocating 'two into one,' it is argued, Mr. Yang is favoring the termination of the class struggle, a reconciliation with the modern revisionists of the Soviet Union and the acceptance of the gradual disappearance of antagonism between Communist and capitalist states.

"The 'one into two' theory insists that the struggle with Soviet revisionists and the East-West conflict are unreconcilable, that class struggle in all forms must be waged to its end."

31. *Voprosy filosofii*, no. 10, 1958.

32. Robert W. Campbell, "Some Recent Changes in Soviet Economic Policy," *World Politics*, October 1956, p. 8.

33. Actually in the theoretical discussions among Western socialist economists in the 1930's, particularly in the writings of Oskar Lange and A. P. Lerner, the idea had long been accepted that a market economy was indispensable to socialist planning. In fact Lange went so far as to argue that under capitalism a true market economy was impossible because of monopolies, and only under socialism would one have the free shifting of resources. These views were rejected in the Soviet Union, where the dogmatism of a centrally controlled economy was frozen under Stalinist practice. See *On the Economic Theory of Socialism*, ed. Benjamin Lippincott (Minneapolis, 1938).

34. N. S. Khrushchev, "Report to the 21st Congress of the C.P.S.U.," in the *Current Digest of the Soviet Press*, vol. XX, no. 5, March 11, 1959. A comprehensive analysis of the Draft Programme and the issues of the future Communist society is contained in *Survey*, no. 38, October 1961. See also George A. Brinkley, "The 'Withering' of the State under Khrushchev," *The Review of Politics*, January 1961.

35. The discussion of parallels, formally in method and substantively in categories, between Soviet philosophy and Catholic scholasticism, while relevant to our problem, is far beyond the scope of this paper. For an outline of these parallels, see Gustave Wetter, *Dialectical Materialism*, pp. 555–56. For a critique, see Franz Borkenau, "A Thomist on Leninism," *The Twentieth Century*, February 1954.

36. For example, an article in *Izvestia*, April 7, 1962, entitled "Economic Reflections: Are Experiments Needed Only in Physics?" by R. Levin. In this article the author remarks that "he envies the engineers, the technicians and designers." When a problem arises in technology, the scientists are allowed to experiment, but when, as he recalls from a meeting of the Estonian economic council, a report was received that a plant had suffered a drop in production because of an innovation in wage incentives, the answer is "We must put an end to experimenting." But, he asks, "can the young economic science of socialism do without experiments" in creating "new forms for the economic organization of society?" And, having established his baseline, the writer proceeds to offer some simple but biting comments on the "extreme centralization of distribution" in the U.S.S.R.

37. The text of Professor Parin's article is worth citing in some detail: "In all

178

this history of science there has probably not been another time as eventful as ours... No sooner is the universe created anew in the mind than it, the 'new' one, turns out to be subject to demolition. Indeed a single generation of mankind has had to assimilate the idea of the theory of relativity, relativistic wave-particles, anti-matter, the key to the 'code' of nucleic acids, the theory of automatic regulation, radiations emanating from distant 'exploding' galaxies, and much else....

"Of course the great innovator in physiology, founder of an original (experimental!) trend in science did not imagine that his works would be turned into a hybrid of a prayer book and a bludgeon to intimidate heretics. In 1950, however, some of I. P. Pavlov's students proclaimed themselves monopoly holders of truth.... The argument was conducted less with facts obtained in experiments than with out-of-context quotations from the works of the great physiologist; and administrative pressure was sometimes used as the chief argument....

"The time is coming when younger researchers will gradually replace the scientists of my generation who now direct the research staffs. We ourselves are training our successors. But to teach a person the methods of experimental work, mathematical calculation and finally the skill of analyzing the collected facts is to stop half-way. Real scientific thought, which it is our duty to develop in every one of our pupils of today, would be based on high ethical principles. Real science is boldly invading the unknown, exploring it, constantly improving the instruments and methods of research. It does not hide beyond the authority of yesterday's great scientists or today's veteran scientific executives.

"... Truth is born in the clash of views, in heated creative discussion. However dear the scientist holds the viewpoint... he must be able for truth's sake to renounce his own reasoning [if necessary]. It is impermissible to enforce it by compulsion, by administrative influence, for in that case the personal clash may develop into a social clash. Science breathes only one air, the oxygen of facts."

In language less hortatory, but even more directly polemical, the famous Russian physicist Peter Kapitza, in an article, "Theory, Experiment, Practice," written about the same time, denounced those dialectical materialists who hampered the development of cybernetics, quantum theory, the resonance theory of chemistry, and the theory of relativity. (*Ekonomicheskaya Gazeta*, March 26, 1962.)

38. Gustave Wetter, *Dialectical Materialism*, p. 556.

39. *Istoriya Velikoi Otechestvennoi Voiny Sov. Soyuza*, I, 439, cited in Alexander Werth, *Russia At War 1941–1945* (New York, 1964), p. 134. My colleague Alexander Dallin, the director of the Russian Institute at Columbia University, has written to me in this connection: "I have been impressed lately by the extent to which 'declassified' disputes and dialogues have been going on in virtually every field of Soviet scholarship and practice. I suspect that the cumulative effect on the young generation must be strikingly different from that of the Stalinist past: no more single answers but licit diversity, uncertainty or reluctant tolerance.... Thomas W. Wolfe in his book [*Soviet Strategy at the Crossroads* (Cambridge, Mass., 1964)] does a fine job of documenting the many basic areas of difference among the military, and between the military and civilian elites, on strategic doctrine, etc. In a recent Soviet book on international law, I found, for the first time in my own experience, the systematic listing in the footnotes of all the disagreements among Soviet specialists (such as: 'Romaskin says...; Tunkin, on the contrary, wrote that...'). There are more

and more areas where the Soviet specialists that one meets are quite frank to say that the official theoretical analysis is of no use, or is not being applied. . . . In regard to Africa, for example, Soviet theorists no longer seem at all concerned about the efforts to demonstrate the rise of class consciousness among the Bantu proletariat, let alone act on the basis of 'class analysis' of African societies." (Private correspondence, October 1, 1964.)

40. *Science and Freedom,* Proceedings of the Hamburg Conference, Congress for Cultural Freedom (London, 1955), pp. 225–26.

41. K. Zeleniskii, "Literature and Future Man," *Voprosy Literatury,* February 1962.

42. There are now at least four Soviet journals devoted to cybernetics. *Problemy Kibernetikii* (ed. A. A. Lyapunov), first published in 1958, appears twice-yearly in hard cover volumes and is the main repository for new work on theoretical cybernetics. (It is now translated into English.) *Kibernetikii Sbornik* contains translations of Western works. *Tekhnicheskaya Kibernetika* is devoted to engineering problems in the information and control areas, and is published in the United States as *Engineering Cybernetics. Probl. Pered. Inf.* ("Problems of the Transmission of Information"), formerly a monograph series, became a journal in 1965.

43. In 1961, the Twenty-Second Congress of the C.P.S.U. emphasized that cybernetics, computers, and control systems must be introduced on a large scale in industry, research, planning and management.

44. For a review of the debates on this question, see C. Olgin, "Soviet Ideology and Cybernetics," *Bulletin* of the Institute for the Study of the USSR, February 1962. I have also drawn on an unpublished essay by Michael Arbib, surveying the development of cybernetics in the Soviet Union.

45. For a comprehensive review of these efforts, as well as a sampling of recent Russian writing, see Patricia Blake and Max Hayward (eds.), *Dissonant Voices in Soviet Literature* (New York, 1961), and, by the same editors, *Half-Way to the Moon: New Writings from Russia* (New York, 1963). See also Priscilla Johnson (ed.), *Khrushchev and the Arts: The Politics of Soviet Culture, 1962–1964* (Cambridge, Mass., 1965). This book contains the resolutions of the special plenum on ideology and the arts held by the Central Committee of the Communist Party in June 1963, as well as a variety of other documents that reflect the cultural debates of that crucial period.

46. Solzhenitsyn is the author of the novel about a Stalinist prison camp, *One Day in the Life of Ivan Denisovich;* it was written in 1959, but was allowed to appear in print only in November 1962. Aksenov, who was born in 1932, has written stories about Soviet youth that have been immensely popular among the younger generation but were attacked by conservative critics as portraying Soviet youth as *stilyagi*—Teddy boys. Dudintsev's novel, *Not By Bread Alone,* drew a startled response in Russia with its unflattering portrait of the Soviet bureaucrats. Paustovsky, one of the older generation of Russian writers, has been probably the most outspoken in his condemnation of the repressions of the past. In a remarkable act, he evaded the regular censorship by gathering an anthology of young Russian writing and having it printed in the provinces as *Tarusa Pages.* Nekrasov, a Stalin Prize novelist, provoked Khrushchev to an open attack when his travel essays *On Both Sides of the Ocean* appeared. He was attacked for mocking the clichés in Soviet movies ("the old worker with greying moustaches who understands all and has a clear answer for everything") and for his plea

for non-ideological descriptions. Voznesensky, a protégé of Pasternak, is among the most popular poets in the Soviet Union. Advance orders for his last book of verse, *The Triangular Pear* (1962), reached 100,000 two months before its publication. Yevtushenko, of course, has become the symbol of the young Soviet writers, passionate in their affirmations about Russia, accusatory about the past, and skeptical about the present. Yevtushenko himself is something of a grandstand player, yet despite his exhibitionist streak there is a deep undercurrent of moral fervor and concern for free expression. (The information in this note is adapted from the notes in the two volumes by Blake and Hayward.)

47. The speech was first reported, in somewhat garbled form, in *Literaturnaya Gazeta* (October 27, 1956) and was later printed in full in the French *L'Express* (March 22, 1957). An English text is available in the volume edited by Hugh McLean and Walter Vickery, *The Year of Protest, 1956* (New York, 1961), pp. 155–60.

48. Alexander Gerschenkron, "The Changeability of a Dictatorship," *World Politics,* July 1964, pp. 597–98. One finds the same attitude in almost all the Communist countries of Eastern Europe. As a Czech writer remarks in *Survey* (No. 51, April 1964, p. 86), "To them [the new generation] ideology and politics, and, indeed, any form of public activity are a lot of bunk, just hollow words with little relation to reality. Not that they are anti-Communists, a meaningless term in their ears; they just could not care less. They were born into socialism and they live in socialism and what they see around *is* socialism. Pretty dull and shabby, and certainly nothing to write here about."

49. Barrington Moore, *Soviet Politics: The Dilemma of Power* (Cambridge, Mass., 1950), especially chapters 7 and 8. For an illuminating discussion of this problem, see, also, Alex Inkeles, "Social Change in Soviet Russia," in Berger, Abel, and Page (eds.), *Freedom and Control in Modern Society* (New York, 1954).

50. Alexander Werth, *Russia at War 1941–1945,* p. 183. Werth (p. 188) tells of meeting a Glasgow Communist, John Gibbons, who since 1939 had been working for Moscow Radio: "During the grim winter of 1941–1942, he was to suffer deeply from having tea without sugar and only a piece of dry bread while his boss on Moscow Radio, with a higher-category ration card, was in the same office eating ham and eggs. *'It's part of the system,'* he would say, 'and no doubt they are right, but it was bloody unpleasant to *smell* the ham and eggs. All the more so as the boss *thought it was quite normal,* and never even offered me a scrap of the ham.'" (First and third italics mine, second in the original.)

51. Robert V. Daniels, "Soviet Thought in the Nineteen-Thirties," *Indiana Slavic Studies,* vol. 1 (1956).

52. There is the story, of course, of the three groups of theologians, one of which argued that there were complete logical proofs for the existence of God, one of which argued that there could be no logical proofs of the existence of God, and one which declared that the truth lay somewhere in the middle.

53. *The New Soviet Society,* annotated by Herbert Ritvo (New York, 1962), p. 115.

54. Many of these difficulties underlay Khrushchev's division of the Communist Party, one part guiding the agricultural sector, the other the industrial sector— a move revoked by his successors.

55. Emile Durkheim, *The Division of Labor,* p. 28.

56. As Talcott Parsons has observed: "In the U.S.S.R. the primary problem

concerns the long-run status of the Communist Party—can this quasi-religious structure remain differentiated from the 'State' and still maintain a tight control over it? This question involves both the status of religion (in the more analytical sense) and the possibilities of relaxing control in the direction of political democratization. The major problem is closely linked to the latter—it is a question of genuine autonomy, relative to both party and state, of non-political spheres of organization; notably both of the economy, and of the professions and the services in which they are involved. At present, the most acute focus of tendencies to seek this type of autonomy is the 'intellectuals'—in what sense may science and the arts be treated as the simple handmaidens of the Party?" Talcott Parsons, "Differentiation and Variation in Social Structures" in *Theories of Society* (New York, 1961), p. 263.

57. For a discussion of the theme of the "end of ideology" as it relates to the Communist world, see the essay by Michael Polanyi, *Beyond Nihilism,* Eddington Memorial Lecture (New York and London, 1960). For a general discussion of the theme, see this writer's *The End of Ideology,* revised ed. (New York, 1965), especially the epilogue.

58. With such a conclusion, this may also be the place to clear up some misunderstandings about the theme. The "end of ideology," as the term has been used by this writer, Raymond Aron, Edward Shils, and others does not mean the end of "belief-systems" or the "end of ideals." If, in the West, ideologies in the form of mobilized creeds have been types of "secular religions," then the end of ideology—either because the creeds have lost their truth value, or because the movements sustaining them have become exhausted—means, in effect, an end to the "war of beliefs," to *politique à outrance*. (As, in a sense, the end of the Thirty Years War signalled an end to the "wars of religion.")

As applied to Western politics, the theme of the "end of ideology" means that the conflicts which characterized these societies—the traditional divisions of "left" and "right"—have changed from "ideological politics" to "civil politics." In fine, it is not that political differences and distinctions no longer exist, but that the *way* in which these differences are fought—in the past often a "war to the death," at least on the rhetorical level—has changed.

Whether a similar change in the "creedal wars" between the Western democratic societies and the Soviet and East European countries is possible, is the underlying problem of this paper. In political fact, such "wars" may diminish because of the rise of a third power, China, which threatens both. But such political questions apart, there is a basis, I think, as the doctrinaire certitudes of ideology fade, for new attitudes to emerge, and for a new form of discussion to appear. For the strongest pull is the intellectual one, the membership in the "open community" of science and the "open community" of literature— the free community of one's peers. And this, I think, is the commitment of scientists and intellectuals in all countries, East and West, who give proud allegiance to those ideals.

Marxist Economics in Retrospect and Prospect

1. *Selected Correspondence of Marx and Engels* (London, 1934), p. 472.

2. Ricardo has been blamed for having prepared the ground for Marx. H. S. Foxwell, the Cambridge economist and famous collector of rare economic books,

wrote inside the cover of his copy of Ricardo's *Principles:* "The first edition of this disastrous book, which gave us Marxian socialism and the class war." The copy is now part of the Foxwell collection in the Kress Library at the Harvard Business School.

3. The English edition of Böhm-Bawerk's essay was republished by Paul M. Sweezy (New York, 1949) together with a reply to Böhm-Bawerk by the Austrian Marxist Rudolf Hilferding (who later went to Germany and served twice as Minister of Finance under the Weimar Republic). Böhm-Bawerk's essay runs to over a hundred pages. As Sweezy points out, the English title is not a correct translation of the German original "Zum Abschluss des Marxschen System." The latter simply means "On the Conclusion of the Marxian System" and does not convey the impression of an obituary.

4. In the third edition of his *Geschichte und Kritik der Kapitalzinstheorien* (Innsbruck, 1914) Böhm-Bawerk refers to Hilferding's reply. He is quite justified in rejecting it as evasive and unsatisfactory. As Paul Samuelson points out ("Wages and Interest: A Modern Dissection of Marxian Economic Models," *The American Economic Review,* vol. 47, Dec. 1957, pp. 884–912), some Marxists seem to believe that L. von Bortkiewicz, who has dealt extensively with the problem of "Value and Price in the Marxian System" (see especially an English translation of his article under this title in *International Economic Papers,* no. 2, 1952), "ended up justifying Marx." Samuelson shows that Bortkiewicz's theory does not "differ essentially from the conventional 'discounted' productivity theories. . . . subscribed to by Taussig, Wicksell, Böhm-Bawerk, and non-Austrians."

On Bortkiewicz compare the volume by Paul Sweezy quoted above and Schumpeter, *History of Economic Analysis* (New York, 1954). For the unwary reader, Bortkiewicz could easily give the impression that he stood on the side of Marx as against his critics including Böhm-Bawerk, because (elsewhere) he criticized the latter's theory of interest unmercifully. Schumpeter remarks (p. 907 n): "The interesting thing about the latter [Bortkiewicz's criticisms of Böhm-Bawerk] is its spirit of uncompromising hostility that differs so strikingly from the spirit he displayed in his famous critical pieces on Marx."

Schumpeter described Bortkiewicz as a "comma hunter" whose criticism often was "directed towards details" (p. 851 n). This certainly was true of Bortkiewicz's criticism of Böhm-Bawerk's theory of interest, which was fully cleared up by Böhm-Bawerk himself in a lengthy reply in the third and fourth edition of his *Kapital und Kapitalzins,* now also available in English.

5. "Wages and Interest . . ."

6. Samuelson's conclusions do not, however, depend on the fixed coefficient and linearity assumption.

7. Böhm-Bawerk did not deal with the dynamic theories of Marx.

8. On the labor theory as a source of inefficiency in Russian planning and the methods actually used see Abram Bergson's authoritative book, *The Economics of Socialist Planning* (New Haven, 1964), especially the concluding chapter.

9. Another area where, in the interest of economic efficiency, the Soviet Government and even more so the European satellites have moved in the direction of bourgeois economics is international trade. For a good discussion of this trend, the discovery or rediscovery, usually in a disguised form, of the principle of comparative cost, see Alan A. Brown, "Centrally Planned Foreign Trade and

Economic Efficiency," *The American Economist,* vol. V, no. 2 (November 1961).

10. Numerous examples of correct and incorrect forecasts can be found in Leopold Schwarzschild's unsympathetic biography, *Karl Marx: The Red Prussian* (New York, 1947), e.g., pp. 308 ff. But the sympathetic and apologetic biography by Franz Mehring, *Karl Marx: The Story of His Life* (the "official" German Socialist biography first published in 1918 with numerous editions and translations) also relates many examples.

11. See William Fellner, *Emergence and Content of Modern Economic Analysis* (New York, 1960), chapter 12, "Marxian Socialism," for a lucid interpretation of the tendencies postulated by Marx in terms of modern economic analysis. Fellner shows what kind of (most unrealistic) factual assumptions one would have to make to deduce a tendency for falling wages.

12. An exception is Jürgen Kuczinski, one of the leading economists of the Soviet zone of Germany. In numerous publications, some of which were written in the United States for the American Federation of Labor, Kuczinski tries to show that the "relative position" of labor has drastically deteriorated from 1860 until now and that the "real" real wages have hardly gone up. See for example *A Short History of Labour Conditions Under Industrial Capitalism,* Volume Two, *The United States of America 1789 to the Present Day* (London, 1943).

13. As a modern example take E. März, *Die Marxsche Wirtschaftslehre in Widerstreit der Meinungen* (Vienna, 1959). Kuczinski shifts back and forth between the absolute and relative interpretation.

14. This has baffled many writers. Some try to give reasons why that should necessarily be the case (e.g., N. Kaldor), others regard it as a statistical accident.

15. All this shows that the Marxist theory of the increasing polarization of society into rich and poor, capitalists and proletariat, is simply not true. In political terms, for obvious strategic reasons, Marxist parties everywhere have tended to broaden the concept of the proletariat so as to attract the votes of the middle classes or even large parts of farmers (small landowners).

16. On this see W. Fellner, *Emergence and Content* . . .

17. See the book by E. März mentioned above for an attempt to uphold the purity of the Marxist doctrine. For a non-Marxist economist it would be easy to specify factual (though hardly realistic) assumptions which would produce the Marxist results. What one has to do is to introduce a third type of income, e.g., Ricardian rent, which can be made to expand at the expense of both wages and profits. But Marx did not do this, because it would clash with other parts of his system.

18. "Marxism: A Talk to Students," *Monthly Review,* October 1958.

19. See his *Development and Underdevelopment,* National Bank of Egypt Fiftieth Anniversary Commemoration Lecture (Cairo, 1956). Needless to say, Myrdal's policy conclusions differ from those of the Marxists.

20. I myself have attempted to review the whole problem and to give a comprehensive criticism of the theory in "Terms of Trade and Economic Development," in *Economic Development for Latin America,* ed. H. S. Ellis (London, 1961), pp. 275–303, and in *International Trade and Economic Development* (Cairo, 1959). A large part of the literature was recently reviewed by T. Morgan, "Trends in Terms of Trade and Their Repercussions on Primary Producers," in *International Trade Theory in a Developing World,* ed. Roy Harrod (London, 1963), pp. 52–95.

The latest careful, statistical analysis of price trends in international trade is contained in Robert E. Lipsey's important book, *Price and Quantity Trends in the Foreign Trade of the U.S.* (Princeton, 1963). This study, carried out with the extreme care concerning the reliability of the basic data, statistical methods, and theoretical analysis which one expects from a National Bureau of Economic Research publication, reaches the following conclusion (p. 76):

"Two widely held beliefs regarding net barter terms of trade found no confirmation in the data for the United States. One is that there has been a substantial long-term improvement in the terms of trade of developed countries, including the United States [which is the implied obverse of the theory criticized in the text]; the other, that there has been a significant long-term deterioration in the terms of trade of primary as compared to manufactured products. Although there have been very large swings in U.S. terms of trade since 1879, no long-run trend has emerged. The average level of U.S. terms of trade since World War II has been almost the same as before World War I."

21. Technically the period 1929–39 covers two severe depressions, 1929–33 and 1937–38. But the business cycle "upswing" in between (1933–37) was not much of a prosperity period and did not reduce the unemployment percentage below fourteen per cent (annual average 1937).

22. I personally think that from the analytical standpoint (abstracting from policy impact and popular influence, including the impact on the economic profession) Keynes' theory did not constitute in Pigou's words, "a revolution," although "Keynes made a very important, original and valuable addition to the armoury of economic analysis." See A. C. Pigou, *Keynes's 'General Theory': A Retrospective View* (London and New York, 1953), pp. 65–66, and my essays, "The General Theory After Ten Years" and "Sixteen Years Later" in R. Lekachman (ed.), *Keynes' General Theory: Reports of Three Decades* (New York, 1964).

23. For some further details see my "Integration and Growth of the World Economy in Historical Perspective," *The American Economic Review,* vol. LIV, no. 2, Mar. 1964, part I, pp. 7–10.

24. On this compare the monumental volume—monumental not merely in size!—of Milton Friedman and Anna J. Schwartz, *Monetary History of the United States 1867–1960* (Princeton, 1964). Their interpretation of those particular episodes should be convincing even for those who do not go along with the authors' bolder and broader generalizations concerning the predominant role of the quantity of money even in mild short-run fluctuations.

Communist Economic Planning vs. Capitalism as a Model for Development

1. H. W. Singer, "The Distribution of Gains Between Investing and Borrowing Countries," *American Economic Review,* May 1950, pp. 473–85.

2. *Ibid.*

3. United Nations, *Yearbook of National Accounts Statistics, 1961* (New York, 1961) and Leon A. Mears, "Indonesia," *Economic Development: Analysis and Case Studies,* Adamantios Pepelasis, *et al.* ed. (New York, 1961), pp. 418–67.

4. Charles P. Kindleberger, *The Terms of Trade; a European Case Study* (New York, 1956).

5. The point is that both the income and the price elasticities of demand

for food are less than one. There are various empirical studies which have demonstrated the truth of this statement. See, for instance, Richard Stone, *The Measurement of Consumer's Expenditure and Behavior in the United Kingdom 1925-1938*, Vol. 1, Cambridge University Press, 1954.

6. Raul Prebisch, *National Policy for Economic Welfare* (New York, 1955), p. 13.

7. Gottfried Haberler, "Critical Observations on Some Current Notions in the Theory of Economic Development," *L'Industria*, no. 2, 1957.

8. A. N. McLeod, "Trade and Investment in Underdeveloped Areas: a Comment," *American Economic Review*, June 1951, pp. 411–19.

9. Haberler, "Critical Observations..." See also Austin Robinson, "The Changing Structure of the British Economy," *Economic Journal*, Sept. 1954.

10. See United Nations, *Economic Development of Latin America and Its Principal Problems* (New York, 1950).

11. Singer, "Distribution of Gains..."

12. Gottfried Haberler in *Review of Economics and Statistics*, Supplement, Feb. 1958, p. 5.

13. See Prebisch, *National Policy...*; the United Nations 1950 study on Latin America cited earlier; and United Nations, *Latin America* and *Relative Prices of Exports and Imports of Under-developed Countries* (New York, 1949).

14. *Economic Development & Cultural Change*, Oct. 1959. Two charts on the British terms of trade in 1876–1948 and 1801–1953 are presented in the Morgan article.

15. *The Terms of Trade...*

16. Nicholas Spulber, *The Economics of Communist Eastern Europe* (Cambridge, Mass., 1957). See also G. Warren Nutter, *Growth of Industrial Production in the Soviet Union* (Princeton, N. J., 1962).

17. Derived from Abram Bergson and Simon Kuznets, eds., *Economic Trends in the Soviet Union* (Cambridge, Mass., 1963) and *Yearbook of National Accounts Statistics*, 1961 (New York, 1961).

18. Y. L. Wu, *The Steel Industry in Communist China* (New York, 1965).

19. C. J. Staller, "Fluctuations in Economic Activity; Planned and Free Market Economies, 1950–60," *American Economic Review*, June 1964, pp. 385–95.

20. A similar story may be told of Communist China. Table 1 below presents measures of fluctuations shown in the data on Communist China which were not available to Staller and which are now computed by the same two methods* used by Staller in order to facilitate comparison. The results are placed alongside the corresponding mean values of the eight planned economies (excluding Communist China). With the exception of construction output, two sets of figures are employed for all three indicators; namely, total output, industrial output, and agricultural production. The first set consists of 1) the "net material product," 2) the gross value output of modern industry, and 3) the gross value output of agriculture, as given in official Communist Chinese statistics and

---

* Method I measures the standard error of the least squares fit of the series Y_t/Y_{t-1} to time. Method II measures the antilog of the square root of the logarithmic variance of the series Y_t/Y_{t-1} with unity subtracted from the antilog, i.e.,

$$\text{antilog} \sqrt{\frac{\Sigma[\log(Y_t/Y_{t-1}) - \frac{1}{N}\Sigma\log(Y_t/Y_{t-1})]^2}{N}} - 1.$$

TABLE 1

	Total Output			Agriculture			Industry			Construction	
	Communist China				Communist China			Communist China			Communist China
	Mean of 8 Planned Economies (Staller) 1950–60	Official Data 1951–57	Estimate of Gross Domestic Product (ours) 1952–62	Mean of 8 Planned Economies (Staller) 1950–60	Official Data of Gross Value Output 1951–57	Estimate of Gross Value-Added (ours) 1952–62	Mean of 8 Planned Economies (Staller) 1950–60	Official Data on Gross Value Output of Modern Industry 1951–57	Estimate of Gross Value-Added (ours) 1952–62	Mean of 8 Planned Economies (Staller) 1950–60	Estimate of Gross Value-Added (Liu & Yeh) 1952–57
Method I	6.5	4.6	15.0	12.3	3.6	6.3	4.2	9.8	28.4	11.9	25.7
Method II	5.7	5.7	17.5	11.5	3.9	7.0	4.2	10.1	44.7	10.7	21.9

Source: Table 2.

TABLE 2

	Official Data					Estimated Data		
Year	Derived Values of Net Material Product [1]	Gross Value Output of Modern Industry [2]	Gross Value Output of Agriculture [3]	Construction (Gross Value-Added) [4]	Year	Gross Domestic Product [5]	Gross Value-Added in Modern Industry [6]	Gross Value-Added in Agriculture [7]
				(Billions of 1952 Yuan)				
1951	50.10	159.1	419.7	...	1952	75.6	9.4	35.9
1952	61.25	220.5	483.9	2.06	1953	78.9	11.8	35.6
1953	69.83	288.1	499.1	2.56	1954	82.2	13.8	35.4
1954	73.75	339.8	515.7	3.01	1955	86.1	15.1	36.4
1955	78.58	370.8	555.4	3.29	1956	96.6	19.8	37.6
1956	89.61	503.4	582.9	5.59	1957	100.0	21.9	38.1
1957	93.71	556.3	603.5	5.20	1958	110.7	27.1	39.3
					1959	119.1	37.7	37.0
					1960	120.7	45.3	31.0
					1961	82.1	17.1	33.6
					1962	109.0	25.6	34.4

Notes: (1) Various official sources cited in Yuan-li Wu et al., *The Economic Potential of Communist China*, Vol. I, Stanford Research Institute, 1963, p. 156.
(2) *Great Ten Years*, 1959, Peking, p. 80.
(3) *Idem.*, p. 104.
(4) Ta-chung Liu and Kung-chia Yeh. *The Economy of the Chinese Mainland: National Income and Economic Development, 1933–1959*, Vol. I, The RAND Corporation, Calif., p. 236.
(5) For the data of 1952–61, see Yuan-li Wu et al., *op. cit.*, Vol. III, p. 241; For 1962 data see, Yuan-li Wu et al., *op. cit.*, Vol. III, p. 120.
(6) *Ibid.*; for 1962, see Yuan-li Wu et al., *op. cit.*, Vol. III, p. 119. See also Fred C. Hung and Yuan-li Wu, "Conceptual Difficulties in Measuring China's Industrial Output" *Industrial Development in Communist China*, Edited by Choh-ming Li, Frederick A. Praeger, Inc., 1964, pp. 56–64.
(7) *Ibid.*

derived from official statements. The second set consists of the author's estimates of the "gross domestic product" and the gross value-added in the sectors of modern industry and agriculture respectively. Details concerning the latter estimates, available elsewhere,** are not given. The first set covers the period of 1951–57 only while the second set spans an eleven-year period—from 1952 to 1962 inclusive—which is identical in length to Staller's series. For construction output, we present a series of gross value-added developed by T. C. Liu and K. C. Yeh for 1952–57 only. Credit should also be given to Liu and Yeh for certain basic estimates which served as a starting point in the longer series worked out since their study. To facilitate reference, the original data (at constant 1952 prices) used in computing the fluctuations are presented in Table 2.

The seven years covered in the first three series of official data without adjustment include the first five year plan (1953–57), as well as two of the first years of the Communist regime (established in 1949) which are usually designated as the period of economic rehabilitation. Excluded are the period of the "Great Leap Forward" (1958 to early 1960) and the subsequent "Great Depression" (1961 to the first half of 1962). These series tend, therefore, to underestimate the degree of fluctuations actually experienced in the Chinese economy. The measures of fluctuation based on them are given here only to offer a rough comparison with Staller's data which are based on similar sources in the other planned economies. Fluctuations based on the 1952–62 series are believed to be a more faithful portrayal of the actual course of Chinese economic development under the present regime since the initiation of centralized planning.

21. Compared with the other planned economies, according to our estimates, Communist China had a fluctuation "index" of 15 (method 1) and 17.5 (method 11) in total output during 1952–62 as against Yugoslavia's 11.8 (method 1) and 11.0 (method 11) respectively, which were closest to the Chinese figures. In agricultural output, Communist China registered the scores of 6.3 (method 1) and 7.0 (method 11) as compared with an equal value of 6.3 for the Soviet Union (method 1) and 6.4 for East Germany (method 11). Communist China left the next contender (Yugoslavia) among the other planned economies far behind in the violence of her industrial fluctuations (28.4 according to method 1 and 44.7 according to method 11 versus Yugoslavia's 6.2 and 7.2 respectively).

22. For a fuller discussion see the *Economic Potential of Communist China* (Menlo Park, Calif.: Stanford Research Institute, 1963).

23. Ye. Liberman, "Once More on the Plan, Profits and Bonuses," *Pravda,* Sept. 20, 1964, as translated in *The Current Digest of the Soviet Press,* vol. XVI, no. 38, p. 20.

24. *Chi-hua Ching-chi* (Planned Economy), no. 8, Aug. 1958, pp. 21–23.

Marxism and the Underdeveloped Countries

---

1. Marxism, Marxism-Leninism, Leninism and communism are closely related but not identical concepts. I shall use Marxism largely to refer to general Marxist ideas; Marxism-Leninism to Lenin's extension of these ideas; Leninism to specifi-

---

** See the sources cited in Table 2.

cally Leninist ideas; and communism chiefly to political, practical and organizational matters. The distinctions are at times imprecise but this nowhere affects the substantive argument.

2. In current usage, which I shall follow, the term underdeveloped, a synonym for poor (generally with political overtones), covers almost the whole of Asia, Africa, and Latin America and also parts of the Mediterranean basin, a vast and heterogeneous aggregate with well over half the world's population.

3. *The Political Economy of Growth* (New York, 1957), pp. 249–50.

4. The most widely used conventional national-income statistics vastly exaggerate the difference in incomes and standards of living between rich and poor countries. This has been known for some time. A systematic discussion, both of the extent of exaggeration and the reasons for it, is to be found in an article by Dr. D. Usher: "The Transport Bias in Comparisons of National Income," *Economica*, May 1963. He writes (p. 140): "For example, the conventional comparison shows that the per capita national income of the United Kingdom is about 14 times that of Thailand. Recomputations made by the author to allow for various biases in the comparison suggest that the effective ratio of living standards is about three to one. Even if the recomputed ratio is doubled, the change in order of magnitude is large enough to affect our way of thinking about the underdeveloped countries." This obviously bears on comparisons of income levels and rates of progress.

5. In recent years local production of some commodities (e.g., cigarettes) has replaced imports; this does not affect the argument of the text.

6. It is certainly true that throughout the underdeveloped world the most backward areas are those outside the market system with few or no external contacts. Yet Baran writes (p. 248): "The dilemma that the majority of mankind faces today is either to liberate itself from both [monopoly capitalism] or to be cut down by them to the size of the crippling clogs."

7. London, 1926. Quotation from pp. 8–9.

8. London, 1942. Quotation from p. 283.

9. Cambridge, 1948. Quotation from p. 297.

10. *Africa Must Unite* (London, 1963), p. xiii. This book is published in a series called Heinemann Educational Books. Elsewhere he wrote: "The contradictions among the various foreign groups and the colonial imperialist powers in their struggle for sources of raw materials and their territories. In this sense imperialism and colonialism become the export of capital to sources of raw materials, the frenzied and heartless struggle for monopolist possession of these sources, the struggle for a redivision of the already divided world—a struggle waged with particular fury by new financial groups and powers seeking newer territories and colonies against the old groups and powers which cling tightly to that which they have grabbed. The contradictions between the handful of ruling 'civilized' nations and the millions of colonial peoples of the world. In this sense imperialism is the most degrading exploitation and the most inhuman oppression of the millions of people living in the colonies. The purpose of this exploitation and oppression is to squeeze out super-profits ... The dominance of finance capital in the advanced capitalist countries; the export of capital to the sources of raw materials (imperialism) and the omnipotence of a financial oligarchy (finance capital) reveal the character of monopolist capital which quickens the revolt of the intelligentsia and the working class elements of the

colonies against imperialism and brings them to the national liberation movement as their only salvation. The increase in the export of capital to the
colonies; the extension of 'spheres of influence' and colonial formation of
capitalism into a world system of financial enslavement and colonial oppression
and exploitation of a vast majority of the population of the earth by a few
handfuls of the so-called 'civilized' nations. The monopolistic possession of
'spheres of influence' and colonies; the uneven development of the different
capitalist countries leading to a frenzied struggle between the countries which
'have' and the countries which 'have not.' Thus war becomes the only method
of restoring the disturbed 'equilibrium'." *Towards Colonial Freedom* (London,
1947), pp. 34–5.

11. *Africa Must Unite,* pp. xiii, 173, 184.

12. In maintaining law and order and establishing a transport system and
public utilities, the colonial powers have fostered material progress in Africa and
Asia by encouraging the inflow of administrative, commercial, and technical skills
as well as capital. These results were explicitly, although somewhat unexpectedly,
recognized by the representative of Liberia at the United Nations on the
accession of Ghana to the United Nations as a sovereign state. He said: "The
remarkable development of the state of Ghana while it was under guardianship
provides a unique example of what can be accomplished through the processes
of mutual cooperation and good will among peoples" (speech at the General
Assembly, March 8, 1957).

13. Moscow, 1962. Quotation from pp. 14–15.

14. To quote Potekhin again (pp. 15–17): "The aim is to close all the channels
through which national income is leaking out of Africa. The governments of
many African countries have already tackled this problem. Let us enumerate
some of the principal measures directed towards the elimination of 'financial
haemorrhage': nationalization of enterprises belonging to foreign companies;
compulsory reinvestment of a part of foreign companies' profits; higher taxation
of profits; establishment of national banks and insurance companies; setting up
of their own maritime shipping and air fleet; and state control over exports,
imports and foreign exchange transactions. Little has been done so far, and this
is quite understandable as the majority of African countries won political
independence just two or three years ago... There is a question pertaining to
both aspects of our problem: which is to be preferred—private capitalist enterprise
or the setting up of state-owned establishments? To our mind, the latter has
every advantage as compared to private enterprises. Briefly, these advantages are
reduced to the following: the establishment of state-owned enterprises ensures an
incomparably higher rate of economic development than private enterprise; it
is the most reliable way of closing the channels for the leakage of national
income abroad and the surest means of eliminating the dominance of foreign
monopolies. Taking into account the extreme weakness of private national
capital in nearly all the countries of the continent, it should be admitted that
it is only the setting up of a state-owned sector in the economy that will ensure
economic independence in a short space of time."

15. As other Marxist-Leninist writers, Academician Potekhin seems to imply
that the absence of a local capital-goods industry in Africa is the result of sup-
pression by Western interests: "The American economists are perfectly aware
of the fact that industrialization of this kind contradicts the interests of the USA,

as well as of other industrially developed countries of the West, and deprives them of the control over underdeveloped areas." *Ibid.*

16. *An International Economy* (New York, 1956), pp. 1–2. And also (p. 318): "The larger part of the rest of mankind forms in this sense a lower class of nations...in contrast to the upper class of advanced countries. As a matter of fact, and considering their actual levels of living, the term 'proletariat' would be more appropriate in such an international comparison than it ever was or, any-how, is now within any of the advanced nations. The 'great awakening' in the backward nations is slowly also creating among them the class consciousness without which a social conglomeration is amorphous and unintegrated." Professor Myrdal adds (p. 319) that he regards effective combination by the underprivileged countries as most important to increase their bargaining power, to raise their standard of living and to promote world integration and democracy. See also his *Development and Underdevelopment* (Cairo, 1956), *passim.*

17. Myrdal, *Development and Underdevelopment*, pp. 62–3.

18. Alexander Erlich and Christian R. Sonne, "The Soviet Union: Economic Activity" in *Africa and the Communist World*, ed. Z. Brzezinski (Stanford, Calif., 1963), pp. 54–55.

19. "Such beliefs as that deliberate control or conscious organization is also in social affairs always superior to the results of spontaneous processes which are not directed by a human mind, or that any order based on a plan laid down beforehand must be better than one formed by the balancing of opposing forces, have in this way profoundly affected political development." F. A. Hayek: "The Intellectuals and Socialism" in *The Intellectuals,* ed. George B. de Huszar (Glencoe, 1960), p. 377.

20. Professor Hayek's remarks (p. 375) apply overwhelmingly to the intellec-tual contacts between the West and the underdeveloped countries. "In no other field has the predominant influence of the socialist intellectuals been felt more strongly during the last hundred years than in the contacts between different national civilizations...It is this which mainly accounts for the extraordinary spectacle that for generations the supposedly 'capitalist' West has been lending its moral and material support almost exclusively to those ideological movements in the countries farther East which aimed at undermining Western civilization; and that at the same time the information which the Western public has obtained about events in Central and Eastern Europe has almost inevitably been colored by a socialist bias."

21. In a general way this situation is familiar. It is perceptively discussed by Prabhakar Padhye, "The Intellectual in Modern Asia" in *The Intellectuals* (pp. 433–34): Western education, he says, has caused an urban minority and the masses in the villages to think different thoughts and speak different languages and even regard each other with a strange incomprehension. Students return from Western universities and find the land of their birth more alien and the ways of life more strange than the West. "They are utterly unable to adjust themselves to the realities here...The Asian intellectual is frustrated because his youthful dreams have cruelly foundered on the rocks of Asian reality ...his alienation from the people completely disenchants him. His inability to function creatively in society drives him to frustration and anger...Psychologi-cally there is a terrible void inside them. There is no faith and no conviction

to sustain them. They suffer from a terrible feeling of alienation and disenchantment, which threatens to make permanent misanthropes of them."

In 1958 I met a highly educated and intelligent Indian academic in Delhi whom I questioned about the legislation which had then been introduced in a number of Indian States prohibiting the slaughter of cattle. He implored me not to discuss this matter with him, because it set up almost physically painful strains within him. He said that I could have no idea of the problems which faced him, and Indian intellectuals generally, who pretended to represent the community but were in fact wholly alienated from the vast majority of their countrymen.

22. As Padhye points out (pp. 434-36), intellectuals believe that they can find a secure and legitimate place in the structure of the planned society the Communists will build. "Our alienated intellectual has been pining for this feeling of integration. He is intensely unhappy about his isolation from the people. Though outwardly he might like to flaunt his 'cultural' superiority, inwardly he is disturbed by a feeling of guilt. Communism gives him a good opportunity to get rid of this feeling. The communist emphasis on modernization and planning places a special value on the talents of the intellectuals, who can thus retain their sense of superiority and yet have the feeling of being integrated with the interests and destiny of the people. More than this, they can retain their white collars and still go around as revolutionaries, as privileged servants of the 'supreme revolution of the times'." Czeslaw Milosz in *The Captive Mind* (London, 1953), makes substantially similar points in the context of Eastern Europe.

23. The determination of the Communists to do so is known in a general way, but for its full appreciation it is necessary to read the literature, notably Marx's *Address to the Communist League of Germany* (1850), and the principal writings of Lenin before 1917.

24. The writings of Orwell, Barzun, and Weaver, though less well known than I think they should be, are at least reasonably accessible. Herbert Lüthy's penetrating discussion on this subject is not available in English. His essay, "Fragmente zu einem Instrumentarium des geistigen Terrors," published in 1945 in Switzerland and included in a recent collection of essays, *Nach dem Untergang des Abendlandes* (Cologne and Berlin, 1964), is a powerful and perceptive discussion of the far-reaching consequences of the decay or debauchment of the language, and of its systematic exploitation in Communist writings.

25. Extensive agricultural, mineral, commercial and industrial complexes have been built up throughout the underdeveloped world with reinvested profits.

DATE DUE

MAR 15 '72